CIRCLE FOR HEKATE
Volume I: History & Mythology

PUBLISHED BY AVALONIA

BM AVALONIA
LONDON
WC1N 3XX
ENGLAND, UK

WWW.AVALONIABOOKS.CO.UK

CIRCLE FOR HEKATE - VOLUME I: HISTORY & MYTHOLOGY
THE CIRCLE FOR HEKATE PROJECT.

COPYRIGHT © SORITA D'ESTE, 2017

ISBN: 978-1-910191-07-1
(PAPERBACK)

FIRST EDITION, NOVEMBER 2017

DESIGN BY ∂ℊℰℊℐ

CIRCLE FOR
Hekate

Volume I:
History & Mythology

Sorita d'Este

PUBLISHED BY AVALONIA

WWW.AVALONIABOOKS.CO.UK

I dedicate this project, in service, to the Goddess I worship
most of all, and who has chosen me as her helper, Ἑκάτη.

Volume I is also dedicated, in life, to my dear friend
Paul Harry Barron, who walked the Ridgeway and survived,
and who has completed many a devoted circle with me.
You are an inspiration.

ACKNOWLEDGEMENTS

This has not been a straightforward circle to complete, my thanks goes out to everyone who listened to my endless excited stories and everyone who encouraged me to not give up.

Blessings to all the Torchbearers of the *Covenant of Hekate* past, present and future. In particular: *Andrea Angelos, Dorn Simon, Francine Derschner, Florian Schlie, Sosanna Renee Olsen, Palladia Soria, Paul Harry Barron, Robert Podmore, Larry Phillips, Mima Cornish, Tinnekke Bebout, Vikki Bramshaw and Hazel*; may your work continue to inspire!

Gratitude to *David Rankine* for being the psychopomp at the start of this journey.

Thank you to *Rosa Laguna* for understanding my vision and words, giving it form with your pen. The sigil of the *Serpent Circle for Hekate* which features on the cover and prominently throughout this series is perfect!

With gratitude to all the various people who made this project possible. The *Andres Mata Private Collection* (New York); *Alexander Gherardi* from e-tiquities.com; *Steve* from antiqueprints.com and *A.S.* (London). In thanks to all those who support and make possible the resources available through the *British Museum* and *Library*, the *Wellcome Library*, *JSTOR*, *MetMuseum*, *CBd Budapest*, *Ashmolean Museum*, the *Campbell Bonner Magical Gems Database*; *theoi.com* and the many other online resources. Also to each and every single one of the researchers and authors listed in the *Bibliography* of this book - without your work this work would not be possible.

Thank you also to *Sophie Childs, Tita M., Carrie Kirkpatrick, Constantinos N., Eirini T., Marcel S., Claudiney Prieto, Katie Gerrard, Vikki Bramshaw, Hannah WM, Georgi Mishev, Francis A., Colin Irving, Melissa A., Mat Auryn* and the members of the *Covenant of Hekate*. You all provided help, inspiration, encouraging reminders and sometimes downright nagging – and without that I may never have found the finishing line with Volume I!

Finally, thank you to *Lokabandhu* who made this project possible in so many ways. Your support carries me, and your wisdom, kindness and calm continue to be an inspiration. *I love you.*

"MUST we then speak of this subject also: and shall we write concerning things that are not to be told, and shall we publish things not to be divulged, and secrets not to be spoken aloud?"
— Julian the Apostate, Oration upon the Mother of Gods,
4th century CE, trans. C.W. King, 1888

Table of Contents

"It is ignorance which leads to profanation. Men ridicule what they do not properly understand."

The Eleusinian and Bacchic Mysteries, by Thomas Taylor

"I call Einodian Hecate, lovely dame,
of earthly, wat'ry, and celestial frame,
Sepulchral, in a saffron veil array'd,
leas'd with dark ghosts that wander thro' the shade;
Persian, unconquerable huntress hail!
The world's key-bearer never doom'd to fail
On the rough rock to wander thee delights,
leader and nurse be present to our rites
Propitious grant our just desires success,
accept our homage, and the incense bless."

Orphic Hymn to Hecate
date unknown, circa 300 BCE – 200 CE.
trans. Thomas Taylor, 1792

Introduction

The goddess Hekate continues to inspire awe today. She is one of the most ancient Pagan goddesses, closely linked to the worship of the Great Mother Goddess Kybele and the Ephesian Artemis, as well as with the Mysteries of the Grain Goddess Demeter and her daughter Persephone. She was worshipped alongside gods such as Zeus, Hermes, Apollo and honoured at the entranceways into cities, temples and homes, as well as crossroads.

In Hesiod's *Theogony*, the earliest and most complete surviving literary account of the Greek Gods, Hekate is given the unique position of being honoured by both Zeus and the other immortal gods.

> *"...Hecate whom Zeus the son of Cronos honoured above all. He gave her splendid gifts, to have a share of the earth and the unfruitful sea. She received honour also in starry heaven, and is honoured exceedingly by the deathless gods..."*[1]

She is described as a benevolent goddess, capable of granting success in many different aspects of life, as well as being a nurse to the young. Hekate is a shapeshifting goddess, manifesting in various forms and faces, single and triple-bodied, and with the heads of maidens as well as those of animals. She wields her torches illuminating the Mysteries, guiding, protecting and defending that which is under her care. She uses her serpents or whips to strike fear in those who are unprepared for her Mysteries, gifting her devotees with the ability to understand the serpent energy and

---

1 The Theogony, circa 8th or 7th century BCE, Hesiod, trans. Evelyn-White, 1914.

knowledge. With her daggers, she cuts away that which is no longer necessary, whether the umbilical cord at birth or life itself upon death.

Numerous other goddesses were syncretised with Hekate, in different geographic regions and at different times in history. Her worship may have originated in the ancient Minoan or Mycenaean cultures, and was well attested throughout the Greek and Roman periods, spreading to the very corners of those Empires with those who travelled there. Evidence for her ancient worship has been found not only in Greece, but also as far apart as Sicily and Southern Italy, Egypt, Libya, Turkey, Bulgaria and Syria.

This book represents only a small part of the historical knowledge we have available about the goddess Hekate. It can be read as a standalone volume by those interested in the history and myths associated with this goddess, and is intended as background reading providing contextual foundations for the practices, including devotional rites, meditations, contemplations and charms, in the subsequent volumes in this series.

Circle for Hekate: Volume I is the first in a series of books on Hekate. In this volume I bring together an overview of Hekate's place in Greek mythology, together with highlighting the most important goddesses she was syncretised with, the most interesting places her worship was attested at, the different physical manifestations she presents herself in, and the symbols she is most often recognised by, as well as the way in which she was worshipped historically. I wanted to avoid repeating too much of what has previously been published in the book *Hekate: Liminal Rites* which I co-authored with David Rankine (Avalonia, 2009).

Some repetition was unavoidable, but I hope that readers of my previous work will understand the necessity. I also decided to only touch upon Hekate's role in the Chaldean Oracles, as this has been the subject of two highly recommended works which between them treat the subject in prodigious detail: *Hekate Soteira* by Sarah Illes Johnston and *The Goddess Hekate* by Stephen Ronan.

Subsequent volumes in *Circle for Hekate* introduce experiential learning through devotion, ritual, meditation, contemplation and other related modern practices. Most, but not all, of the practices presented in this series take their inspiration from historical sources. By learning from history and aiming to repeat the triumphs and avoiding the failings of those who went before, I believe that we are able to progress. This is possibly the closest thing to a real and viable shortcut available to us on our spiritual and magical journeys.

Each volume in this series is a *circle* I dedicate to the goddess Hekate. A *Circle* of learning and understanding I have gone through, and one which I now offer to you the reader to do with as you are guided to. It is my hope that it will be a circle of new discoveries, new experiences and new friendships for you, as it has been for me.

The circle is a place from where to start your next journey.

Sorita d'Este, 2017

1 - AESOPUS IN EUROPA, AMSTERDAM 1701, MARKED AS BEING BASED ON A "ROMAN COPY"
IN THIS SATYRICAL DEPICTION HEKATE IS DEPICTED HERE WITH ONE BODY, THREE HEADS, RIDING
A GOAT, HER FEET ARE EAGLE CLAWS, HOOFS, AND SHE HAS ONE NAKED BREAST.

SHE HOLDS A HOOK IN ONE HAND, AND A TORCH IN THE OTHER AND APPEARS TO BE SCREAMING.
HEKATE IS SHOWN WITH NEMESIS (WITH HER IN THE CIRCLE) WITH THE CHARACTERS OF BUSY BODY
AND TURBULENT SPIRIT OUTSIDE. IN THE ACCOMPANYING TEXT THERE IS A DISCUSSION ABOUT THE
DECLINE OF MAGIC IN EUROPE AND ITS SURVIVAL THROUGH SUPERSTITION WITH EXAMPLES
INCLUDING HAPPENINGS IN THE ROYAL HOUSES OF TUSCAN AND MANTUA.

BUSY BODY TELLS HEKATE THAT, THAT THE WHOLE OF EUROPE WOULD SOON BE UNDER HER
AUTHORITY, IF SHE SUCCEEDED IN INTRODUCING HERSELF INTO ENGLAND AND HOLLAND

Theogony: Divine Ancestors

"Again, Phoebe came to the desired embrace of Coeus. Then the goddess through the love of the god conceived and brought forth dark-gowned Leto... Also, she bare Asteria of happy name, whom Perses once led to his great house to be called his dear wife. And she conceived and bare Hekate whom Zeus the son of Cronos honoured above all..."[2]

Hekate is an extraordinarily universal goddess, with an extensive history of worship in many parts of the world. The oldest known historical record of Hekate in literature can be found in Hesiod's *Theogony* dated to the 8th or 7th century BCE. The *Theogony* is one of the earliest surviving texts of the Greek language and the oldest known cosmology of the Hellenic pantheon. Using the *Theogony* as a starting point, this chapter examines Hekate's divine ancestors and their respective roles.

Hesiod was writing after the end of the Greek Dark Ages, a time when the Mycenaean world was being forgotten and a new world was being forged. Researchers are still piecing together information about the history of the preceding centuries when civilisation in the region went into a sudden and steep decline. What we know is that within just a few decades an immense amount of knowledge, including the use of writing, was lost. The cause of the decline, which led to the Greek Dark Ages, was likely due to a combination of war and earthquake-related natural disasters in the region.

---

2 The Theogony, circa 8th or 7th century BCE, Hesiod, trans. Evelyn-White, 1914.

Hekate's exact historical origin remains obscured by the corridors of time, just like that of many, if not most, of the other deities she interacts with. It is unlikely that we will ever have a clear and definite explanation for the origin of the Gods that will satisfy all scholars and contemporary devotees. However, by examining the family tree placement given to her by Hesiod, we can create an interesting, albeit incomplete, mosaic with the available information, through which we can garner glimpses not only of her possible origins but also of the way in which she was understood by her ancient devotees. Using the *Theogony* as a starting point, it is viable to explore the place she was given among the other deathless gods, as well as the possible origins for some of the qualities and roles attributed to her.

Hesiod was a Greek poet and probably a contemporary of Homer. Both were believed to have lived around 750 – 650 BCE, or thereabouts. The work produced by Hesiod and Homer had a lasting influence on subsequent Greek religious writings, and as such their work is considered by some scholars to be key foundational texts. Hesiod's *Theogony* and Homer's *Iliad* and *Odyssey* continue to be studied and inspire new generations of creative thinkers today. The work of both authors is also frequently debated, and there are different opinions regarding the origins and the exact authorship of the works attributed to them. However, these texts were and are relevant. They informed subsequent views, and provide us with a snapshot of the time and place they were written in. Today both authors' work continues to be essential reading for students seeking a basic knowledge of Greek religion and history.

Hesiod's description of Hekate makes it clear that he held this goddess in very high regard. Some scholars argue that the exalted position he attributes to Hekate indicates a bias and suggest that Hesiod may have been a devotee of Hekate, someone who was trying to elevate her cult. It is equally possible that Hesiod was simply writing from the perspective of the time and place he lived in, and that his writings merely reflect the manner in which the goddess Hekate was perceived at the time.

Some of the evidence I present in this volume supports Hesiod's view of Hekate, suggesting that he was writing from an established perspective. Hekate was held in high regard in many places across a broad geographic region, for many centuries. Moreover, the evidence indicates that she was frequently worshipped alongside the god Zeus, sometimes seemingly as his equal or companion. While Hekate was not generally worshipped as one of the Twelve Gods, she was a well-known major goddess throughout the Hellenic world.

2 - GREEK TETRADRACHM COIN FROM BACTRIA (MODERN AFGHANISTAN) 185-170 BCE, SHOWING ZEUS PRESENTING HEKATE WITH TWO TORCHES ON HIS RIGHT HAND. WITH THANKS TO A.S., PRIVATE COLLECTION.

The *Hymn to Hekate* in the *Theogony* is a liminal point between the old regime (the Titans) and the new regime (the Olympians) with Zeus as the new ruler. Hekate is the bridge from the old to the new regime of Gods. She is a Titan goddess, the daughter of Asteria and Perses, but when Zeus takes a stand against his father, Kronos, Hekate fights against the old regime, in favour of the new. She is shown on friezes depicting the battle against the Giants, fighting alongside the other deities by using her torches as weapons. Her actions unquestionably contribute to Zeus' victory, and in the past I agreed with the speculation that Zeus honoured Hekate in the *Theogony* as a result of her support for him in the Titanomachy. However, Hekate was not alone in supporting Zeus in this war, and there is no special mention or honours given to others who helped, which casts doubt on the idea of her involvement in the Titanomachy being the reason for the exalted position she is given.

A more plausible explanation is that an existing, but currently unknown, relationship existed between Hekate and Zeus prior to the war with the Titans. This is supported by evidence showing that Hekate and Zeus continued to be worshipped alongside one another in subsequent centuries. Alternatively, it is possible to postulate that Hekate's cult was dominant or influential at the time and that an alliance between those who supported Hekate and the new regime was necessary in order to forge a successful future. Here it is interesting to note that this mythical battle was said to take place in Thessaly, one of the traditional regions associated with Hekate's worship.

Hesiod's cosmology is older than those given by subsequent writers, who sometimes present Hekate with alternative parentage. We sometimes find for example that Zeus is given as her father[3], rather than Perses, with Asteria; or that Hekate was the daughter of Nyx[4]. Or that she was the daughter of Aristaios[5] or that she was the daughter of Demeter[6], equating her with the goddess Persephone, Queen of the Underworld.

Ultimately, all cosmologies are best viewed as stories through which we can understand the qualities, authority and other attributes of a deity. Mythology sometimes arises naturally, but occasionally is also purposefully created to explain a situation or to encourage specific responses in contemporary society. Stories are still being created today, and they still have the power to evoke changes in the psyches of those listening.

By examining Hekate's position in cosmology more carefully, we can investigate her family tree, and gain insights into the qualities she may have inherited from her Titan ancestors. And by looking at it from a different perspective, interesting and new connections may reveal themselves, allowing new insights and understandings to emerge.

---

3 Orphic Frag, Scholiast on Apoll. Rhod
4 Bacchylides Frag 1B, Scholiast on Apoll. Rhod.
5 Schol. on Apoll. Rhod. ap Pherecydes
6 Orphic Frag, Scholiast on Apoll. Rhod.

Hekate's Family Tree (According to Hesiod)

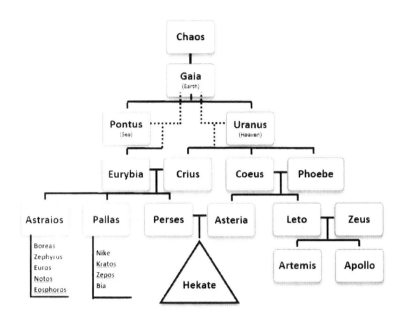

MOTHER: ASTERIA

> *"Also she [i.e. Phoebe] bare Asteria of happy name, whom Perses once led to his great house to be called his dear wife. And she conceived and bare Hekate..."*[7]

The goddess Asteria is associated with divination by dreams (oneiromancy), the starry sky, falling stars and divination by stars (astrology). Hesiod names her as the mother of Hekate, and this is repeated by later writers including Pseudo-Apollodorus and Cicero. Asteria is the sister of Leto (*Latonia*), and aunt of Apollo and Artemis.

Asteria may have her origins as an oracular goddess who was known as Brizo (*Slumber*), worshipped on the ancient island of Delos and associated with dream oracles. Though very little is known about the practices on the island at the time, it is possible that the women visiting it might have done so seeking safety or

---

7 The Theogony, circa 8th or 7th century BCE, Hesiod, trans. Evelyn-White, 1914.

news for their husbands and sons who were out at sea[8].

> *"The women of Delos offered sacrifices to her in vessels of the shape of boats, and the sacrifices consisted of various things; but fishes were never offered to her. Prayers were addressed to her that she might grant everything that was good, but especially, that she might protect ships ..."*[9]

Brizo was worshipped as an oceanic goddess who would protect ships and sailors, and presumably what the ships carried; as such the offerings may have included petitions for the safety of husbands, sons and others working at sea. It is plausible that Hekate's own later association with protection at sea may have been influenced by the activities on this island.

Pliny the Elder in his *Natural History* described the island of Delos (Greece) as also having been named variously:

- *Cynthia* (Cynthia is the name of a Moon Goddess, sometimes conflated with Artemis, Hekate and Selene)
- *Ortygia* (Quail)
- *Asteria* (Star)
- *Lagia* (Hare)
- *Chlamydia* (Cloak)
- *Cynethus* (Dog)
- *Pyripile* (Fiery) (According to Pliny, this name may have been given to the island because fire was first discovered there.)

All the names given by Pliny, except *Lagia*, have an ostensibly direct connection to Hekate. This is not a surprise since according to the mythologies associated with Delos, the island is the body of Hekate's mother, Asteria.

We are told that Asteria, in her efforts to escape the sexual advances of the god Zeus, fled across the land. Zeus transformed himself into an eagle to gain an advantage over her, but Asteria was keen to guard herself against Zeus, and turned herself into a quail (*Ortygia*) and threw herself into the ocean, becoming an island. This excerpt from Callimachus provides more detail:

---

8 See *Where Dreams May Come*, ed. Renberg, 2017.
9 Dictionary of Greek and Roman Biography and Mythology, Smith, 1844

*"But no constraint afflicted thee, but free upon the open sea
thou didst float; and thy name of old was Asteria, since like a
star thou didst leap from heaven into the deep moat, fleeing
wedlock with Zeus. Until then golden Leto consorted not with
thee: then thou wert still Asteria and wert not yet called Delos.
Oft-times did sailors coming from the town of fair-haired
Troezen unto Ephyra within the Saronic gulf descry thee, and
on their way back from Ephyra saw thee no more there, but
thou hadst run to the swift straits of the narrow Euripus with
its sounding stream. And the same day, turning thy back on
the waters of the sea of Chalcis, thou didst swim to the Sunian
headland of the Athenians or to Chios or to the wave-washed
breast of the Maiden's Isle, not yet called Samos – where the
nymphs of Mycalessos, neighbours of Ancaeus, entertained
thee..."*[10]

Having failed to woo Asteria, Zeus later turned his advances
towards her sister, Leto, impregnating her with the twins Apollo
and Artemis. Hera, Zeus' wife, was enraged and particularly
resentful of Leto. As a result, Hera decreed that the pregnant
goddess should not be allowed to give birth anywhere on land. Leto
was ubiquitously turned away wherever she sought refuge. In one
version of the story, Hera even commands the Python of Delphi
to chase the pregnant Leto across the land, preventing her from
having a place to rest and give birth. The wandering Leto is
ultimately guided to the drifting island of Asteria (Ortygia) by her
unborn son, illustrating his future role as god of prophecy, and is
welcomed there.

*"But mark thou, mother: there is to be seen in the water a tiny
island, wandering over the seas. Her feet abide not in one place,
but on the tide she swims even as stalks of asphodel, where the
South wind or the East wind blows, whithersoever the sea
carried her. Thither do thou carry me. For she shall welcome
thy coming. When he had spoken thus much, the other islands
in the sea ran away. But thou, Asteria, lover of song, didst
come down from Euboea to visit the round Cyclades – not long
ago, but still behind thee trailed the sea-weed of Geraestus ...,
seeing the unhappy lady in the grievous pangs of birth: 'Hera,*

10 Callimachus, Hymn 4 to Delos, Trans Mair, 1921

do to me what thou wilt. For I heed not their threats. Cross,
crossover, Leto, unto me.'... [11]

Callimachus continues the story, saying that the messenger goddess Iris informed Hera that Leto is in labour on Ortygia. Hera expresses her anger towards Leto, cursing all those who are impregnated by Zeus to give birth in places worse than those in which underprivileged mill-women give birth. However, when Hera hears that it is Asteria (as Ortygia) who is providing shelter to Leto, she softens because she knows the star goddess successfully avoided sexual relations with her husband:

> *"But against Asteria am I no wise angered for this sin, nor*
> *can I do to her so unkindly as I should – for very wrongly has*
> *she done a favour to Leto. Howbeit I honour her exceedingly*
> *for that she did not desecrate my bed, but instead of Zeus*
> *preferred the sea."* [12]

Leto births the sacred twins, first Artemis and then Apollo, on Ortygia. This marks a very dear relationship between the sisters and one for which Asteria is richly rewarded. Asteria receives adamantine pillars, anchoring her to the seabed and the island becomes Delos, a site of major religious pilgrimage for many centuries to follow.

There are some who believe that Ortygia, and therefore the birthplace of Artemis and Apollo, was the Sicilian Ortygia, a small islet off the coast of Syracuse, rather than Delos. Both are small rocky islands, preventing them from having any agricultural significance, and both had significant temples to Apollo. Sicily was a considerable region of the Greek empire, and Syracuse a major city during that period. Delos is however the more famous and better known of the two islands, and therefore more often credited as being the birthplace of the twins.

There is a third Ortygia claiming to be the place of the twins' birth. This Ortygia is near the site of the Temple of Artemis of Ephesus.

---

11 Callimachus, Hymn 4 to Delos, Trans Mair, 1921
12 Callimachus, Hymn 4 to Delos, Trans Mair, 1921

3 – RUINS OF THE TEMPLE OF APOLLO, ORTYGIA (SYRACUSE, SICILY) AT NIGHT

In addition to having possible origins as a goddess associated with the island of Delos, Asteria is sometimes given Phoenician beginnings. Some of the associations made by this nineteenth-century author are questionable, but there are some interesting parallels worth exploring for readers with interest in this aspect of mythology:

> *"This goddess, who is sometimes called Astarte, was the most important female deity of this early pantheon. The Persian form of the word is Astara. In Phoenician it is Astaroth, and according to Dr Oppert all the Phoenician goddesses were included under this general name. Another form of the name afterwards appeared in Greek mythology as Asteria, and it was applied to the beautiful goddess who fled from the suit of Jove [Zeus], and, flinging herself down from heaven into the sea, became the island afterwards named Delos."*[13]

Phoenicians did live and trade with Delos, but during the later Hellenistic period (circa 323 – 31 BCE), by which time the Temple of Apollo was already firmly established there.

Asteria is not known to have other children attributed to her, and Hekate is specifically named as an only child.

> *"So, then. albeit her mother's only child, she is honoured amongst all the deathless gods"*[14]

---

13 Persian Literature: Ancient and Modern,. Reed, 1893.
14 The Theogony, circa 8th or 7th century BCE, Hesiod, trans. Evelyn-White, 1914.

FATHER: PERSES THE DESTROYER

"The maiden daughter of Perseus,
Brimo Trimorphos [Hekate] " [15]

In the *Theogony*, Perses is the son of Eurybia (Wild Force) and Crius (Ram/Ruler), husband to the star goddess Asteria and father to Hekate. His name is usually taken to mean *destroyer*, and sometimes as *from Persia*. Hekate is also occasionally said to be *Persian* – a reference either to being her father's daughter, or possibly indicative of having Persian origins.

"…only tender-hearted Hekate, bright-coiffed,
the daughter of Persaios, …" [16]

Perses is sometimes confused with the similar Perseis (Perse), one of the three thousand Okeanides nymph daughters of Okeanos. Both are said to be Persian, sharing the meaning of destroyer. Perseis, the Okeanid Nymph, is also given as the wife of the sun god Helios, and with him the mother of Aeetes and Perses – the magician-kings. Aeetes who ruled Colchis is also named as the father of Medea.

"The Kholkians who were ruled by Aeetes, the son of Helios
and Perseis, and brother of Kirke and Minos' wife
Pasiphae." [17]

Hesiod, in this *Theogony*, also mentions this, 800 or so years before Pseudo-Apollodorus:

"And Perseis, the daughter of Okeanos, bare to unwearying
Helios Kirke and Aeetes the king." [18]

Paternal Cousins

Following Hesiod's *Theogony*, Hekate has several cousins on her father's side of the family who are rarely discussed. Because it is clear from the evidence that Hekate's connection with her maternal cousins, Artemis and Apollo, is so imperative, I thought it would be interesting to also highlight her paternal cousins here.

---

15 Alexandria, Lycophron, trans. Mair, 1921
16 Homeric Hymn to Demeter, trans. Evelyn-White, 1914.
17 Pseudo-Apollodorus, Bibliotheca, trans. Aldrich, 1975.
18 The Theogony, circa 8th or 7th century BCE, Hesiod, trans. Evelyn-White, 1914.

Perses' brother Astraeus is associated with the stars and planets, and, like Perses' wife Asteria, is a stellar deity. With Eos, the goddess of the dawn, he fathered the Anemoi. These are the four winds: Boreas, Zephyrus, Notus, Euros, and also Eosphoros (Morning and Evening Star), associated with the planet Venus. This is interesting because Pausanias recorded that Hekate was worshipped with offerings in four pits by the altar to the Four Winds in Sikini.

Perses' other brother, Pallas, was married to Styx, goddess of the underworld river and the personification of hatred. Together they bore Nike (Victory), Kratos (Strength), Zelos (Rivalry) and Bia (Force). Pallas was vanquished by Athena, who also held the title Pallas as an epithet.

This makes Boreas, Zephyrus, Notus, Euros, Eosphoros, Nike, Kratos and Zelos paternal cousins of Hekate according to Hesiod's cosmology.

MATERNAL GRANDPARENTS: COEUS AND PHOEBE

Phoebe, whose name is translated as bright or shining, was the grandmother of Hekate and mother of Asteria according to Hesiod. Like her daughter Asteria, and her grandchildren Hekate, Artemis and Apollo, she was closely associated with prophecy. Phoebe is named as the goddess of the Oracle at Delphi before Apollo. In the Aeschylus's play *Agamemnon*, we hear the Pythia speak:

> "First, in this my prayer, I give the place of chiefest honour among the gods to the first prophet. Earth; and after her to Themis; for she, as is told, took second this oracular seat of her mother. And third in succession, with Themis' consent and by constraint of none, another Titan, Phoebe, child of Earth, took here her seat. She bestowed it, as birth-gift, upon Phoebus [Apollo], who has his name from Phoebe."[19]

Coeus was a benevolent god, considered to be the axis of the world, as well as being one of the brothers who played a part in the

---

19 Agamemnon, Aeschylus, 6th or 5th century BCE, trans. Smyth, 1930

castration of Uranus. It is likely that he was also associated with oracles and prophecy. Coeus was also considered to be one of the gods who discovered things which were beneficent to humanity.

PATERNAL GRANDPARENTS: CRIUS & EURYBIA

Crius is one of the brothers of Coeus and likewise participated in the castration of Uranus, taking the part of the Southern Pillar. He is linked to the Ram and the constellation of Ares. His sons include Perses, and his stellar brother Astraios.

> *"And goddess of the sea Eurybia, bright goddess, was joined in love to Crius and bare great Astraios, and Pallas, and Perses who also was eminent among all men in wisdom…"[20]*

Eurybia, daughter of the sea god Pontos and Gaia, was said to have mastery over the sea, as well as over other natural forces such as the winds and constellations.

GREAT-GRANDPARENTS: EARTH, HEAVEN & SEA

Going back another generation, Gaia (Earth) is Hekate's great-grandmother on both sides of her family lineage. With Uranus (Heaven) Gaia birthed Phoebe, and with Pontus (sea) she birthed Coeus. Her great-grandparents, therefore, are the three domains associated with her in the *Theogony*: Gaia (Earth), Ouranos (Heaven) and Pontos (Sea).

This gives a different understanding of the way in which Hesiod attributes a share of each of the three domains of Earth, Heaven and Sea to Hekate (underline is my emphasis):

> *"Hekate whom Zeus the son of Kronos honoured above all. He gave her splendid gifts, to have a share of the <u>earth</u> and the unfruitful <u>sea</u>.*
>
> *She received honour also in <u>starry heaven</u>, and is honoured exceedingly by the deathless gods . . . For as many as were born*

---

20 The Theogony, circa 8th or 7th century BCE, Hesiod, trans. Evelyn-White, 1914.

> *of Gaia [Earth] and Ouranos [Heaven] amongst all these she*
> *has her due portion.*
>
> *The son of Kronos [Zeus] did her no wrong nor took anything*
> *away of all that was her portion among the former Titan gods:*
> *but she holds, as the division was at first from the beginning,*
> *privilege both in earth, and in heaven, and in sea.*
>
> *Also, because she is an only child, the goddess receives not less*
> *honour, but much more still, for Zeus honours her."*[21]

Gaia, Ouranos and Pontos are primordial gods, with each of them in turn, being the physical Earth (Gaia), Heavens (Ouranos) and Ocean (Pontos). They are not just associated with the respective domains, rather they are the domains themselves.

Gaia was the original goddess of the Delphic Oracle and was closely connected with prophecy, as early as 1700-1400 BCE. The earth, her body, is the realm of the dead, and calling on the dead for insight and predictions was a common practice in antiquity.

Another daughter of Gaia, Themis, also occupied the role of the goddess of Delphi for a period, before the function passed to Phoebe, mother of Asteria and Leto and eventually to Apollo. Delphi, just like the gift of prophecy, was in a manner of speaking 'in the family'.

VIRGIN, WIFE, MOTHER OR LOVER?

Hekate is never explicitly described as the wife of any of the gods, as such she remains an independent and wandering goddess, free from the ties of marriage. She is frequently described as a virgin or maiden goddess, but she is also sometimes linked to male gods and said to have offspring with some of them.

These contradictory descriptions should be understood in the context of the culture, time and place. Hekate was a goddess of many forms, and her cult subsumed that of other deities along the way, incorporating aspects of their histories and worship in the process. For example, Persephone was the Virgin (Kore) before she was abducted by Hades, becoming his wife as well as the Queen of the Underworld. Yet, Persephone, for some, remains a symbol

---

21 The Theogony, circa 8th or 7th century BCE, Hesiod, trans. Evelyn-White, 1914.

of virginity and youth, whose yearly return to the world of the living is closely linked with the agricultural growth cycle.

Hekate continued to be described as a virginal goddess throughout the history of her worship. In the third century CE Lycophron Hekate is described as:

"The maiden daughter of Perseus, Brimo Trimorphos..."[22]

In the PGM, dated to between 200 BCE and 500 CE, we find references to virginity in several invocations involving Hekate. For example, in the *Charm of Hekate Ereschigal against fear of punishment*, we read:

"I saw the other things down below, virgin, bitch, and all the rest"[23]

And in the Chaldean Oracles of the second century CE:

"I come, a virgin of varied forms..." [24]

Hekate is also named as a maiden by Pindar (522-443 BCE) in his Paeans, where he includes a proclamation by the goddess in an oracle. The extract may have been a song sung at her shrine to remind locals of a victory[25] or as part of a festival honouring Apollo:

"The virgin with the red border, kindly Hecate, was the messenger for the word which wanted to come true. "[26]

Depictions of Hekate before the twentieth-century ordinarily show her as a young woman, or a lady of indeterminate age. She takes on many forms, single, triple and sometimes zoomorphic. She is even named as the mother of Skylla, as well as the sorceresses Kirke and Medea, but regardless of this appears to have maintained her maiden status.

---

22 Lycophron, Alexandra, trans. Mair, 1921.
23 PGM LXX.4-25, Betz, 1997.
24 Hekate Soteira, Johnston, 1990.
25 In relation to Abderans, colonialists from Tean in Thrace.
26 Pindar's Paeans, Rutherford, 2001.

Skylla: Daughter of Hekate?

*"Nor let them go too near the hateful den of Ausonian Skylla,
that wicked monster borne to Phorkys by night-wandering
Hekate, whom men call Kratais."*[27]

Speaking these words in the Argonautica, the sorceress Kirke
equates Hekate with Kratais (Kharybdis). The latter is also named
as *Skylakagetis*, meaning leader of dogs, Lamia (from Shark) and
Trienos (the Thrice). Trienos is a reference to three high and low
tides, which were ascribed to Skylla's ability to suck the water in
and spit it out again three times a day. The number three is also an
important symbol associated with Hekate.

4 - SKYLLA, DAUGHTER OF HEKATE. IN THE ARCHEOLOGICAL MUSEUM, ATHENS.

Skylla is depicted as having the torso and head of a female and
a body with multiple legs, sometimes part canine and part fish. She
is closely associated with both the island of Sicily and with the Strait
of Messina, a narrow and treacherous strip of ocean between Sicily

27 Argonautica, Apollonius Rhodius, 3rd century BCE, trans. Seaton, 1912.

and mainland Italy, where she is said to live.

> *"Half-way up the cliff is a murky cave, facing Erebos, and doubtless it is past this, Odysseus, that you and your men will steer your vessel... Inside lives Skylla, yelping hideously; her voice is no deeper than a young puppy's but she herself is a fearsome monster; no one could see her and still be happy, not even a god if he went that way. She has twelve feet all dangling down, six long necks with a grisly head on each of them, and in each head a triple row of crowded and close-set teeth, fraught with black death..."*[28]

Kirke's advice to Odysseus is that he should invoke Kratais for her help against the perils of Skylla:

> *"Will you not bow to the deathless gods themselves? Skylla is not of mortal kind; she is a deathless monster, grim and baleful, savage, not to be wrestled with. Against her there is no defence, and the best path is the path of flight. If you pause to arm beside that rock, I fear that she may dart out again, seize again with as many heads and snatch as many men as before. No, row hard and invoke Krataiis; she is Skylla's mother; it is she who bore her to plague mankind; Krataiis will hold her from darting twice."*[29]

There are some parallels between Skylla and the Nereids, female creatures who lived in the Aegean Sea, which included Thetis, a goddess of the waters. Thetis is sometimes equated to Metis, who is described as the first of the wives of Zeus.

> *"Now Zeus, king of the gods, made Metis his wife first, and she was wisest among gods and mortal men. But when she was about to bring forth the goddess bright-eyed Athene, Zeus craftily deceived her with cunning words and put her in his own belly, as Earth and starry Heaven advised."*[30]

She was associated with the art of magic, as well as with wisdom. She was also described as the goddess of wisdom, wise counsel and prudence, qualities which were highly valued in the Mycenaean era.

> *"The general resemblance between the myths of Metis and*

---

28 The Odyssey, Homer, circa 8th or 7th century BCE, trans. Shewring, 1980.
29 The Odyssey, Homer, circa 8th or 7th century BCE, trans. Shewring, 1980.
30 The Theogony, circa 8th or 7th century BCE, Hesiod, trans. Evelyn-White, 1914.

Thetis is unmistakable. Metis, like Thetis, was a sea-power.
Metis like Thetis was a shape-shifter. Metis, like Thetis, was
loved by Zeus. Metis, like Thetis, was destined to bear a son
that should oust his father - a danger averted in either case by
an oracular utterance and consequent guile."[31]

While Zeus desired Thetis, he avoided intercourse with her due to an oracle and according to Ovid instead sent Peleus to be with her. He went looking for her in a cave, and to escape his embraces Thetis variously shapeshifted into a bird, a tree, a tiger and hundreds of other forms[32]. However, with the help of the gods of the sea, Peleus was able to have his way with the shape-shifting virgin Nereid in the end.

"...you will have the bride you desire, if you bind her,
unawares, with nooses and tight cords, while she is lulled asleep
in the rocky cave. Though she deceives you with a hundred
counterfeit shapes, hold her to you, whatever she becomes, until
she is again what she was before."[33]

Thetis is depicted as a young naked woman riding a dolphin, or astride a hippocampus, a mythical sea monster. The hippocampus has the body of a horse, but the tail of a fish, and is sometimes simply named as a sea-horse.

Medea, Kirke and Aigialeus

"We are told that Helios had two sons, Aeetes and Perses,
Aeetes being the king of Kolkhis and the other king of the
Tauric Khersonese, ... Perses had a daughter Hekate ... she
married Aeetes and bore two daughters, Kirke and Medea,
and a son Aigialeus."[34]

In the above quote from Diodorus Siculus, Hekate is given as the granddaughter of Helios, wife of the mortal king Aeetes, and mother to Kirke and Medea, as well as a son Aigialeus. This is a very different genealogy from that given by Hesiod around 500 years before, and although it is a later addition, it none the less provides us with a fascinating perspective of a first-century BCE

31 Zeus. A Study In Ancient Religion. Volume 2, Part 1, Cook, 1925.
32 Metamorphosis, Ovid, 43 BCE – 18 CE, trans Kline, 1903.
33 Metamorphosis, Ovid, 43 BCE – 18 CE, trans Kline, 1903.
34 Library of History, Diodorus Siculus, C1st BCE, trans. Oldfather, 1933.

perspective.

Kirke was a shapeshifting goddess or sorceress who is only defeated by Odysseus when the latter is given help from the trickster god Hermes. Hers is a story of magic, lust and power – and from very early on she is considered as divine. The Homeric Hymn describes her as:

> *"Kirke, a goddess with braided hair, with human speech and with strange powers; the magician Aeetes was her brother, and both were the radiant sun-god Helios' children; their mother was Perse, Okeanos' daughter."* [35]

Based on the legends told of her, Kirke had an exceptional knowledge of magic. Not only was she adept at using herbs and plants, but she could control the weather, move the unseen and control the weather. She also practised love magic and knew the secrets of necromancy.

Hekate is named explicitly as the teacher of the young Medea in the Argonautica:

> *"There is a maiden, nurtured in the halls of Aeetes, whom the goddess Hecate taught to handle magic herbs with exceeding skill all that the land and flowing waters produce."* [36]

Medea's story is one of prodigious power and love, a story which ultimately ends in tragedy. She is associated with Hekate as a Priestess, describing the goddess as *"the mistress whom I worship above all others and name as my helper"* [37]. She also attributed her power to Hekate saying that *"provided the triple-formed goddess helps and by her presence assents to my great experiments."* [38]

When, in the Metamorphoses, Medea seeks to protect Jason from a fire, she invokes the pure rites of Hekate Triformis, the spirits of place (in the grove), and Helios as her grandfather. Medea is also positioned as a devotee of Hekate, who calls upon her at shrines, for example in the Argonautica we find:

> *"...the chariot to bear her to the beauteous shrine of Hecate. Thereupon the handmaids were making ready the chariot; and*

---

35 The Odyssey, Homer, circa 8th or 7th century BCE, trans. Shewring, 1980.
36 Argonautica, Apollonius Rhodius, 3rd century BCE, trans. Seaton, 1912.
37 Medea, Euripides, 431 BCE, trans. F. Graf, 1979.
38 Metamorphoses, Ovid, 8 CE, trans. C.E. Newlands, 1997.

> *Medea meanwhile took from the hollow casket a charm which*
> *men say is called the charm of Prometheus. If a man should*
> *anoint his body therewithal, having first appeased the Maiden*
> *[Hekate], the only-begotten, with sacrifice by night..."*[39]

Medea is specifically named as a priestess and devotee of Hekate in the Argonautica:

> *"As a rule she [Medea] did not spend her time at home, but*
> *was busy all day in the temple of Hekate, of whom she was a*
> *priestess."* [40]

Medea was also considered to be an outstanding and accurate Oracle. She predicted the colonisation of Thera (Santorini), a prediction which was subsequently repeated by the Delphic Oracle. As a result of this Pindar described Medea as speaking words from her *"immortal mouth"*[41] promoting her, in part at least, to divine status.

Aigialeus is an alternative name for Absyrtus, the brother of Medea. In one version of the myth he travels with Medea on her journey with Jason, and Medea kills him brutally. In another, he is sent in pursuit of Medea by their father, and Jason kills him on an island sacred to Artemis. In different versions of the legend he is given different mothers, with Apollonius saying his mother is Asterodeia, who is equated with the goddess Asteria.

Evidence from various sources links Kirke, Medea and Aigialeus with both Helios and Hekate in different ways. In most instances, Kirke and Medea are named as witches or sorceresses who call on Hekate as a goddess, and to Helios as both a god and ancestor.

Much is made in the way both Medea and Kirke are named as 'daughters' of Hekate. It is possible that the term 'daughter' was used as an allegory, or even as a title, to denote the close relationship these women had with Hekate. Terms like 'son' and 'daughter' to describe a relationship to a deity are used in a variety of spiritual traditions. For example, followers of the deities (*orishas*) of the Yoruba traditions believe that they are born as the sons and

---

39 Argonautica, Apollonius Rhodius, 3rd century BCE, trans. Seaton, 1912.
40 Argonautica, Apollonius Rhodius, 3rd century BCE, trans. Seaton, 1912.
41 Pythian Ode 4, Pindar, 462 BCE, trans. Krevans, 1984.

daughters of a particular Orisha. Christians are often described as the 'children' of their God. They also use the term 'father' to refer to a priest, 'mother' in the Roman Catholic Church is used to refer to Mother Superior. Monks refer to each other as 'brother' and nuns name each other as 'sister'. Familial terms are also lovingly used by some contemporary Pagans, who describe themselves as, for example, 'Daughters of the Goddess'.

The idea that someone is a 'daughter of Hekate' (or insert appropriate gender) would then simply be a declaration that the individual's bond with Hekate is like that of a parent to a child. It is a bond that can never be broken, and it is for life.

Many-Named
Mother of the Gods

"Hail, many-named Mother of the Gods,
whose children are fair,
Hail, mighty Hekate of the Threshold."[42]

Hekate is a goddess of many names. This is emphasised in both the PGM and in Proclus' *Hymn to Hekate and Janus* where she is referred to as *many-named*. Nonnus similarly alludes to Hekate as being a goddess of many names, in his fifth century CE Dionysiaca:

"If thou art Hekate of many names, if in the night thou doest
shake thy mystic torch in brandcarrying hand, come
nightwanderer..."[43]

The understanding different groups of people hold of a deity often change over time. These changes are frequently natural adaptations to an ever-evolving culture, or variations reflecting a changing landscape due to industrialisation or migration. Religious and ritual practices evolve with what is available. For example, as different foods and plants become available the aesthetics and ingredients of offerings will change, albeit in a way which preserves something of the original.

Similarly the names and epithets given to a deity will change with successive generations of people encountering their worship. The Greeks and Romans travelled within a vast geographical

---

42 Hymn to Hekate and Janus, Proclus, circa 5th century CE, trans. S. Ronan, 1989.
43 Dionysiaca, Nonnus, 5th century CE, trans. Rouse, 1940.

region, conquering, trading and spreading their religious practices and beliefs. They were fond of equating the deities they encountered in different parts of their respective empires to gods in their own pantheon. Sometimes their own deity would with time also take on some of the qualities of the local deity, as the conflation between the two deities become complete. Occasionally a particular cult became more prevalent, and absorbed other smaller, local cults into itself.

Names and epithets associated with a deity therefore provide us not only with information on how to invoke or praise a deity, but also with information about their history. Epithets are windows back in time to how people in different places and times understood a deity, whilst simultaneously telling us about the history of deities whose cults influenced that of the god we are examining.

THE NAME *HEKATE*
(Εκατη)

The origin and meaning of the name *Hekate* remain obscured by history. There are however several plausible explanations.

Hekate may have the same root as *Hekatos*, which is the masculine version of the name and means 'worker from afar'. *Hekatos* was a prevalent cult title of Apollo. This title denotes Apollo's skilled use of his bow and arrows, and there is no reason why *Hekate* as the female version of the name should not be taken as having the same meaning. Artemis was famous for her skills as a huntress, using her bow and arrows – which she used to hunt, but also to punish wrongdoers by sending disease. Apollo used his bow to protect and also initially to revenge wrongdoers. Both Artemis and Apollo were considered deities associated with archery. Hekate is on occasion shown with a bow and arrows, but such depictions are rare, and no explanation is offered in surviving myths.

If this is the meaning of the name, it would further strengthen the existing association between Hekate and Apollo. It would also support the notion that the goddesses Hekate and Artemis, who are frequently conflated, may have originally been the same goddess, or at the very least had common origins.

Alternatively, *Hekate* may be a foreign name, with an unknown meaning, but with a likely connection to the region of Caria (in Anatolia) where names with the same root were commonly used as a first name. However, this is a chicken-and-egg argument. It seems more likely that children may have been named after Hekate/Hekatos, both of whom were popular deities in the region. The name *Hekate* might then still be foreign to the region. It is possible that a local deity with an existing cult was conflated with an incoming cult of *Hekate,* and that the incoming cult incorporated local ideas and practices at that time.

Another theory is that the name *Hekate* may have been derived from the Greek word εκατό (*ekato*) meaning hundred.

Hecate (with a c) is the Roman Latin transliteration of Ἑκάτη. Using *Hekate* rather than *Hecate* is a personal preference. Both transliterations are correct, and could be used interchangeably.

DIVINE MERGERS

Any attempt to try and understand Hekate by putting her in a tidy box and mark it with her name, will only lead to complications and a lot of (needless) headaches. In her role as goddess of the threshold and of gateways, Hekate uniquely interacted with a multitude of other deities, as she was often worshipped at city gates and at the entranceways to the temples of other gods. Gateway and entranceway shrines may have been smaller, however they would have been a constant reminder of the presence of the deity to all who entered and left. They were not insignificant.

As previously noted, both the Greeks and Romans had a penchant for renaming the local deities they encountered after their own deities, usually based on shared qualities they perceived. Unfortunately, this means that sometimes the local names were lost and replaced with the Greek or Roman name. Again, this makes it difficult to provide a clearly labelled box into which to put Hekate, or indeed any of the deities encountered by these nations. The religious plurality and polyonymy of antiquity do not care much for the fixed labels we are so very fond of in the twenty-first century CE.

The understanding we have today of Hekate was strongly influenced by the different deities she was equated to, conflated with and otherwise merged with over many hundreds of years. For this reason it is important to be aware of at least some of the goddesses who may have influenced Hekate, because by doing so we can enrich our own understanding and connection to her today.

5 - KYBELE, WITH HEKATE (BOTTOM RIGHT) AND HERMES (BOTTOM LEFT). IN THE ACROPOLIS MUSEUM, ATHENS.

Kybele, The Mother of the Gods

Hekate was intimately linked to the cult of the Phrygian Kybele, especially in Anatolia. She was equated to the Phrygian mother, and shown as being her attendant. The title *Mother of the Gods* is occasionally given to Hekate emphasising this connection.

In religious art, Kybele was shown as being accompanied by Hekate, and the god Hermes. In these depictions, Kybele is usually shown as being larger, with Hekate and Hermes being smaller and standing either side of her. Alternatively, Hekate and Hermes are seen as leading and following Kybele who is shown riding on her chariot, or seated on a lion. A stucco now in the Cairo Museum collection, which is believed to have been found in Smyrna (Anatolia) shows Kybele, seated with lions in the central position, flanked by Hekate and Hermes. It was mounted on a podium with depictions of the Twelve Gods.

Hekate and Kybele share a strong association with bulls. Hekate was frequently described as being bull-horned and sometimes bull-faced. The Great Mother goddess' cult stronghold in Çatalhöyük (Southern Anatolia) abounded with bull symbolism, to the extent that some writers refer to the people of Çatalhöyük as *The People of the Bull*[44].

Here figurines showing an enthroned voluptuous woman flanked by lions were found which strongly resemble that of later depictions of Kybele. Çatalhöyük is believed to have been occupied from at least 8000 BCE, suggesting that the Phrygian Mother's cult may have existed in the region for many thousands of years.

An enthroned statue of Kybele in the *Archaeological Museum of Corinth* shows a triple Hekate depicted on the right-hand side of the throne. On the left is depicted branches of pine with pan flutes, both symbols of the god Pan.

Artemis

"...Artemis Hecate watch over the child-bed of women."[45]

Hekate and Artemis are frequently conflated from the fifth century BCE onwards. Sometimes they were merged as Artemis-Hekate, and at other times they were simply thought to be the same goddess. They both also maintain their independence as individual goddesses, being cousins in Hesiod's *Theogony*, and portrayed as taking different parts next to each other in selected myths.

When Hekate gains an association with the Moon in later literature, she is paired with Apollo, the brother of Artemis, who then becomes equated to the Sun. In so doing Hekate and Apollo

---

44 See Taking the Bull by the Horns, Twiss & Russel, 2009
45 Aiskhylos, Suppliants, 5th century BCE, quoted in Murray, 2015.

replace Selene (Moon) and Helios (Sun) as the deities of the Moon and the Sun.

Artemis and Hekate share several important cult titles in common, including *Soteira, Enodia, Eileithyia , Perseia, Tauropolos, Kore, Parthenos, Phosphoros, Phoebe*. They were celebrated as Artemis-Hekate at Mounykhia, a Full Moon festival on the 16th Mounykhion[46] at Piraeus. Small cakes called *amphiphontes* meaning *shining on both sides*, were offered to the goddess here. The same cakes, decorated with small torches, formed part of crossroad offerings which may also have been dedicated to Hekate. They additionally share numerous symbols in common including bees, dogs, hunting bows, torches, serpents, the polos, modius and trees.

Based on available evidence, it is possible to speculate that they are aspects of the same earlier goddess who survived from the Greek Dark Ages into the Hellenic period; or that Hekate may have been an aspect of Artemis which gained popularity in its own right. Similarly, they may have been closely connected with an earlier cult, likely that of the Phrygian Great Mother. It might also be pure coincidence and the various associations could be explained by similarities they held in common with subsequent syncretising.

Bendis

"We find the undoubtedly Thracian goddess Bendis with many points of likeness to Hekate. The epithet Dilongchos (two-fold) that belonged to the former is explained by Hesychius as describing the goddess who, like Hekate, had power in more than one sphere of nature; and the torch seems to have been the special symbol of both."[47]

The Thracian Bendis shares symbols such as spears, horses and crossroads in common with Hekate. Both were also considered to be benevolent Mother Goddesses. Like Hekate, Bendis was equated with or merged with Artemis, and was sometimes called the Thracian Artemis.

Bendis was a Lunar Goddess and the mother of the god Sabazius, who is likened to Dionysos. She was depicted with two

---

46 April/May in the modern calendar.
47 The Cults of the Greek States, Farnell, 1896-1909.

spears, and Hekate also bears a spear, the best-known example being from the fifth century BCE play by Sophocles *The Root-Cutters*.

"The spear of Hekate of the Crossroads
Which she bears as she travels Olympus
And dwells in the triple ways of the holy land"[48]

By the fifth-century BCE, when Bendis' worship spread to Athens, Hekate's cult was gaining in popularity in the city. If Thrace was Hekate's homeland, the Indo-European and Middle Eastern influences associated with Hekate might be explained by the influence of Bendis on the torchbearers' cult.

6 - THE THRACIAN GODDESS BENDIS, WITH A HOUND. SHE IS WEARING A PHRYGIAN CAP.
BELIEVED TO BE FROM TANAGRA, ATTICA. TERRACOTTA, CIRCA 350 BCE.

Mishev asserts that Hekate fits into the Thracian idea of a Mother Goddess writing that:

"The depiction and the idea of the Thracian Mother Goddess

---

48 The Root-Cutters, Sophocles,5th century BCE, Trans. Yardley, 2009.

39

as Hekate, i.e. as the one who gives birth to the divine son, shouldn't seem strange to us because of the images found in the territory of Bulgaria of Hekate with a little child in her hands, again accompanied by her sacred dogs-wolves, which are a second naming of the divine son in his winter hypostasis, at the time of his birth."[49]

Other authors have also made this connection between the Thracian Mother Goddess and Hekate. Janouchová writes that:

"Under the oriental influence, Bendis was often also identified with deities of the night – Cottyto, Cybele, and Hekate. These deities were often associated with the life cycle and fertility of women and were famous for orgiastic night dances and celebrations. These goddesses are also known for their connection to dark magic and the underworld."[50]

Dogs were sacrificed to Bendis, an uncommon practice which was also associated with both Hekate and Enodia. All three of these goddesses were equated and thought to be the same by ancient writers. Bendis has also been equated to Hekate at Neapolis and the Parthenos of the city there.

Also see: *The Wandering Goddess, Neapolis*

Bona Dea

"Others again hold the view that she is Hecate of the Netherworld."[51]

Hekate was equated to the Roman virgin goddess Bona Dea (*the good goddess*). Hekate and Bona Dea are both associated with snakes, knowledge of pharmakeia and healing and both are named explicitly as virgin goddesses. The genuine identity of Bona Dea was considered an initiatory secret, and the knowledge of her true name was closely guarded.

Bona Dea was linked to the worship of Hekate, Demeter, Ceres as well as to Medea, and many other goddesses. Based on the available evidence it is conceivable that Hekate was somehow associated with this Roman cult.

49 Thracian Magic, Mishev, Avalonia, 2012.
50 The Cult of Bendis In Athens And Thrace, Janouchová, 2013.
51 Macrobius, quoted in Bona Dea, Brouwer, 1989.

Brimo

"The maiden daughter of Perseus, Brimo Trimorphos"[52]

Brimo was a name given to a Thessalian goddess of the underworld. Her name was invoked and used in conjunction with that of Hekate from the fifth century BCE, and was also given as an epithet for Persephone, Demeter and Kybele. Brimo can be translated as *terrifying*.

In the Orphic Gold Tablets, Brimo is used as a name for a goddess forming a trio with Demeter and Persephone[53] and is most likely a reference to Hekate, who usually completes the Eleusian trio. If this is so, then it opens up interesting avenues for speculation about Hekate's role at Eleusis.

7 - THE TRIANGLE FOUND AT PERGAMON DATING TO CIRCA 3RD CENTURY CE.

We are told that Brimo gives birth to Brimos at the climax of the ceremonies of Eleusis, which is most often interpreted by contemporary scholars as Persephone giving birth to Iacchos, her son and the primary male torchbearer of Eleusis. If the Brimo of Eleusis is Hekate, then this echoes the role of Bendis giving birth to Sabazius in the Thracian legends. Both Sabazius and Iacchos are equated to Dionysos. In the Mysteries of Samothrace Sabazius was

---

52 Lycophron, Alexandra, 3rd century BCE, trans. Mair, 1921.
53 Pherae tablet 27, circa 4th century BCE.

worshipped alongside Hekate-Brimo[54] providing additional strength to the argument that Hekate, not Persephone, was the Brimo of Eleusis.

The PGM equates Hekate to Brimo, and it is a title used for Hekate on defixiones. The ceremonial triangle which forms part of a curious set of magical tools found at Pergamon, depicting Hekate at the three corners, names her as Brimo. The name is also used in the context of katabasis, a function associated with Hekate, as well as with Orpheus. The mysteries of Eleusis, were according to some ancient writers, established by Orpheus, the Thracian mystic.

Medea, in addition to invoking Hekate, also invokes the goddess as Brimo in the Argonautica[55].

Despoina

Despoina (*Lady*) was an Arcadian goddess associated with fertility, and sometimes said to be the daughter of Demeter with Poseidon. She was linked to the Eleusinian mysteries, and her real name, according to some records, could not be revealed to non-initiates.

Nevertheless, Aeschylus specifically calls her Despoina-Hekate.[56] Despoina is also given doorway and gateway attributes usually reserved for Hekate. Despoina was additionally used as a title for Hekate at Didyma, where Hekate was venerated at the gates of the Temple of Apollo, as well as in Colophon – another city in Ionia.

Demeter and Persephone

Demeter, Persephone and Hekate form a formidable trio of goddesses synonymous with the Mystery Cults of Greece, especially at Eleusis. The three goddesses each maintained their own separate identities were also conflated with one another. Hekate is equated with Persephone, and also with Demeter. It is possible that some of the conflations were due to

---

54 See Ancient Greek Divination, Johnston, 2009.
55 Argonautica, Apollonius Rhodius, 3rd century BCE, trans. Seaton, 1912.
56 Fragment 216, Aeschylus, 5th century BCE, trans. Weir Smith, 1926.

misunderstandings due to the goddesses' close relationship at major cult centres such as Eleusis, Selinunte and Samothrace, and frequent depictions of them together.

Tempting as it is to speculate that Hekate's triplicity is somehow linked to the connection between Demeter, Persephone and Hekate, there is no evidence to support this. If there were a connection, three-form images of Hekate would be expected to somehow reflect this connection, which they don't. Historical triple images of Hekate always shows three similar, often identical women, even when they are holding different objects.

All three are depicted with torches, and although Hekate is more often shown with two torches, this is not exclusively so. All three are also associated with the poppy, the modius (grain measure) and grain. Persephone and Hekate are both shown with the pomegranate, they are both named as daughters of Demeter and Zeus, and until Persephone's abduction they are both described as virgin goddesses.

Also see: *The Wandering Goddess, Hekate at Eleusis.*

Diana

> *"In Nemi Diana/Artemis was venerated as a goddess of the crossroads, as a triple goddess, trivia, and as such had several functions. She was a nature deity, ...but also of the moon and the darker sides of nature, and she was also venerated as a protector of women and childbirth"*[57]

Diana's cult became one of the most loved and wide-spread cults of the Roman Empire. Hekate and Artemis are both persistently equated with Diana, just as they are with one another.

In Aricia Diana shared the title of *Trivia* with Hekate, giving her a three-fold nature. Horace named her as *Diva Triformis* and Catulus (149–87 BCE) named her as *Diana Trivia*.

The triple form of Diana was not confined to Nemi. A fresco in the House of Livia on the Palatine Hill shows a sanctuary with a monument believed to be a baetylic (meteoric) stone, shaped like

---

57 Diana and Her Followers, Molteson, in From Artemis to Diana: The Goddess of Man and Beast, 2009.

the omphalos at Delphi. The depiction is accompanied by the heads of a boar, goat and stag which indicate that this is a sanctuary of Diana-Hekate. A depiction on the wall behind the stone depicts three small female figures, believed to be Diana-Hekate, holding torches surrounded by large trees.[58]

8 - COIN SHOWING DIANA NEMORENSIS: DIANA, HEKATE AND SELENE.

Diana's most famous cult centre was on the shores of Lake Nemi (Aricia), about 40 kilometres from Rome. At this volcanic lake, which Virgil named *Speculum Dianae* which means *The Mirror of Diana*, the goddess was worshipped continuously for at least a thousand years. The legendary *Rex Nemorensis* (King of the Woods) served the goddess here as both Priest and Guardian of the temple. The Nemoralia, the famous festival of Diana which started at Lake Nemi, lasted for three days, during the mid-August period (13th to 15th). The poet Ausonius remarks in his *Idyll*, that the Ides of August is dedicated to Hekate of Latonia [Leto]:

"Sextiles Hecate Latonia vindicat Idus."[59]

These dates are also associated with Hekate at her temple in Lagina, Caria.

At the feast of the Nemoralia lights were floated out onto the lake by devotees. This widespread festival was adopted by the later Roman Catholics and became the *Feast of the Assumption of the Virgin*

---

58 Sanctuaries of the Goddess of the Hunt, Poulsen, From Artemis to Diana: The Goddess of Man and Beast, 2009.
59 See Ausonius, Idyll 5.23

Mary. Some contemporary worshippers honour Hekate on the 13th or the 16th of August as a likely continuation of this feast.

Evidence for Diana's association with Artemis suggests that it started before the Roman era, as the Etruscans were already in part Hellenised before they settled in Italy. If this is the case, it accounts for the varied depictions of Diana, showing her like the huntress depictions of Artemis, as well as in the form of the Ephesian Artemis and the Lady of the wild animals, *Potnia Theron.*

The Etruscans are best known as being associated with the Tuscany region of Italy, but new evidence (including DNA) suggests that they had their origins in Anatolia. If this is so, then some of the religious views held by the Etruscans may have travelled directly from Anatolia, or other regions such as Thrace, to Italy long before the Greek and Roman influence.

Etruscan society had social views related to the role of women which were significantly different from that of the Romans and Greeks. This frequently led the latter to believe that the Etruscans were outrageously promiscuous. Women were given much higher social status in Etruscan society, for example mothers, rather than just fathers, were named on graves.

Diana and Hekate both continue to be associated with the practice of magic and witchcraft. Diana is, for example, the goddess of *The Aradia, or the Gospel of the Witches* by Charles G. Leland, a text which had a monumental, but sometimes overlooked, influence on the development of initiatory Wicca and subsequent Goddess and Pagan traditions of the 20th century. The first part of *The Charge of the Goddess,* which is one of the key texts of Gardnerian Wicca, is taken nearly verbatim from this 1899 text:

> *'When I shall have departed from this world,*
> *Whenever ye have need of anything,*
> *Once in the month, and when the moon is full,*
> *Ye shall assemble in some desert place,*
> *Or in a forest all together join*
> *To adore the potent spirit of your queen,*
> *My mother, great Diana. She who fain*
> *Would learn all sorcery yet has not won*
> *Its deepest secrets, them my mother will*
> *Teach her, in truth all things as yet unknown.*

And ye shall all be freed from slavery,
And so ye shall be free in everything;
And as the sign that ye are truly free,
Ye shall be naked in your rites, both men
And women also: this shall last until
The last of your oppressors shall be dead"[60]

Leland's work is part of a long history of Diana being associated with the survival of paganism and magic in Italy. Here are a few examples:

- 1576: Bartolo Spina wrote of witches gathering at night to worship Diana in his work, *Quaestio de Strigus* (*"An Investigation of Witches"*).
- 1647: Peter Pipernus wrote *De Nuce Maga Beneventana & De Effectibus Magicis* (*"Six Books of Magic Effects and of the Witch Walnut Tree of Benevento"*) of Diana.
- 1749: Girolamo Tartarotti published a book called *Del Congresso Notturno Delle Lammie* (*"Of the Nocturnal Meeting of Spirits"*) which declared that *"The identity of the Dianic cult with modern witchcraft is demonstrated and proven"*.

Diana's worship spread throughout the Roman Empire. In Britain, for example, there is evidence for Diana's worship during the Roman era, including inscriptions[61] and engraved gemstones dating to between the second-and fourth-centuries CE in the south of England and Welsh borders. Diana found a foothold in Britain and centuries after the Roman Empire ceased to exist stories of Diana were still being told and passed down successive generations. Diana became the *Goddess of Witches*, and the *Faerie Queen* and was linked to the practice of magic, superstition and the occult. But where there are stories of Diana, there are whispers of Hekate – and like Diana, Hekate appears as the Faery Queen in Scottish folklore[62]:

"In Scottish lore, Hekate was often equated with the Faery Queen of the Unseelie court, Nicneven, who dwelt in the mountain Ben Nevis…"[63]

The continuous association of Diana with witchcraft, together

---

60 The Aradia, Leland, 1899.
61 For examples see Roman Inscriptions in Britain 138, 316, 1126, 1209 ,2122, 2174
62 Also see Hekate wears Tartan!, Rankine, Hekate; Her Sacred Fires, 2010.
63 Digging Deeper, Carding, The Faerie Queens, 2012.

with the conflation of Diana with Hekate most likely contributed to some of the associations Hekate has with witchcraft today.

Enodia

"'Enodia' expressed Hekate's connection with roads –
specifically places where three roads meet." [64]

Enodia is the name of an ancient goddess, associated with the underworld and roads, who was worshipped in Pherai, Thessaly, alongside Zeus, before the fifth century BCE. Her name translates to *'in-the-road'*. Worship at Pherai may have started out-of-doors and predated the building of the sanctuary, which is why it is difficult to establish a foundation date for the site. However, the more than 3500 finds linked to this sanctuary attests that it was in regular use over a long period of time. Many of the figurines deposited at the site represent animals including bulls, snakes, dogs and horses – animals which are all also associated with Hekate.

From Pherai Enodia's name spread to other parts of the Greek world. She was worshipped in Larissa (Thessaly), Macedonia and Athens. Although Enodia may originally have been a separate goddess, her cult became synonymous with and indistinguishable from that of Hekate.

In Hippocrates' work Hekate-Enodia is named as being associated with the nocturnal attacks of ghosts and bad dreams (nightmares). Under this name she was also frequently named as being associated with the souls of the dead[65], and witchcraft.

Dogs were sacrificed to Enodia, and it may also be through this divine fusion that dog-sacrifices came to be associated with Hekate. Purificatory and scapegoat rituals frequently featured dog sacrifices, and it is important to note that these practices were performed in the names of several deities, not just that of Hekate.

Some of the more sinister ideas associated with Hekate such as ghosts, dog sacrifices and hostile witchcraft can be found prominently in the cult of Enodia. Nevertheless, when Enodia was included as one of the Olympian Twelve Gods her association with

---

64 Hekate Soteira, Johnston, 1990.
65 Restless Dead, Johnston, 1999.

ghosts and magic was not always highlighted.

In addition to being used as an epithet for Hekate, the name Enodia was also occasionally used for the goddesses Artemis and Persephone.

As a title Enodia was linked to Hekate since at least the fourth-century BCE, but not exclusively.

Also see: *The Wandering Goddess, Hekate of Thessaly.*

Selene

From the second century BCE the Moon Goddess Selene became increasingly syncretised with Hekate. In the *Greek Lyric Fragments*, we find *"Artemis is Selene"*, and this idea continued into the much later PGM. Completing the trio is Hekate.

9 - DETAIL OF ENDYMION AND SELENE, BY SEBASTIANO RICCI 1713,
CHISWICK HOUSE, LONDON

By the fifth century CE Nonnus was confident enough to write:

*"O Selene, driver of the silver chariot! If thou art Hekate of
many names ... if thou art staghunter Artemis ..."* [66]

Hekate is also referred to and equated to Mene, one of the fifty daughters of Selene. Mene was the name of the daughter who presided over the months, which were calculated by the phase of the Moon. This group of goddesses were so closely associated with

66 Dionysiaca, Nonnus, 5th century CE, trans. Rouse, 1940.

each other that on occasion they were considered entirely interchangeable. Kotansky emphasises this, writing that:

> *"By the time of the writing of the Greek Magical Papyri, in fact, Artemis-Hekate-Selene-Mene-Persephone were so intimately intertwined that any differentiation between them as archetypal moon goddesses and earthly, netherworld figures was impossible."*[67]

Isis

In the *Metamorphoses* Hekate is mentioned as one of the many names of the Greco-Egyptian Mother Goddess Isis. The same text ascribes long lists of qualities to Isis, many of which are also attributable to Hekate.

> *"I am she that is the natural mother of all things, mistress and governess of all the Elements, the initial progeny of worlds, chief of powers divine, Queen of heaven! the principal of the Gods celestial, the light of the goddesses: at my will the planets of the air, the wholesome winds of the Seas, and the silences of hell be disposed; my name, my divinity is adored throughout all the world in divers manners, in variable customs and in many names...*
>
> *...to others Bellona and Hecate and Rhamnusia..."*[68]

However, the *Metamorphoses* names many goddesses as being Isis, reflecting a very particular religious perspective, where all the names refer to the same deity and as such it is not that surprising to find Hekate listed. Furthermore, Isis' cult was a popular one and fused with that of many other Greek and Roman goddesses. However, Hekate and Isis had many points of commonality and became merged into Isis-Hekate. Jackson discusses one example of such an amalgamation in her book *Isis*:

> *"Magic is a major aspect linking Isis to Hekate. There is a bronze statue in Rome that depicts Hekate wearing the lunar crown of Isis, topped by lotus blossoms, and carrying a lighted torch in each hand. The statue is dedicated to Hekate and Serapis from someone who was saved by them from an*

---

67 Antiquity and Humanity: Essays on Ancient Religion & Philosophy, Kotansky, 2001.
68 Metamorphoses, The Eleusinian and Bacchic Mysteries, Taylor,1891.

unnamed danger. Both Isis and Artemis are shown carrying a torch as is Torch-bearing Hekate who illuminates the secrets of the underworld.[69]

This is not an isolated example. Isis-Hekate was shown on coins, including lead tesserae from Memphis. Minted during the Roman period one such example depicts Isis-Hekate with three faces, crowned with a horned crown, next to the Apis bull and another smaller human figure – possibly a daimones. Isis had acquired the horns during her own conflation with the cow-headed Hathor, and Hekate was often described as being bull or cow-headed. The uraeus-serpent also appears on coins showing Isis-Hekate, again highlighting the serpent symbol shared by both goddesses.

Isis-Hekate similarly appears on intaglios (engraved gemstones) in triple form, holding serpents, swords and torches, items associated with Hekate.

10 - STATUE OF HEKATE HOLDING A CHILD, WITH A DOG NEXT TO HER.
IN THE ARCHEOLOGICAL MUSEUM SOFIA, BULGARIA

The two goddesses are also both depicted as Mother Goddesses, holding a child. Isis is shown holding her son Horus (or Harpocrates), in both seated and standing positions. Hekate is likewise shown holding a child, likely the baby Dionysos (Sabazius),

---

69 Isis: Eternal Goddess of Egypt and Rome, Jackson, 2015.

though it is possible that it might also represent Apollo or Zeus, as there are hints connecting her to the birth of both these gods (albeit not as their mothers). One extant example of this can be found in the Archaeological Museum Sofia, Bulgaria (see fig.10).

11 - PLANTAE PEDUM, WITH ADDITIONAL MAGICAL MARKINGS, ON THE STEPS OF THE TEMPLE OF HEKATE, LAGINA, TURKEY (ANCIENT CARIA, ANATOLIA)

The carving of feet onto the steps of the Temple of Hekate in Lagina may have been due to contact with the Cult of Isis. The practice of carving *Plantae pedum* as ex-votos at temples was specific to initiates of Isis, and subsequently spread around the Roman Empire alongside her cult. Outside of Egypt Osiris became Serapis, the companion of Isis. Their child Horus, became the god Harpocrates, associated with secrets.

There is evidence for Serapis' presence at the Temple of Hekate in Lagina, suggesting that a small sanctuary to Serapis stood at the site. This, combined with numerous inscriptions from other sites linking Isis-Hekate and Hekate with Serapis, and depictions on crystal talismans showing Hekate with Harpocrates shows that Hekate and Isis' connection went deeper.

The Egyptian collection in the *National Archaeological Museum of Athens* features a bronze statue of Isis entitled *Isis-the-Magician*. This image, which shows Isis with three faces. is likely a Hellenic depiction inspired by Isis' conflation with Hekate.

As an interesting aside, Jackson[70] notes that Isis became associated with dogs outside of Egypt. Isis' temple in Rome showed an image of Isis on a dog, as well as an image of Isis with

---

70 Isis: Eternal Goddess of Egypt and Rome, Jackson, 2016.

a dog beneath her throne. Outside of Egypt processions honouring Isis were frequently led by a priest of Anubis wearing a jackal mask.

12 ISIS THE MAGICIAN, NATIONAL ARCHAEOLOGICAL MUSEUM OF ATHENS.

Trio of Fates: The Erinyes

"In fact Hekate appealed to the later imagination more as an infernal power than as a lunar; she borrows her whip and cord from the Furies..."[71]

The *Erinyes* (or Furies) are depicted as three unpleasant looking women, sometimes robed in black. They are not part of the heavenly gods of Olympus. Instead they dwell with Hades and Persephone alongside the spirits of the dead. The primary function

---

71 The Cults of the Greek States, Farnell, 1896-1909.

of the Erinyes is to uphold natural balance, protect strangers and firstborn children, and to punish oath-breakers. They are primordial forces of nature.

The goddess Hekate in her triple form and the Erinyes, in addition to both being shown as three women, also share a remarkable number of important symbols. If there is an unknown syncretisation between Hekate and the Erinyes, this may provide additional clues to Hekate's three-form nature.

The Erinyes hold torches, swords, whips – and sometimes spears and snakes, all of which are objects the three-fold Hekate is also depicted with. The tools wielded by the Erinyes represent natural balance and justice. If there is a connection between the implements of the Erinyes and those of Hekate, then the same meaning and purpose could be assigned to Hekate's tools, which are after all identical.

13 - THE REMORSE OF ORESTES (1862) BY WILLIAM-ADOLPHE BOUGUEREAU (1825-1905).

In the Sudas,[72] the Erinyes are described as *Aei Parthenos* (*Eternal virgins*). This was to ensure that they would be incorruptible and that their powers would not be affected by bribes. Hekate is also described as a Virgin Goddess, and given the titles of both Kore and Parthenos.

Both Hekate and the Erinyes are described as being crowned

---

72 Byzantine Greek lexicon, 10th century CE.

with the coils of wild serpents. Von Rudloff highlights this connection saying that the "...*portrayal is reminiscent of the Erinyes, as Aischylos reputedly first described them...*"[73]

Physis

Physis is a goddess who may have been derived from Hekate, representing a lower aspect of the Feminine Divine, represented by Hekate, in the *Chaldean Oracles*.

> *"Boundless Physis is suspended from the back of the goddess [Hekate]."*[74]

According to the Oracles, Physis represented the moon as well as the functioning of the material world, which the theurgists sought to rise above. She was associated with earthly daimones who were considered to be deceptive, but she herself was not evil. The Oracles advise the theurgists to avoid Physis:

> *"Do not invoke the self-manifesting image of Physis! Do not look at Physis! For her name is like Fate!"*[75]

Physis was described by the early fifth-century CE Greek bishop Synesius as the mother of daimones.[76] In this he was drawing on the *Chaldean Oracles*, which stated:

> *"Physis persuades us to believe that the daemones are pure, and that the products of evil matter are propitious and good."*[77]

EPITHETS

There are hundreds of epithets associated with Hekate. Epithets are like surnames, generally added to that of the deity, but in some instances used instead of the primary name the deity is known by. Epithets are frequently employed in hymns and invocations, and provide both scholars and devotees with insights into the nature of a deity.

It is useful to consider the different reasons epithets may have

---

73 Hekate in Ancient Greek Religion, Von Rudloff, 1999.
74 Chaldean Oracles, 2nd century CE, from Hekate Soteira, Johnston, 1990.
75 Chaldean Oracles, 2nd century CE, from Hekate Soteira, Johnston, 1990.
76 Hymn 5, Synesius, 5th century CE.
77 Chaldean Oracles, 2nd century CE, from Hekate Soteira, Johnston, 1990.

been given to Hekate:

- Syncretisation with another deity, where the cult of Hekate merged with that of another deity. Examples include *Isis-Hekate, Hekate-Selene, Artemis-Hekate, Diana-Hekate*.
- Related to a specific cult role held by the deity. For example, *Hekate Kourotrophos*, where the epithet describes something about the function fulfilled by the deity.
- Honorific titles, earned by the deity or given to them to emphasise something powerful about them. *Hekate Soteira* (Saviour) was used at locations where Hekate was said to have contributed to safeguarding a city or its people.
- Epithets can be descriptive, recording something of the appearance of the deity. *Hekate Phosphoros* (light), describes the goddess manifesting as (mysterious) luminous light.
- Epithets may indicate a link to a particular location. *Hekate Propylaia* (by the gate) is a reference to the placement of shrines to the goddess in gateways.
- Polyonymy, the use of many names for the same thing. A good example of this can be seen in the Metamorphosis[78] where the names of dozens of goddesses, including Hekate, are said to simply be other names for Isis.

Hekate has hundredsof epithets attributed to her at different times, and in different places, during her long history of worship. With a thriving international cult today new attributes and with them new epithets continue to emerge.

There are several websites dedicated to gathering together Hekate's historical epithets, together with evidence for their use. In particular see the websites of *Sara Neheti Croft, Renee Olson* and the *Covenant of Hekate* for examples. [79]

The following table provides a short list of just some of the many titles associated with Hekate.

---

78 Metamorphoses Book 11.47, Apuleius, C2nd CE.
79 There are several online projects working to gather all the known names, notably wicketicons.blogspot.co.uk/2013/04/hekates-many-names-part-1-of-3.html by Sara Neheti Croft, and byherfires.blogspot.co.uk/2014/02/names-and-epithets-of-goddess-hecate.html by Renee Olson. Also see www.hekatecovenant.com for the website of the Covenant of Hekate. Also see the blog by Mat Auryn, http://www.patheos.com/blogs/matauryn/2017/07/19/many-epithets-hekate/

Epithet	Meaning
Angelos	Messenger
Dadophoros	Torchbearer
Enodia	In the Road
Epipurgidia[80]	On the Tower
Chthonia [81]	Of the Earth / Underworld
Kleidouchos	Key-bearer / keeper
Kore	Maiden
Kourotrophos	Child's Nurse
Kynegetis	Leader of dogs
Lampadephoros / Lampadios	Bearer of a lamp
Mastigophorous	Whip-bearer
Melinoe	Possibly 'quince-coloured'. a yellow colour associated with death, or 'dark-minded'
Meter Theon	Mother of the Gods
Parthenos	Virgin
Pege Psychon	Source of Souls
Perseian	Daughter of Perses
Physis	Nature
Phosphoros	Light / luminous light
Propolos	Guide / Companion
Propylaia	Before the Gate
Soteira[82]	Saviour
Skylakitis	Protector of Dogs
Tauropolos	Bull-faced
Trimorphos, Triformis	Three-formed
Trioditis	Three-roads
Trivia	Three-ways

---

80 A reference by Pausanias to a statue of Hekate in Athens.
81 A title shared with Demeter and Gaia.
82 A title shared with other deities – including Artemis and Athena, and Zeus (Soter). Sports Games, the *Soteria* were held in different locations, including Delphi, in honour of Soteira, or sometimes Kore Soteira. It is used for Hekate in places she was attributed with protecting a city, and also in the Chaldean Oracles.

The Wandering Goddess

"...night-wandering Hekate..."[83]

Historians continue to piece together the silent history of the Greek Dark Ages (circa 1100-700 BCE) and the mysterious, culturally, and scientifically advanced Mycenaean and Minoan civilisations which preceded it. We have no real evidence for Hekate before the early Archaic Period (circa 800-700 BCE), but we do know that during this period her worship appears to be already well established in some regions.

There are many debates aimed at determining which region Hekate was originally from. It is possible to argue that Hekate originated in Asia Minor (especially from Caria in Anatolia), or that she is Thracian, hails from Thessaly, or that she was Attic or more specifically Athenian. Scholars have, and will continue to debate the matter as new evidence and different ways of thinking surface.

Hekate makes her literary debut in Hesiod's *Theogony* which was written only a few decades after the end of the Greek Dark Ages. In it, Hesiod provides an overview of the Titanomachy[84] as well as the first cosmology of the gods. Hesiod was writing about gods who preceded his writing, and as such Hekate was not a new deity to him. Rather, she is recognised as being a Titan whose previous status and rulership was acknowledged by Zeus. This gives Hekate pre-Archaic Greek, rather than non-Greek, origins.

---

83 Argonautica, Apollonius Rhodius, 3rd century BCE, trans. Seaton, 1912.
84 The Theogony is the only account of the war against the Giants to survive. At least one other did exist, known as the *Titanomachy* or the *Epic Cycle*, however unfortunately only very small fragments of it survives.

Today Greece, or *Hellas*, is a defined area of land in the southern part of the Balkan peninsula, at the crossroads of Asia, Europe and Africa. We speak of Greece as being the cradle of Western civilisation, but where was the historical Greece? Macedonia, Bulgaria, France, Southern Italy, Sicily, parts of Turkey bordering onto the Aegean sea, Syria, Egypt and parts of North Africa; and briefly parts of modern Pakistan and Afghanistan were all once part of the Greek Empire.

14 - DETAIL OF HEKATE TRIFORMIS, WITH THREE NYMPHS IN THE LOUVRE. DATE UNCERTAIN, BUT EITHER 188 BCE OR 389 BCE. FROM GREATER SYRIA/ PHOENICIA. LIKELY AN EX-VOTO AS IT BEARS A DEDICATION OF THANKS FROM FLAVIUS GERONTIUS.

Several of the most eminent Greek philosophers were from geographical areas outside of what we think of as Greece today. For example:

- Empedocles - Agrigento, Sicily (Italy)
- Parmenides – Campania (Southern Italy)

- Anaxagoras – Anatolia (Southern Turkey)
- Pythagoras – Anatolia (Southern Turkey)

These philosophers are all considered to be quintessentially Greek, even though they were all from outside the borders of mainland Greece. Likewise, if Hekate is shown to have roots outside of mainland Greece, this does not automatically make her non-Greek.

This aim of this chapter is to introduce a selection of locations at which Hekate was historically worshipped, with the hope of illustrating the diversity of reverence, as well as interesting similarities, and curious practices which are usually overlooked.

"...wandering through the heavens..."[85]

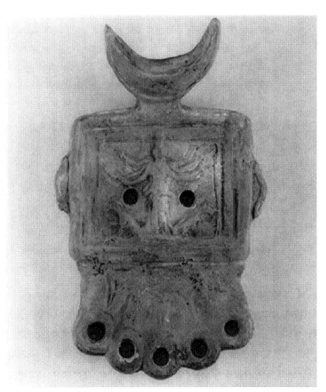

15 - OIL LAMP BELIEVED TO BE FROM ASIA MINOR DEPICTING HEKATE TRIFORMIS, FLANKED BY TWO DOGS. DATED LATE FIRST OR EARLY SECOND CENTURY CE. DIGITAL IMAGE COURTESY OF THE GETTY'S OPEN CONTENT PROGRAM.

---

85 Chaldean Oracles, C2nd CE, trans. Johnston.

MINOAN CRETE

The island of Crete, the largest of the Greek Islands today, was home to one of the earliest advanced civilisations in the world, the Minoans. The Minoan culture flourished between 2000BCE and 1400BCE, they developed writing and birthed the legends of King Minos, the Minotaur and Theseus (founder of Athens). Scintillating snippets of information provide possible links between Hekate and Crete. According to Herodotus, the Carians were believed to be of Minoan descent. Ancient Caria in Anatolia, home to The Temple of Hekate in Lagina, is believed by some scholars to be the homeland of Hekate due to the prevalence her cult had in the region.

> *"Of these, the Carians have come to the mainland from the islands; for in the past they were islanders, called Leleges and under the rule of Minos, not (as far as I can learn by report) paying tribute, but manning ships for him when he needed them. Since Minos had subjected a good deal of territory for himself and was victorious in war, this made the Carians too at that time by far the most respected of all nations."*[86]

Eileithyia, who was, like Artemis, equated to Hekate, also had a presence on Crete. Homer noted that this birth goddess was worshipped in a cave on the coast, and his work enabled archaeologists to find the remains of the shrine centuries later.

> *"What was more natural than to find a tablet at Knossos recording the despatch of a jar of honey to Eleuthia at Amnisos? Eleuthia is a known form of the name Eileithyia, the goddess of child-birth."*[87]

The Minoans produced the figurines we now know simply as the Minoan Snake Goddesses, images which bear a striking similarity to Hekate. However, it often comes as a surprise that the familiar image we have today of the *Minoan Snake Goddess* was an informed, but creative reconstruction by Sir Arthur Evans and his team.

Fig. 16 shows what the figurine looked like before restoration.

---

86 Hdt. 1.171, Godley translation.
87 The Decipherment of Linear B, Chadwick, 2014.

16 – THE FAIENCE FIGURE BEARING A SNAKE-LIKE OBJECT FOUND IN THE PALACE OF KING MINOS AT KNOSSOS. FROM THE BOOK THE PALACE OF MINOS, ARTHUR EVANS, 1921

17 - RECONSTRUCTED 'SNAKE GODDESSES' FROM THE TEMPLE OF KNOSSOS, MINOAN CRETE. LEFT IMAGE SHOWS FIG.16 ABOVE CREATIVELY RESTORED. THE IMAGE OF THE RIGHT IS OF ANOTHER SNAKE GODDESS FIGURE FOUND AT KNOSSOS, ALSO RESTORED. (WITH THANKS, PECOLD, FOTOLIA)

What the figure originally held in her other hand, what the face and headdress looked like and what the original purpose and symbolism of these figurines were are unknown. After reconstruction, the figurine becomes the recognisable figurine, shown in Fig.17 on the left. This is the popular image widely venerated by devotees in the Goddess Spirituality and Pagan revival movements today, as an ancient image of the Divine Feminine.

A further likely connection between Crete and Hekate can be found in the writings of Pausanias. He noted that Theseus founded a temple to *Artemis Soteira* following the slaying of the Minotaur[88] on Crete. Soteira (*saviour*) is a title frequently applied to Hekate and used to indicate that the goddess provided protection.

18 - SECTION OF THE FRIEZE FROM THE TEMPLE OF HEKATE, LAGINA.
IN THE ISTANBUL ARCHEOLOGICAL MUSEUM, TURKEY

Hekate was also equated to Diktynna the Cretan Virgin Goddess associated with hunting and fishing. To escape the advances of King Minos, who fell in love with her, she threw herself into the sea. Rescued by fishermen she was taken to the island of Aegina, where it is likely her cult continued as that of the goddess *Aphaia*. Aegina, was also recorded as being the site of an important Mystery cult dedicated to Hekate. Like Diktynna, Aphaia was equated to Artemis and also to Britomaris, all of whom are associated with dogs.

88 See Description of Greece, Pausanias, 2nd century CE, trans. Jones, 1918.

HEKATE AT LAGINA AND STRATONICEA

(near present-day Yatağan, Turkey – Ancient Caria, Anatolia)

The Temple of Hekate at Lagina, Caria, Anatolia was the last major temple built during the Hellenistic period. The temple was constructed on the site of an older settlement, which may have included an earlier temple. Lagina is the largest known temple which was dedicated entirely to Hekate and is famous for being the site of a key-bearing procession. In this procession, a key was carried by a young girl along the *Sacred Way*, an 11km road which connected the temple at Lagina to the nearby city of Stratonicea. Unfortunately, we don't have reliable information on the purpose of the ceremony. Johnston writes that:

> *"None of our sources explain what it was supposed to accomplish, but if it took its name from a key that was carried, then that key must have been of central importance - it must have been used to lock or unlock something significant."* [89]

Johnston further explains that although we don't know what the key opened, the number of inscriptions naming the festival indicates that it was a significant festival. We can speculate that it was the key to the city, the key to the temple at Lagina, or the key to another (unknown) precinct. Considering Hekate's ability to traverse between the worlds of the living and the dead, it is conceivable that the key opened the way to some form of ritual katabasis. At Lagina, the goddess Hekate was given the epithet *Kleidouchos* (key-bearer), so it is also possible that the young girl who carried the keys in the procession represented the goddess in the ceremony.

The friezes, which once decorated the temple, depict scenes which chronicled events which were significant at Lagina. Interpretation of the friezes is however incomplete, and some aspects of them appear to be unique to Caria.

North: The frieze from the north portion of the temple depicts the war against the Amazons. It shows a meeting between the Amazon and Greek warriors, with Hekate being the central figure sanctioning a pact. The position of her body in this particular frieze

---

89 Restless Dead, Johnston, 1999.

has been interpreted as being indicative that while she brought the sides together and sanctioned the pact, she sided with the legendary female warriors of Anatolia.

East: The eastern frieze depicts scenes from the life of Zeus, including a version of his birth in which Hekate takes the role of midwife. She assists the goddess Rhea in swaddling the baby and protecting it from his father Kronos' paranoid madness.

West: The western side shows a version of the war against the Giants. Like that of the famous friezes of Pergamon, it depicts Hekate as fighting on the side of Zeus.

South: The south side shows a selection of Carian deities gathering for a feast. This has been interpreted as a gathering for the Hekatesion or another significant festival.

Here it is interesting to note that the front of the temple (East) depicted the birth of Zeus and the back his battle and victory over the Titans. These are pivotal points in Greek religious history, Zeus' birth and his victory in the battle which enables him to ascend to the throne. At both these points, Hekate is present. Both these themes are also found in the *Theogony* more than 500 years before.

Hekate assists in childbirth:

> *"And the son of Cronos made her a nurse of the young who after that day saw with their eyes the light of all-seeing Dawn. So from the beginning she is a nurse of the young..."*[90]

And Hekate decides who wins in battle:

> *"And when men arm themselves for the battle that destroys men, then the goddess is at hand to give victory and grant glory readily to whom she will."*[91]

> KARIA.—**TEMPLE NEAR STRATONIKEIA.**—A large temple of Hecate was found last year in Caria, near the ancient Stratonikeia (Eski Hissar). Hamdi Bey, the director of the museum at Constantinople, has been carrying on excavations. He has secured about 160 ft. of the sculptured frieze complete, and has repaired the road to the coast ready for its shipment. A member of the *École Française* has been invited by him to assist him, and the results will be published by the School.— *Athenæum*, Oct. 1.

19 – 1893 ANNOUNCEMENT IN THE AMERICAN JOURNAL OF ARCHAEOLOGY ETC, VOL. 8.

90 The Theogony, circa 8th or 7th century BCE, Hesiod, trans. Evelyn-White, 1914.
91 The Theogony, circa 8th or 7th century BCE, Hesiod, trans. Evelyn-White, 1914.

The friezes were taken from Lagina in the late 1800's and are on display in the *Archaeological Museum of Istanbul* in Turkey. In a curious twist, the exhibition is near to where a Temple to Hekate Phosphoros once stood when Istanbul was the ancient city of Byzantium. In recent years there has been a renewed interest in both Lagina and the nearby city of Stratonicea from archaeologists.

20 - A SMALL BRONZE HEKATE ICON DISCOVERED AT LAGINA, CIRCA 200 BCE.

A small bronze icon showing Hekate in a form similar to that of Artemis of Ephesus was found during early twenty-first century excavations at Lagina. The goddess is depicted as standing on what is believed to be the stern of a boat, the rest of the ship may have been made from wood or another material which has long since perished. In the Chaldean Oracles, there is a reference to Hekate as holding *"the helm of the All"* which Ronan suggests that this hints at the conflation of Hekate with Isis, as the latter is frequently depicted with a rudder and ships.[92]

Depictions of Aphrodite in the same region shows her with the same decorated pillar-like torso. This suggests that all three goddesses, i.e. the Ephesian Artemis, the Carian Aphrodite and Hekate, were influenced by an earlier and probably local cult. Another surviving example of Hekate depicted on the stern of a boat can be seen in a fragment of a Roman oil lamp, found in the temenos of a temple of Demeter and Persephone, near Bodrum, Turkey (ancient Halicarnassus) and now in the British Museum collection.

In the Hellenistic period, Hekate was given titles which included *megiste* (greatest), *epiphanestatē thea* (most manifest goddess)

---

92 The Goddess Hekate, Ronan, 1992.

and *saviour* (Soteira) in Caria. This according to Johnston suggests that she was the leading goddess of her own city and also that Hekate played the same roles in Caria as Kybele did for Phrygia, taking the part of a city goddess and benefactress[93].

21 - THE STOA OF THE TEMPLE OF HEKATE, LAGINA.

22 - MODEL RECONSTRUCTION OF THE TEMPLE OF HEKATE, LAGINA.
IN THE ARCHEOLOGICAL MUSEUM OF ISTANBUL, TURKEY

93 Restless Dead, Johnston, 1999.

THE CLASSICAL REVIEW.

METRICAL INSCRIPTION FROM LAGINA.

THE following inscription from Lagina, in Caria, was published by MM. Charles Diehl and Georges Cousin in the *Bulletin de Correspondance Hellénique* of the present year (xi. pp. 160 foll.) from a copy and an impression taken by themselves, and a copy of M. Benndorf :—

```
. . . . . . . . . . . . . . . . AT . . . . . . . . . . . .
    ΣΗΣΙΕΡΗΣ . . . . . . ΑΙΔΙΜΟΕΝΤΙΠΟΘΩΙ
    ΟΥΓΑΡΜΟΙΠΛΟΥΤΟΙΟΜΕΓΑ . Θ . ΟΣΑΜΦΙΜΕΜΥΚΕΝ
    ΔΩΜΑΠΕΡΙΣΤΙΛΠΝΑΙΣΛΑΜΠΟΜΕΝΟΝΣΤΑΜΙΣΙΝ
5   Ο . ΔΕΠΡΟΘΥΜΙΗΣΤΕΑΣΑΝΤΟΣΟΝ . . . ΟΝΑΡΕΤΗ
    ΕΥΣΕΒΙΗΝΙΕΡΗΝΕΣΤΕΛΟΣΕΙΡΓΑΣΑΤΟ
    ΠΑΝΤΑΔΕΣΕΙΟΘΥΩΡΟΣΟΣΟΝΣΘΕΝΟΣΑΧΗΝΕΣΣΙΝ
    ΕΛΛΑΧΕΝΕΜΜΕΝΕΩΣΟΜΠΝΙΑΚΥΔΑΛΙΜΗ
    ΚΑΙΤΕΣΟΙΑΡΗΤΕΙΡΑΝΕΜΗΝΑΛΟΧΟΝΜΕΝΕΘΗΚΑ
10  ΜΟΣΧΙΟΝΕΞΑΣΙΗΣΗΓΕΝΟΣΕΣΤΙΦΙΛΟΝ
```
NO. XIX. VOL. II.   U

```
    ΚΛΩΔΙΑΝΗΝΔΕΠΙΟΙΚΛΗΔΟΥΧΟΝΠΑΙΔΕΡΑΤΕΙΝΗΝ
    ΚΛΗΙΔΟΣΡΑΔΙΝΙΙΙΣΧΕΡΣΙΝΕΦΑΠΤΟΜΕΝΗΝ
    ΟΠΠΟΣΑΔΕΝΔΑΙΤΗΣΙΚΑΙΕΙΛΑΠΙΝΗΣΙΝΕΡΕΞΑ
    ΟΙΔΕΠΑΤΡΗΣΓΛΥΚΕΡΗΣΠΟΛΛΑΚΙΜΑΡΤΥΡΙΗ
15  . . . ΤΑΔΕΡΕ . ΑΣΑΜΟΙΣΘΕΝΟΣΩΠΑΣΕΝΟΙΑΛΙΠΕΡΝΗΣ
    . . ΜΑΣΕΚΑΙΤΟΝΣ . ΔΑΙΜΟΝΑΠ . ΕΙΟΙΙΝΗΝ
    . . . . . ΚΑΙΡΟΙΟ . . . . . . . Ο . . . . . ΤΕ . . . . . . . . . .
    . . . . . Α . ΣΠΑΛΛ . . . . . . . . . . . . .
```

The editors, in their cursive transcript, have made only a very slight and unsuccessful attempt to restore the text, although the poem is pretty enough to be worth making out. It is incomplete at the beginning and end ; but the surviving lines read evidently as follows :—

```
        . . . . . . . . . . . . . . . . at . θω .
        σῆς ἱερῆς [τιμῆς φ]αιδιμόεντι πόθῳ.
        Οὐ γάρ μοι πλούτοιο μεγά[ν](ὀ)[ρ]ος ἀμφιμέμυκεν
        δῶμα πέρι στιλπναῖς λαμπόμενον σταμίσιν·
5       ο[ὐ]δὲ προθυμίη σ(π)ε(ύ)σαντος ὅ(μι)[όφρ]ονα ῥέ(ζει)[ν]
        εὐσεβίην ἱερὴν ἐς τέλος εἰργάσατο.

        πάντα δὲ σεῖο θυωρός, ὅσον σθένος ἀχήνεσσιν,
        ἔλλαχεν ἐμμερέως, 'Ομπνια κυδαλίμη·
        καί τέ σοι ἀρήτειραν ἐμὴν ἄλοχον μὲν ἔθηκα
10      Μόσχιον, ἐξ 'Ασίης ἣ γένος ἐστὶ φίλον·
        Κλωδιανὴν δ' ἐπὶ οἱ κληδοῦχον παῖδ' ἐρατεινὴν
        κληῖδος ῥαδιν(α)ῖς χερσὶν ἐφαπτομένην·
        ὁππόσα δ' ἐν δαίτησι καὶ εἰλαπίνησιν ἔρεξα
        οἶδε πάτρης γλυκερῆς πολλάκι μαρτυρίη·
15      πάν]τα δ' ἐρε[ξ]α [ὅ]σα μοι σθένος ὤπασεν οἷα λιπερνής,
        καὶ] μά σε καὶ τ(ὴ)ν σ[οι] δαίμονα πει[θ]ο(μέ)νην.
        . . . καίροιο . . . . . . . . . . θ . . . . . τε . . . . . .
        . . . . α . σπαλα . . . . . . . . . .
```

In line 3 we have an echo of the opening of Pindar's first Olympian ode, ὁ δὲ χρυσὸς αἰθόμενον πῦρ | ἅτε διαπρέπει νυκτὶ μεγάνορος ἔξοχα πλούτου—, and of Homer's description of Circe's palace filled with her singing (*Od.* x. 227) : δάπεδον ἅπαν ἀμφιμέμυκεν. 'Ομπνια in line 8 is Hecate, whose temple at Lagina was very famous. It will be observed that the dialect is Ionic throughout. The date of the poem is hard to guess ; but the name Κλωδιανή points to the first Christian century at the earliest. A translation is often the best of commentaries, and therefore I append one here :—

——"with singular desire for thy holy worship. For around me echoes no palace of splendid wealth, gleaming with polished columns all about ; nor could my zeal, when I strove to do (or 'offer') what my heart desired, carry my pious devotion into effect. Yet thy priest, so far as we poor had power, received all dues infallingly, thou glorious Ompnia. Yea and I gave thee as priestess my wife Moschion, who is a dear daughter of Asia ; and Clodiana beside her, my sweet child, as thy key-bearer, grasping thy key with slender hands. And how great things I did in banquets and feastings, the record of my dear fatherland knows full oft. Yea, all things have I done, for a poor man, to the best of my power, so help me thou and the goddess that obeys thy will (*i.e.* Demeter and Persephone)——"

E. L. HICKS.

23 - METRICAL INSCRIPTION FROM LAGINA, BY E. L. HICKS IN THE CLASSICAL ASSOCIATION
THE CLASSICAL REVIEW, VOL. 2, NO. 9 NOV. 1888

67

Based on inscriptions found at the site, it is evident that the priesthood at Lagina was hereditary, and that the girls who carried the key in the official processions were from a particular priestly family. For example, in the preceding article in *The Classical Review, 1888,* the author provides a transcription of one inscription found at Lagina, together with his translation. This provides a unique and personal insight into life at Lagina, a small but precious window through to a time where the Priest's wife and daughter both served at the temple. For convenience here is a transcript of the translation:

> "…. *With singular desire for thy holy worship, For around me echoes no palace of splendid wealth, Gleaming with polished columns all about; nor could my zeal, when I strove to do (or 'offer') what my heart desired, carry my pious devotion into effect. Yet thy priest, so far as we poor had power, received all dues unfailingly, thou glorious Ompnia, yea and I gave thee as priestess my wife Moschion, who is a dear daughter of Asia; and Clodiana beside her, my sweet child, as thy key-bearer, grasping thy key with slender hands. And how great things I did in banquets and feastings, the record of my dear fatherland knows full oft. Yet, all things have I done, for a poor man, to the best of my power, so help me thou and the goddess that obeys thy will (i.e. Demeter and Persephone)…."* [94]

There is evidence that eunuchs also served at the temple in some capacity. It is not clear what role they held at Lagina, but the evidence shows that they were not present at this temple in the capacity of Hekate's priesthood[95].

Serapis, Isis and Feet

Archaeological evidence from Lagina reveals that the god Serapis also had a presence at this temple. A relief which may have formed part of the pediment of a small temple shows Serapis wearing a modius, the grain measure associated with agricultural deities. In Egypt the god Osiris was consort to the goddess Isis (Aset), but as her worship spread into Europe Osiris was replaced

---

94 Inscription from Lagina, translation by E.L. Hicks, 1888.
95 See Cybele, Attis and related cults, Vermaseren and Lane, 1996.

with Serapis. This Greco-Egyptian god is a syncretization of Osiris and Apis, the Sacred Bull of Memphis and son of the goddess Hathor. Serapis also took on some of the qualities of Hades and Dionysos. As discussed in an earlier chapter, the goddesses Hekate and Isis were conflated, and there are examples where Hekate replaces Isis entirely in inscriptions, becoming Serapis' companion. This may account for Serapis' presence at Lagina.

During a visit to the site in 2015 I was struck by the extent of pilgrim graffiti at the site, which included magical symbols, writing and numerous carved footprints. Frustrated that I was unable to find further information in the context of this temple, I embarked on my own research into the subject.

24 - EXAMPLES FOOTPRINTS (AND OTHER MARKINGS) ON THE STEPS OF THE TEMPLE OF HEKATE IN LAGINA, TURKEY. FOR AN ADDITIONAL EXAMPLE SEE: *MANY NAMED MOTHER OF THE GODS, DIVINE MERGERS, ISIS*

Giant footprints are venerated in India and Sri Lanka as being the footprints of the Buddha and are also frequently recognised as part of the cult of various goddesses, including that of the goddess Kali Ma in Kolkata, India. Likewise, giant footprints, measuring nearly a metre each, also feature at the Syro-Hittite temple *Ain Dara*[96]. This temple is believed to have been dedicated to the goddess Ishtar or Astarte and was in use in the period between 1300 BCE and 740 BCE. These giant footsteps, their original purpose being unknown, are significantly different from the human-sized *plantae pedum* at Lagina.

Feet were also carved as ex-voto offerings on the steps of temples of the goddess Isis in Egypt. This practice subsequently spread into the Hellenic world alongside the cult of Isis. One theory is that feet were carved in this way with the hope that this would allow the devotee to have continued attendance in the company of their deity.[97]

Examples of feet carvings, showing one small and one larger foot can also be found in the context of the cult of Artemis Lochia at Delos. Likewise, four sets of plantae pedum dating to around the second century CE have also been found in the context of a temple of *Isis Lochia* in Dion, a site which previously was dedicated to Artemis Eileithyia until it was usurped by the cult of Isis around the third or second century BCE[98].

The reason for the presence of *plantae pedum* at Lagina is unknown, and I have been unable to find any study documenting the carvings to date. Based on the photographs I took at the site in 2015 I would estimate that there are at least a dozen sets of feet, probably more. There are also additional single feet carvings. The quality of the carvings vary, and some are accompanied by other inscriptions and symbols.

It is most likely that the carvings are somehow connected to the presence of the god Serapis at the site, having travelled to Lagina from temples where he was venerated alongside Isis. It is

---

96 This temple is believed by some to be similar to the famous Temple of Solomon, but predates it by a few centuries.
97 Theban Desert Road Survey in the Egyptian Western Desert, Darnell & Darnell, 2002
98 See Footsteps in Stone: Variability within a Global Culture, Beyond Boundaries, Revell, 2017

also possible that the practice is linked to Hekate's association with Artemis, or her association with Isis.

Also see: *Many Named Mother of the Gods, Divine Mergers*

Agathos Daemon

Lagina was also home to a curious cult altar dedicated to the daemon of Leros, a benefactor of Lagina. Cult altars honouring the daemones of benefactors are not unique, but this one is peculiar as it implies that Leros was still alive when the altar was dedicated. This is highly unusual as such altars were usually created for the dead. The inscription is ambiguous as to whether the altar was dedicated to the wife; or the wife and husband team as one *Agathos Daemon*[99].

Hekate and Zeus Panamoros

At a cult sanctuary dedicated jointly to Hekate and Zeus Panamoros existed in the nearby city of Stratonicea. Here thirty boys from noble families were expected to process daily, dressed in white and carrying boughs in their hands, singing hymns to Hekate and Zeus.[100] Equality meals were offered as part of the cult of Zeus Panamoros. For this, food was presented on a communal table, and everyone, regardless of social status, was invited to participate on an equal basis.

In some later texts the goddess worshipped with Zeus Panamoros is named as Hera. This suggests that the goddess was viewed as the consort of the god in this location.

Also see: *Symbols of Her Mysteries, Paeans-Songs for the Goddess.*

HEKATE AT ANTIOCH

(present-day Antakya, Turkey/ nr.Syria border)

Antioch was a prosperous place during the Hellenic and Roman periods and went on to become one of the most significant

---

99 See Notes on Sacred Laws, Rigsby,2009
100 Roman Festivals in the Greek East: From the Early Empire to the Middle Byzantine Era,Graf, 2015.

places for Christianity during the Roman era. It is sometimes referred to as the cradle of Christianity. Peter evangelised the first Pagans to Christianity there, and Paul's first mission was to Antioch, where his converts were the first to be named specifically as 'Christian'. Christianity and the older religions of the region co-existed here for several centuries, but by the time Emperor Julian visited in 362 CE the presence and influence of the pagan religions had been greatly reduced.

Antioch was also home to an underground temple dedicated to Hekate which could be reached only by descending 365 steps. The temple was constructed and dedicated by Emperor Diocletian (244-312 CE). Hints of secrecy, combined with the number of steps in the staircase, suggests that it may have been associated with an initiatory or otherwise Mystery related cult.

THE RELIGIOUS ANTIQUITIES OF ASIA MINOR : THE GODDESS OF ANTIOCH AS HEKATE.

25 – THE PHOTO ABOVE IS FROM A 1911 ARTICLE BY RAMSAY ENTITLED 'SKETCHES IN THE RELIGIOUS ANTIQUITIES OF ASIA MINOR' PUBLISHED IN THE ANNUAL OF THE BRITISH SCHOOL AT ATHENS, VOL. 18. THIS SMALL, 15CM HIGH MARBLE STATUE, FROM ANTIOCH DATES TO THE ROMAN PERIOD AND SHOWS HEKATE IN TRIPLE FORM.

HEKATE AT EPHESUS

(near present-day Selçuk, Turkey)

> *"An Ephesian tradition relates that Hekate was admitted to Ephesos only after she agreed to assume the dress of Artemis."*[101]

Long before the building of the famous temple which became one of the *Seven Wonders of the Ancient World*, the site where the Temple of Artemis of Ephesus stood was considered sacred ground. Evidence shows that the site had been in use since at least the Bronze Age (3200-1000 BCE) when according to Callimachus an Amazonian temple occupied the site. This bronze age temple was destroyed by floods during the archaic period and then rebuilt around 550 BCE at the expense of the King of Lydia.

This second temple burned to the ground during an arson attack in 356 BCE. According to legend, this happened on the night of Alexander the Great's birth. It was said that the goddess Artemis was unable to save her temple as she was away attending to the future leader's birth. The temple was rebuilt once again, with the resulting temple becoming one of the best-known buildings of the ancient world. It was the only temple dedicated to a goddess which became one of the Seven Wonders of the Ancient World.

It remained in use until 401 CE when it was finally destroyed.

26 - VISITING THE RUINS OF THE TEMPLE OF ARTEMIS OF EPHESUS IN OCTOBER 2015.

---

101 The Mother of the Gods and a Hellenistic Bronze Matrix, Reeder, 1987

Today very little remains visible of this once magnificent place, the ruins of which lie on the outskirts of what is today Selçuk, in Turkey. One pillar constructed by the excavation team from debris found at the site stands as a strange and miserable reminder of what once was. What is left of this once famous temple is today adorned with wild birds and turtles, perhaps a fitting sanctuary to remind visitors that Artemis is the protectress of animals and the Lady of the wild beasts.

27 - GREAT ARTEMIS OF EPHESUS, SELÇUK MUSEUM OF EPHESUS, TURKEY.

The pillars which once adorned the temple are said to have been taken from Ephesus and incorporated into the famous Hagia Sophia, in Istanbul. Among these is believed to be the now famous weeping or wishing column, where visitors queue to make a healing petition.

The Artemis worshipped at Ephesus is pointedly different from the Hellenic Artemis, enough to consider them separate goddesses regardless of their shared name. The Ephesian Artemis, unlike Artemis the virgin huntress, shares many commonalities with the cult of the Phrygian Mother Goddess, Kybele. The pillar-like body of the Ephesian Artemis is also found on other Near-Eastern deities. Likewise, the headdress depicting the walls of the city is similar to that worn by the Phrygian Kybele. At Ephesus, a hereditary Priestess served the goddess, together with a group of holy women, a group of virgin girls and the legendary Megabyzoi.

It is thought that the Megabyzoi may have been eunuch priests who served Artemis of Ephesus exclusively. The evidence for this is however inconsistent. The Megabyzoi may also have been the name of a family whose men served the goddess, and who were of royal Persian descent, again indicating a hereditary priesthood.

Hekate also had a significant presence at the Temple of Artemis of Ephesus, albeit in a slightly unusual place. Hekate's shrines are usually found by or in front of entranceways, but at Ephesus, her shrine stood behind the temple. Here visitors were warned to not gaze upon the image of the goddess made by the sculptor Menestratus:

> *"...and there is a Hecate of his at Ephesus, in the Temple of Diana [Artemis] there, behind the sanctuary. The keepers of the temple recommend persons, when viewing it, to be careful of their eyes, so remarkably radiant is the marble..."*[102]

It is conceivable that this statue was of Hekate as Phosphoros, the form in which Hekate appeared as luminous light. Could the unusual characteristics associated with the radiance of this statue have been the reason for Hekate's shrine having a place behind the temple, rather than by its entrance way? Maybe Hekate's shrine was part of an older temple or sanctuary, which survived or continued on after the historic fire.

Additionally, there is some evidence suggesting that the Temple of Hekate at Ephesus was in, or otherwise contained, an underground chamber or cave.

---

102 Natural History, Pliny, 1st century CE.

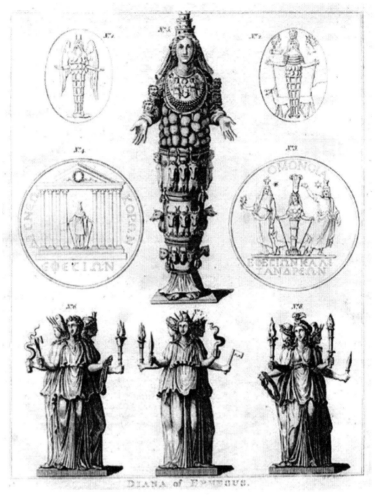

28 - DIANA OF EPHESUS, FROM CALMET'S FRAGMENTS 1800, SHOWN WITH IMAGES OF HEKATE IN HER TRIPLE FORM. IMAGE COURTESY OF ANTIQUEPRINTS.COM, WITH THANKS.

Hekate also had a presence in the city of Ephesus, which is about four kilometres from the Temple of Artemis. An image of Hekate formed part of the decorations on the *Gate of Persecution*, so named by Christians who misunderstood the image of Achilles dragging Troy around the city as being an example of the persecution of Christians.

> *"...The two principal bas-reliefs [from the Gate of Persecution] are said to be removed to Russia, though it is stated that one of them is in the possession of the Duke of Bedford: the third*

*represented a head of Hecate, with a serpent on the one side
and a bow on the other."*[103]

Today the gateway leading to the ruins of the Library of Celsus, in Ephesus, is home to a crude carving of Hekate in her triplicate form. The age of the carving is unknown, and it is one of several such amateur images around the city. It is a reminder that Hekate was honoured here, in her traditional gateway role, and possibly at a time when the city had already officially converted to Christianity.

29 – CARVING OF HEKATE IN A GATEWAY LEADING TO THE LIBRARY OF CELSUS, EPHESUS.

Hekate was also sometimes depicted in a form similar to that of the Ephesian Artemis. One such example is the small bronze from Lagina previously discussed, which is not an isolated example:

*"…we see three heads and shoulders and six hands, but the
lower part of her body is single, and closely resembles that of the
Ephesian Artemis. We have probably here a real reminiscence*

103 Ephesus and the Temple of Diana, Falkener,1862.

of this cognate cult, and as we find bulls' heads wrought on the idol of Ephesus, so here on the gem we see bulls at the feet of Hekate." [104]

Also see: *The Wandering Goddess, Hekate at Lagina and Stratonicea.*

Hekate in the life of Julian the Apostate

Julian the Apostate (331-363 CE) is remembered today for his attempt to return the Roman Empire to polytheism. His achievements and writings continue to inspire people today, but very few people seem to know that the goddess Hekate, at Ephesus, stood smiling with torches aflame (literally) at a pivotal point in the young Julian's life.

The celebrated philosophers Eusebius and Chrysanthius had the young Julian entrusted to them for their mentorship. Eusebius was adamant that the theurgists and their magic were to be avoided and was keen to illustrate the follies of these things to his student. When the theurgist Maximus invited him to attend a ceremony at the Temple of Hekate, Eusebius seized the opportunity. They arrived at the temple where they were welcomed by their host. Maximus proceeded by burning a grain of incense and reciting a hymn, and we are told that he:

"was so highly successful in his demonstration that the image of the goddess first began to smile, then even seemed to laugh aloud." [105]

The ceremony continued, and soon after the goddess' torches, according to accounts, spontaneously burst into flame[106].

Julian was so impressed by Maximus that he abandoned Eusebius and Chrysanthius as teachers, and studied with Maximus at Ephesus instead. In due course he received initiation into the Mysteries, we are told at Ephesus. An underground chamber is mentioned and it is assumed that at least part of the ceremony took place in the Temple of Hekate.

---

104 The Cults of the Greek States, Farnell, 1896-1909.
105 Lives of the Philosophers and Sophists, Eunapius, quoted from Trombley, 1995.
106 It is possible that some of what Julian witnessed was cleverly engineered temple special effects designed by inventors who followed in the footsteps of the famous Heron of Alexandria (10-70CE). Stage magic tricks powered by engineered gadgets were employed to keep worshippers in awe, and were closely guarded secrets.

Presently Julian became Emperor, and a few years later assumed the position of sole Emperor of the Roman Empire.

During his short reign, Julian made many daring social changes and is today primarily remembered for his attempt to restore Paganism to the Roman Empire. In 362 CE Julian issued his *Edict of Tolerance*, which aimed to give all religious traditions equal legal standing. Julian ordered the rebuilding and opening of temples which had been destroyed or abandoned, and also confiscated temples which had been (illegally) appropriated by wealthy citizens. Julian's Edict also allowed dissident Christian bishops to return to the Empire.[107]

His rule would not last. Julian died in 363 CE from either battle wounds or, according to some, injuries sustained by a Christian soldier in his own army who assassinated him. Maximus was executed soon after, and Christianity was restored as the official religion of Rome, to the exclusion of all others.

HEKATE IN CYRENE

(near present-day Shahhat, Libya, North Africa)

The city of Cyrene was the largest and most influential of the Greek cities on the Mediterranean coast of North Africa. Cyrene was founded on the advice of an Oracle by people from the island of Thera (Santorini) possibly as early as the seventh century BCE. It was established following instruction from the *Oracle of Delphi*. Herodotus[108] recorded that the inhabitants of Thera ignored the first Oracle. Many years passed, and when Thera experienced crop failure following a severe drought, the Oracle was consulted again. According to Pindar, the mythical founder of Cyrene, Battus approached the Oracle of Delphi for help with his stutter, when he was ordered to found the city of Cyrene.

> *"Seventeen generations later, when Euphamus' descendant Battus approached the Delphic Oracle, asking for help with his defective speech, he was ordered by the Pythia to found Cyrene, and did so successfully..."*[109]

---

107 See Lives of the Philosophers and Sophists, Eunapius,
108 See Herodotus' Histories IV.
109 The Song of the lynx: Magic and Rhetori, Pythian 4, Johnston, 1995

30 - DECAPITATED STATUES OUTSIDE THE TEMPLE OF DEMETER IN CYRENE, LIBYA.
LAPAS77 / SHUTTERSTOCK.COM

Hekate's temple in Cyrene stood inside the precinct of the temple of Apollo. In the second century BCE, a law was passed which prohibited the burning of incense at this Temple of Hekate, but no explanation is offered. The temple is believed to have been destroyed or at least severely damaged during the Jewish Revolt of the early first century CE, and we know from an inscription dating to 119 CE that it was ordered to be rebuilt suggesting continued worship and use in subsequent years.

Cyrene is also the location where Jason used the iynx wheel to cause Medea to fall in love with him. According to Pindar Jason did this to ensure that Medea would follow him back to Athens. **Also see:** *Symbols of Her Mysteries, Magic Wheels & Whirlings.*

HEKATE AT DIDYMA AND MILETOS

(near present-day Didim, Aydin Province, Turkey)

Didyma was home to a renowned oracle of Apollo, which was almost as famous as that of Delphi. Evidence from the site shows that there was also a connection to Zeus, Kybele and Artemis here, with a temple dedicated to the latter in her association with water.

Visitors to Didyma travelled via a Sacred Way, and the Milesian priests had to walk the route in full, praying and singing as they progressed.

"The Sacred Way was adorned with sculptures and shrines at various points along its length where the Molpoi were required to stop and sing Paeans (hymns). The first stop for the Molpoi was at the image of Hekate at the Sacred Gate of Miletos..."[110]

The Molpoi carried two mysterious cubic stones or *gulloi* in a procession, treating the stones as altars or icons. They garlanded and sprinkled it with wine in honour of Hekate. One of the stones was placed at the image of Hekate by the gates, and the other by the threshold of the temple, marking the beginning and end of the Sacred Way. They offered the first song of this famous procession at Hekate's shrine.[111]

31 - ANCIENT MILETOS, THE SACRED WAY.
DUZEN : SHUTTERSTOCK.COM

An inscription at Didyma dating to the first century CE attests to the worship of the goddess as *Angelos*, believed in this context to be a title of Hekate. The text states that a father and son financier team constructed an enclosure to Angelos, and also acted charitably in some other ways:

"And they also constructed the enclosure of Angelos at their own expense and set up an altar to Apollo. Because of the lack of water in the place, they dug new wells".[112]

Another inscription at Didyma records the cutting of stones for a *Phosphorion*[113], which may have been built for Hekate. Phosphoros

---

110 Miletos: Archaeology and History, Greaves, 2005.
111 See Hekate Soteira, Johnston, 1990.
112 The Colossian Syncretism: The Interface Between Christianity and Folk Belief at Colossae, Arnold, 1995.
113 See Didyma: Apollo's Oracle, Cult, and Companions, Fontenrose, 1988.

is however also a title given to two of Hekate's cousins, the god Heosphoros (morning star), and on occasion to the goddess Artemis.

A number of other finds related to Miletos highlight Hekate's presence there. She is named as Despoina, on a statue of a seated female found on the road connecting Didyma to Cape Monodendri. Hekate is also attested to in an inscription on a bowl decorated with rays found at Didyma. This bowl formed part of the Seleukid offerings of 288/7 CE[114].

Hekate was also known and worshipped in other parts of Ionia, and was closely linked to both the goddesses Kybele and Antaia throughout the region.

> *"Strabo tells us that Hekate is related to Cybele, and at Colophon Hekate was closely linked with the Mother Antaia."*[115]

Antaia or *Mater Antaia* was considered to the same as the goddess Demeter. She is the Ceralian Mother of Orphic Hymn number 40, in which the reason for her conflation with Demeter is evident:

> *"Ceralian [Antaia] queen, of celebrated name, from whom both men, and Gods immortal came;*
>
> *Who widely wand'ring once, oppress'd with grief, in Eleusina's valley found'st relief,*
>
> *Discovering Proserpine [Persephone] thy daughter pure in dread Avernus [Aides], dismal and obscure;*
>
> *A sacred youth while thro' the world you stray Bacchus [Dysaulos], attending leader of the way;*
>
> *The holy marriage of terrestrial Jove [Zeus Khthonios] relating, while oppress'd with grief you rove;*
>
> *Come, much invok'd, and to these rites inclin'd, thy mystic suppliant bless, with fav'ring mind."*[116]

---

114 See Didyma: Apollo's Oracle, Cult, and Companions, Fontenrose, 1988.
115 The Mother of the Gods and a Hellenistic Bronze Matrix, Reeder, 1987
116 Orphic Hymns, trans. Taylor, 1792.

In Colophon, black bitches and puppies were sacrificed to Hekate as Enodia in night-time rituals according to Pausanias.[117]

There was also a small island near Colophon which was dedicated to Artemis. Here it is said pregnant women swam with the belief that it would help them towards an easy birth.

HEKATE OF PAPHLAGONIA

(Black Sea coast, Turkey – Ancient Anatolia)

In his Argonautica, Apollonius Rhodius describes how the Argonauts land at the mouth of the river Halys, on the Paphlagonia coast. They were instructed to do this by Medea, who offered a ritual and sacrifice to the goddess there.

We are told that the details of the ritual are secret, but that the altar built to Hekate by the Argonauts on the beach there remained visible for several generations.

HEKATE IN COLCHIS

(present-day Georgia)

> *"In this river grows a reed, which is called leucophyllus, or the reed with the white leaf. This reed is found at the dawning of the morning light, at what time the sacrifices are offered to Hecate, at the time when the divinely inspired paean is chanted, at the beginning of the spring; when they who are troubled with jealous heads gather this reed, and strew it in their wives' chambers to keep them chaste. And the nature of the reed is such, that if any wild extravagant person happens to come rashly in drink into the room where it lies, he presently becomes deprived of his rational thoughts, and immediately confesses whatever he has wickedly done and intended to do."*[118]

Plutarch links this reed with Hecate, and in particular rites celebrated to her in the spring in or near the river Phasis. Colchis, the kingdom of King Aeetes the father of Medea, was on the banks of the same river. It was here where Medea was first taught the secrets of working natural magic by the goddess Hekate, and where

---

117 Description of Greece, Pausanias, 2nd century CE, trans. Jones, 1918.
118 Plutarch, Plutarch's Morals, vol. 5, trans. Goodwin, 1878.

Jason came to find her.

The reed is most likely *Arundo donax*, commonly known as Giant Cane or Giant Reed, and is native to Europe. Mixed with the seeds of another plant, *Peganum harmala*, this reed allegedly produces a concoction with psychedelic qualities similar to that of the South American ayahuasca brew. It is also believed by some that this mix is the soma of the Vedas.

Rutherford highlights that the purpose was to induce paean cries:

> *"The reed called leukophullos grows on the river (Phasis).*
> *During the mysteries of Hecate at the start of spring it is*
> *sought out at dawn for the purpose of inducing a paian-cry*
> *under its influence"*[119].

Giant Cane also appears in mythology as the reed that the panpipes of the god Pan were made from, which provides a connection to the Temple of Artemis in Ephesus, and the Temple of Hekate which stood behind it. It is here that the nymph Syrinx fled to preserve her virginity from the desire of the god Pan. It is said that she entered a cave by the Temple of Artemis where she hid in the reeds and that Pan in his desperate search for her cut the reeds. He then became convinced that Syrinx had metamorphosed into the reeds and thought that he killed her by mistake. He brought a bundle of the reeds to his mouth to kiss it, and as he did so his breath produced a sound on the reeds and his panpipes were invented.

Syrinx continued to take shelter in this cave, into which only virgins could enter. We know that Artemis was served by virgin nymphs and priestesses, and that virginity (in this instance, *virgo intacta*) was imperative to her cult. The cave may have been the same, or otherwise connected to the same underground chambers as those believed to have formed part of the Temple of Hekate at Ephesus.

Also see: *The Wandering Goddess, Hekate at Ephesus*

The river Phasis is known today as the Rioni.

---

119 Pindar's Paeans, Rutherford, 2001

The chanting and singing of paeans are often associated with Dionysos and Apollo, but also formed an important part of celebrations to Hekate.

Also see: *Symbols of Her Mysteries, Paeans – Songs for the Goddess.*

HEKATE OF RHODES

(Greek Island)

> *"Like the goddess of Lagina, Hecate was sometimes invoked as Soteira on Rhodes and Kos, and in Phrygia to the east"*[120]

Hekate was worshipped alongside Zeus on rock-cut throne sanctuaries in the island of Rhodes. It appears that Hekate was worshipped here as an invisible goddess with no form, though it is possible that removable icons or black stones were placed on the thrones to represent the deities.

The throne in Rhodes was dedicated to Hekate as *"hiera soteira euekoos phosphoros Enodia"*. (*Holy, Saviour, utterances, Light Bringer, of the Road*). Soteira, Phosphoros and Enodia are all titles of Hekate. Zeus was invoked with the title of *"Zeus Kronides Anax"* and depicted with a double axe, or labrys. The labrys is associated with Zeus at other locations, especially in Anatolia and frequently at sites where Hekate was worshipped alongside him – examples can be found at Lagina.

The labrys was further associated with an unnamed goddess who presided over the palaces of Minoan Crete, sometimes referred to as the *Lady of the Labyrinth* and therefore suggestive of a Minoan connection. Priests serving in Apollo's temple at Delphi were called the Servants of the Labrys.

It is possible that the Cult of the Empty Throne originated in Anatolia. Stratonicea and other parts of Caria were under the control of the Rhodians for a short period during the second century BCE. Empty thrones dedicated to Hekate and Zeus can also be found at Chalke, an island near Rhodes in the Dodecanese.

In Rhodes, the plant asphodel was offered to Hekate in the form of wreaths[121]. Asphodel was used as an expensive flavouring

---

120 Berg in Hecate: Greek or 'Anatolian?,1974
121 Suidas s.v. Asphodelos

for a particular local delicacy of roasted figs, making it a valuable offering. In other parts of Greece asphodel was associated with the dead and planted near tombs.

Evidence for the worship of Hekate Propylaia, alongside Hermes Propylaios and Apollo Apotropaios, can also be found at Rhodes. A large three-sided archaic styled sculpture of Hekate was found on the Acropolis of Rhodes, on which Hekate is depicted as wearing a polos headpiece.

Hekate is further allied to Hermes on Rhodes through a grave inscription dating to the second century BCE. The inscription was for a man described as a secretary who taught for more than fifty years.

> "…Now the plain of the Pious holds him,
> For Plouton and Kore have given a place to swell,
> Hermes and Hecate the torch bearer made him beloved,
> Of all, and supervisor of the mysteries,
> Because of his faithfulness."[122]

Rouse suggests that Hekate's title of Soteira (Saviour) might be connected to her role as a healing goddess, referencing, in particular, the rock-cut thrones in Rhodes and Chalce as examples:

> "...Hecate, indeed, with or without a consort, had sometimes a special power in this department. A throne cut out of the rock is dedicated to her in Rhodes as Saviour, and in the island of Chalce a similar throne is ascribed to her." [123].

Also see: *The Body of the Goddess, The Invisible Goddess.*

HEKATE OF ATHENS

> "I have heard it foretold, that one day the Athenians would dispense justice in their own houses, that each citizen would have himself a little tribunal constructed in his porch similar to the altars of Hecate."[124]

Aristophanes may have been exaggerating the popularity of porch shrines in Athens dedicated to Hekate in order to prove his point, but we know that Hekate was a very popular goddess in the

---

122 Lattimore; Rhodes, 2nd century BCE, Sources for Greek Religion. 2012
123 See Greek Votive Offerings, Rouse, 1902.
124 The Wasps, Aristophanes, 420 BCE, trans. anon.

ancient city. In addition to the household shrines, Hekate received worship and honours at numerous public sanctuaries and shrines. By the 1960's evidence for twenty-two Hekataia and Hekate-Herms have been found in the Agora during excavations[125].

32 - SANCTUARY OF HEKATE, IN THE ANCIENT AGORA, ATHENS.

The earliest known statue dedicated specifically to Hekate in Athens is a terracotta figurine of a seated goddess dated to the sixth century, with an inscription: "*Aigaion dedicated to Hekate*". This is believed to also be the oldest known depiction of Hekate.

According to Pausanias, the first statue showing Hekate as three-formed stood next to the *Temple of Nike* on the Parthenon in Athens.

> "*It was Alcamenes, in my opinion, who first made three images of Hecate attached to one another, a figure called by the Athenians Epipurgidia (on the Tower); it stands beside the temple of the Wingless Victory...*"[126]

Although the fate of the original icon described by Pausanias is unknown, three-formed images of the goddess became very popular in subsequent centuries.

> "*There was a great demand for small Hekataia in Athens at the end of the fifth and in the fourth centuries, and the influence of Alkamenes' recent work would not have been small.*"[127]

> "*It has generally been recognized that the representation of*

---

125 Harrison, Archaic and Archaistic Sculpture, 1965
126 Description of Greece, Pausanias, 2nd century CE, trans. Jones, 1918.
127 An underworld scene on a black-figured Lekythos, Karouzou, 1972.

> *Hekate in triple form is an Attic invention. Pausanias specifically names the Athenian sculptor Alkamenes as the first to portray the goddess in this way, and the triple Hekataia known from Attica have consistently outnumbered those from other sites. The finds from the Agora maintain this proportion.*"[128]

An excellent example of a Hekate-Herm believed to be from Athens shows a triple Hekate crowned with a polos on a pillar body. It is believed to date to the fifth or early fourth century and in the collection of the Benaki Museum, Athens.

The Triangular Shrine, in the Athenian Agora must be one of Hekate's most impressive shrines in the city, certainly one of the oldest. It is located at the crossroads outside the south-west corner of the ancient Agora, and is, as the name suggests, triangular in shape. Activity on the site is believed to date to around 700-800BCE, with the construction of the final triangular shrine dating to around 450 – 400 BCE. The shrine remained in use well into the Roman period. In addition to being at a crossroads, its proximity to the cemetery may indicate a connection to ancestor worship.

Another sanctuary or temple to Hekate in Ancient Athens stood at the site which is now home to the church of Saint Photini. This is located near the Temple of the Olympian Zeus and the Athens Gate. *Photini* means *Enlightened One* and this Saint is said to have been the first to proclaim the gospel of Christ.

33 - THE CHURCH OF SAINT PHOTINI, AS SEEN FROM THE ACROPOLIS.

---

128 Archaic and Archaistic Sculpture, Harrison, 1965

34 - TRIPLE HEKATE MARBLE, IN THE ACROPOLIS MUSEUM, ATHENS.

In Athens, Hekate was syncretised with the cult of the goddess Enodia, whose name became a favourite epithet used for Hekate. The Thracian Bendis, whose festivals became established in Athens around the fifth century BCE, may likewise have had a strong influence on Hekate in Athens.

Plutarch, critiquing the work of the fifth century BCE historian Herodotus' work, mentions a feast to Hekate:

> "*And professing to write more particularly and carefully of the affairs of Athens, thou dost not so much as say a word of that solemn procession which the Athenians even at this day send to Agrae, celebrating a feast of thanks-giving to Hecate for their victory. But this helps Herodotus to refel the crime with which he is charged, of having flattered the Athenians for a great sum of money he received of them.*"129

---

129 Plutarch, *De Herodoti malignitate (The Malice of Herodotus)*, trans. Bernardakis, 1893.

Plutarch appears to be using the name Hekate here to describe *Artemis Agrotera* (Huntress), who was celebrated on Agrae (Attica) where 500 goats were sacrificed to her yearly in thanksgiving for their victory at Marathon

Insights on how Hekate was understood in Athens can also be garnered from the way she was petitioned for assistance on defixiones. One first century CE example features a crudely drawn image of a triple formed Hekate, combined with various magical symbols. Hekate is invoked by name, alongside Hades, Persephone, the Fates, the Furies and Hermes to help with an issue concerning stolen property.

> *"Because there seemed no likelihood of public justice, the registering and transferring of the unknown thieves to infernal deities must mean that they, rather than human judges, will mete out the punishment."*[130]

Amongst the pleas, Hekate is asked to cut out the hearts of the thieves:

> *"...Lady Hekate of the heavens, Hekate of the underworld, Hekate of the crossroads, Hekate of the triple-face, Hekate of the single-face, cut the hearts of the thief or the thieves who took the items contained in this deposition. And let the earth not be walkable, the sea not sailable; let there be no enjoyment of life, no increase of children, but may utter destruction visit them or him."*[131]

A lead tablet believed to date the fourth century CE, and thought to be from the Athens or wider Attic region, also calls on Hekate and Hermes. The spell appears to be for a legal matter concerning a man and a woman, the latter probably a prostitute.

> *"......be bound before Hermes of the underworld and Hekate of the underworld. ... and just as this lead is worthless and cold, so let that man and his property be worthless and cold. And those who are with him who have spoken and counselled concerning me."*[132]

Hekate had numerous sanctuaries throughout the Attic region. Erchia, for instance, was home to a Sanctuary to Hekate where

---

130 Curse Tablets and Binding Spells from the Ancient World, Gager, 1992.
131 Curse Tablets and Binding Spells from the Ancient World, Gager, 1992.
132 Curse Tablets and Binding Spells from the Ancient World, Gager, 1992.

offerings were made to *Kourotrophos* (child's nurse) as Hekate[133]. Offerings were also made to her in Thoricus, a city of Southern Attica. Hesychius wrote that Hekate was worshipped by the title of *Propylaia* (at the gateway) at the Propylaea of the Acropolis of Athens.

The ancient goddess Eileithyia also had a presence in Athens according to Pausanias. Eileithyia may have been the name of an ancient birth goddess who was syncretised with Hekate and Artemis, or whose name was an epithet both goddesses were given at times.

> *"[At Athens] is a temple of Eileithyia, who they say came from the Hyperboreans to Delos and helped Leto in her labour; and from Delos the name spread to other peoples."*[134]

Pausanias goes on to say that three wooden statues of Eileithyia stood in her Athenian temple. Two of which he was told originated in Crete, while the third and oldest was brought from Delos. Considering the numerous examples where Hekate and Eileithya are thought to be same, it is interesting to note the use of three statues in this temple, especially with Athens being the likely location of the first three-formed images of Hekate.

There is some evidence that the Semnai (*'the dread ones'*), very ancient female divinities, worshipped in groups of two or three, were worshipped in Athens before the archaic period. These beings were sometimes equated to the three Erinyes, and may have influenced the early worship of Hekate in Athens. The last three days of the month were dedicated to the Semnai, who were sometimes believed to dwell in caves or other subterranean spaces. The Athenians held annual nocturnal torchlit processions in their honour.

HEKATE IN THERA

(Santorini, Greek Island)

In the third-century Artemidorus the Oneiromancer (dream interpreter) set up a statue to *Hekate Phosphoros* amongst his shrines

---

133 See Kourotrophos, Price, 1978.
134 Description of Greece, Pausanias, 2nd century CE, trans. Jones, 1918.

at Thera in the southern Aegean Sea. Alongside that of Hekate he also built altars to Priapus, the Dioscuri and the Samothracian gods on Thera, inscribing them with his verses.

There were three dedications carved into the rock to the left of the complex: an eagle for Zeus of Olympus, a lion for Apollo the Crown Wearer and a dolphin for Poseidon of the Sea. The inscriptions dedicate the votives both to the deities and the people of Thera. Hekate's altar was to the right, alongside that of Priapus.

> "... cut like steps into the rock, are statue bases for Hecate, whom Artemidorus tells us, "the rural people honor" and for Priapus, who himself says in his epigram that he, from Lampsacus, a city on the Hellespont, 'has come to Thera bringing imperishable wealth.'".[135]

The people of Thera, on the instruction of the Oracle of Delphi, celebrated Artemidorus by crowning him and setting up a memorial to him which they hoped would be remembered for as long as the stars shone, and the earth remained solid[136].

Another extant votive relief, dated to 200 BCE and believed to be from Thera, shows Hekate, with a dog and with two long torches in her hands, crowned with a polos. It is in the collection of the National Archaeological Museum in Athens.

A marble statue from Thera of a goddess holding a child may represent the birth goddess Eileithyia who elsewhere was conflated with Hekate or Artemis. She may also have had a sanctuary on the island.

HEKATE AT DELOS

(Greek Island)

Also see: *Theogony, Mother: Asteria*

When Hekate's mother flung herself into the ocean to escape the advances of Zeus, she became an island named Ortygia. Today Delos and the Sicilian Ortygia (Syracuse) both lay claim to the mythology associated with Ortygia, especially that of being the

---

135 Ancient Greek Religion, Mikalson, 2011.
136 See Greek Votive Offerings, Rouse, 1902.

birthplace of the Divine Twins, Artemis and Apollo.

In the straits between Delos and its neighbouring island, Rhenaia, there is an islet which was named by writers as being the *Isle of Hekate*. These rocks were sometimes called Rematiari after rheumatism, due to the island being regularly flooded and therefore constantly wet. It was also known as Psammite after the ritual cakes offered to Hekate.

> *"The Ancients held this Rock in great veneration, and consecrated it to Diana under the name of Hecate: for we read in the Suidas, that it was called the Island of Hecate, or Psammite, from the name of certain Cakes there offered in sacrifice to that Goddess."*[137]

35 - STONE CARVING AT ELEUSIS - SHOWING THREE IMPORTANT SYMBOLS ASSOCIATED WITH THE SITE: SHEAF OF WHEAT, POPPY AND MODIUS (GRAIN MEASURE)

HEKATE AT ELEUSIS

> *"... these goddesses [Demeter, Persephone and Hekate] stood for traditional values of stability and order, which in themselves produced fertility and promised a better life..."* [138]

Eleusis was the foremost centre of worship for the goddess Demeter and her daughter Persephone. It was an important and influential religious centre and one of the most celebrated of the

---

137 A Voyage into the Levant, Tournefort and Midwinter, 1741.
138 The Running Maiden from Eleusis and the Early Classical Image of Hekate, Edwards, 1986.

sites where the initiatory Mysteries were held. Eleusis was well-established before the *Homeric Hymn* dated to 650 BCE. Some scholars claim that the Mysteries of Eleusis predate the Greek Dark Ages and that the centre was already established and active during the Mycenaean era, with a potential foundation date of 1600-1100 BCE. The Thracian Orpheus was credited, in some sources, as being the founder of the Mysteries at Eleusis.

Hekate is frequently depicted alongside Demeter and Persephone, forming a trio of goddesses, who when shown together are synonymous with the Eleusinian mysteries. This is how they are depicted on reliefs found at Eleusis, on Attic red-figure vases with themes related to Eleusis, and in many other locations where the Eleusinian mysteries were influential. The three goddesses are also recurrently mentioned in literature as being associated with the mysteries at Eleusis. There can be no doubt that all three these goddesses were essential to Eleusis and the Mysteries celebrated there.

36 – THE CROSSED TORCHES IS ANOTHER IMPORTANT SYMBOL OF ELEUSIS.

At Eleusis, participants took vows of secrecy as part of their initiations through which they were oath-bound to not reveal the secrets of the Mysteries. They evidently valued the Mysteries of Eleusis enough to keep its secrets safe, as very little was ever revealed. Today it is possible only to make attempts at piecing together what we know with educated guesswork, intuition and creative thinking based on the evidence available. It is like trying to piece together a very large puzzle, with only a fraction of the pieces and no idea of what the end result is meant to look like.

The experience of being initiated at Eleusis was an important one for all participants, who spent lots of time and resources travelling there and preparing themselves through acts of purification and fasting. The public Mysteries were centred on this preparation and on the story of Demeter and her daughter Persephone.

The initiation rituals remain shrouded, and numerous works have tried to decipher and piece together what may have happened there. It is believed that initiates gained a different understanding of death and the afterlife through their experiences at Eleusis. With hints that the ritual had an element of katabasis, it is likely that it contained further aspects of the story of the descent and ascent of the goddess Persephone.

It is plausible that the teachings centred around concepts which highlighted the immortality of the soul, and taught that death (like life) was a transformation, a crossroads in life – rather than an ending. Similar beliefs are expressed on the Orphic Gold Tablets, and on tombstones elsewhere in the context of initiates of the Orphic Mysteries attributed to Orpheus.

37 - DETAIL OF A RELIEF SHOWING HEKATE WITH TWO TORCHES, ARCHEOLOGICAL MUSEUM IN ELEUSIS, GREECE.

Kykeon and Psychedelics

There are several theories centred around the idea that the Eleusinian Mysteries involved the use of a psychedelic or otherwise mind-altering drug as part of the Kykeon drink. Participants drank this drink, which the goddess Demeter also drank, ending their fast. Opinions on what it contained vary wildly and include the use of alcohol, magic mushrooms, ergot[139], and opium.

Hekate has a close association with herbal knowledge and use, and for this reason, I include an overview of the most prevalent theories here.

Ergot is a fungus which grows on some grains including wheat and barley. Ingestion of ergot causes ergotism (also known as *St. Anthony's Fire*) in which burning sensations are felt all over the body. It also frequently leads to loss of consciousness, uncontrolled hysteria, convulsions, gangrene, limb loss and death. For these reasons, the use of ergot at Eleusis is highly unlikely. There are no records hinting at of any of the above being the result of participation in the Mysteries.

Magic mushrooms' dosage is easier to control, and it is less likely to have induced such extreme side effects. However, there is no clear visible evidence of mushrooms as symbols at Eleusis, which makes the use of magic mushrooms unlikely.

The poppy was one of the symbols of Eleusis, and therefore the most likely to have been employed for its active ingredients in ritual. Poppy plants produce an enormous number of seeds, and as such became used as a symbol of fecundity. Hekate and Demeter are habitually depicted as holding, or otherwise decorated with, poppy heads in the context of Eleusis. Both goddesses are also shown with the modius (grain-measure) on their heads, indicating that they were agricultural deities, so the association with fertility would have been essential.

Poppies were well known for their medicinal use in the ancient world, the Mesopotamians referring to it as the *joy plant (Hulgil)* and it may have been in use in Greece and other parts of Europe as early as 3500 BCE. The Greeks used it as a sleep-inducing drug, to

---

139 A fungus that grows on grains.

relieve pain and for other medicinal purposes, and would have been aware of its narcotic properties.

The recipe for Kykeon is given in the *Homeric Hymn to Demeter*. In the hymn, Demeter explicitly turns down red wine, which would not necessarily exclude other types of alcohol. However as there is no mention of the Kykeon being fermented, it seems less likely. The description also does not make mention of any of the ingredients discussed above.

> *"Then Metaneira filled a cup with sweet wine and offered it to her* [Demeter]; *but she refused it, for she said it was not lawful for her to drink red wine, but bade them mix meal and water with soft mint and give her to drink. And Metaneira mixed the draught and gave it to the goddess as she bade. So the great queen Deo received it to observe the sacrament* [Kykeon]."

The soft mint is *Mentha pulegium,* pennyroyal, which was a popular flavouring ingredient in food. It was also well attested as an abortifacient, for gynaecological problems, and as a method of birth control by women wishing to prevent pregnancies.

Kykeon was ingested by initiates after a nine-day fast, as part of their preparation for participating in the Mysteries. It is interesting that Demeter explicitly turns down red wine, as this may indicate that it was somehow either sacred or taboo in the Mysteries and abstaining from it formed part of the pre-ritual fast. My presumption would be that red wine was sacred, especially considering the enigmatic involvement of the god Dionysos at Eleusis.

Ancient Eleusis

A small Doric temple dated to the second century BCE stood outside the greater entranceway to Eleusis. It acted as the first entranceway, after which visitors passed through the greater gateway of Eleusis. This propylaia has been attributed to both Artemis and Diana Propylaia. However, neither of these goddesses had a reason to have such a presence at Eleusis. Considering Hekate's role as Guardian of the Gate, and her association with purification, this temple is more appropriately attributed to Hekate or Artemis-Hekate.

The *Running Maiden of Eleusis* sculpture dates to circa 490-480 BCE. Edwards[140] interprets the image to be that of Hekate, based on the posture of the figure, the clothing and draping, which matches that of other Eleusian depictions of Hekate leading Persephone back from Hades.

> *"Hekate's dress, an open ungirt peplos, is characteristic of young girls. Vase paintings show that in the Early Classical period, and particularly in an Eleusinian context, this image of Hekate was standard..."*[141]

38 - THE RUNNING MAIDEN OF ELEUSIS, BELIEVED TO BE A DEPICTION OF HEKATE.

Hekate is shown in a pose implying movement or running in several instances. There is an example of this on a later Roman glass paste gemstone engraved with Hekate, holding two torches aloft, where she is shown in the same pose. The intaglio is dated to around 1-3 CE and is currently in the British Museum collection.

---

140 The Running Maiden from Eleusis and the Early Classical Image of Hekate, Edwards, 1986
141 The Running Maiden from Eleusis and the Early Classical Image of Hekate, Edwards, 1986

39 – ELEUSIS (2015), VIEW TOWARDS THE SEA WHERE INITIATES ONCE BATHED.

With the popularity of the Eleusinian Mysteries and the importance placed on it, it was, in due course, established at other locations. Bowden[142] shows that Demeter Eleusinia, the epithet given to Demeter at Eleusis, was also recorded in association with other later Mysteries, throughout Southern and Central Greece, Rome and in Asia Minor. This illustrates the popularity and importance of Eleusis but also raises questions about how, and indeed if, the centres were connected.

Hekate's role at Eleusis deserves a study of its own. There are so many mesmerising contradictions and tiny fragments of information hinting at some extraordinary things.

In Orphic texts, Hekate is sometimes named as the daughter of Demeter by Zeus, or the daughter of Rhea by Zeus, her son. This makes Hekate the sister of Persephone, rather than a distant relative. There are further hints that Hekate may have been an older Mother Goddess worshipped at the site, or that she was connected to the secrets of the Mysteries more intimately. Melinoe, a mysterious daughter, born to Persephone after Zeus rapes her (in the form of a snake or disguised as Hades) is also equated to Hekate.

The term *Orphic* was applied to many different texts associated with the Mysteries, possibly as a way of providing them with additional mystical kudos. Orpheus was credited as being the founder of the mysteries at Eleusis, as well as those of Hekate at

---

142 Cults of Demeter Eleusinia and the Transmission of Religious Ideas, Bowden, Mediterranean Historical Review, vol.22, 2007

Aegina. The Orphic Mysteries were also prevalent in Crete and in the South of Italy, where the Mysteries of Diana (in triple form, syncretized with Hekate) were celebrated. Unfortunately, many texts only survive in fragmentary form today.

Persephone's Abduction

The Abduction of Persephone, perhaps one of the most famous myths of the Greek world, took centre stage at Eleusis. The first version of the story was recorded in the seventh century BCE Homeric Hymn to Demeter. Here is a brief summary:

~ ~ ~

Hades, Lord of the Underworld, falls in love with the maiden daughter of Demeter, the Kore (Persephone). Knowing that Demeter would not give her consent, Hades conspires with Zeus, the girl's father, to kidnap Persephone. Hades successfully kidnaps Persephone, taking her into his kingdom to become his wife and queen. The Grain Goddess Demeter is distraught over the disappearance of her daughter and takes to wandering the earth:

> *"Then for nine days queenly Deo wandered over the earth with flaming torches in her hands, so grieved that she never tasted ambrosia and the sweet draught of nectar, nor sprinkled her body with water."*[143]

Finally, on the 10th day Demeter speaks to Hekate:

> *"But when the tenth enlightening dawn had come, Hecate, with a torch in her hands, met her, and spoke to her and told her news: "Queenly Demeter, bringer of seasons and giver of good gifts, what god of heaven or what mortal man has rapt away Persephone and pierced with sorrow your dear heart? For I heard her voice, yet saw not with my eyes who it was. But I tell you truly and shortly all I know."*[144]

Hekate then accompanies Demeter to Helios, who tells her that her daughter is with Hades. Hermes, the messenger god, travels to Hades and returns Persephone to her mother. However, Hades had persuaded her to eat a pomegranate seed, and as a result, she has to return to Hades for a third of every year. On her return,

---

143 Homeric Hymn to Demeter, C7th BCE, trans. Evelyn-White
144 Homeric Hymn to Demeter, C7th BCE, trans. Evelyn-White

Hekate embraces Persephone and becomes her companion[145] and her guide *'from that time'*, being both her preceder and follower[146].

~ ~ ~

This might seem like a contradiction, as it is not possible to be both preceding and following someone. Also, although Hekate has the ability to manifest in more than one body, which might account for this idea, she is not usually shown in triple form at Eleusis. By being both in front of and behind Persephone, Hekate takes the role of both protector and guide towards the Queen of Hades.

This role held by Hekate is strangely overlooked by many contemporary scholars. Persephone's journey is one of katabasis, travelling from the world of the living down into that of the dead, and back to the surface and the world of the living again. Hekate's role as her preceder and follower enabling Persephone's journey is not a simplistic role, rather it is as Johnston puts it:

"one of the most difficult and significant journeys imaginable."
147

Hekate's role towards Demeter is that of benevolent mediator. She intercedes and encourages Demeter to speak with Helios, who provides Demeter with the news she was seeking so desperately.

40 - DETAIL FROM A HYDRIA, SHOWING HEKATE (RIGHT) AS PART OF A SCENE DEPICTING THE DESCENT OF PERSEPHONE. CIRCA 340-330 BCE. SOUTHERN ITALY.
THE METROPOLITAN MUSEUM OF ART, NEW YORK

The story of Demeter's sorrow and search, and Persephone's journey was enacted as part of the yearly public Mysteries at Eleusis. It is likely that the roles of the various deities would have

---

145Hekate is also named as "the golden-shining attendant of Aphrodite." In the 6th century BCE poem Sappho or Alcaeus, Fragment 23.
146 See Homeric Hymn to Demeter.
147 Hekate Soteira, Johnston, 1990

been played by priests and priestesses in the ceremonies.

After many hundreds, maybe thousands of years, the Mysteries at Eleusis fell silent in around 392-395 CE. Some of its secrets may never be revealed.

HEKATE AT SAMOTHRACE

(Greek Island)

> *"The female side of the royal line was particularly devout to Dionysos, and Alexander's mother, Olympias, was well known for her exceptional loyalty to him. She was initiated into the service of Dionysos at Samothrace where the chthonic mysteries of Hekate-Brimo and her consort Dionysos/Sabazios were celebrated and the sanctuary was thereafter taken into Macedonia's protection."* [148]

Samothrace was home to the *Sanctuary of the Great Gods* and had a pantheon of deities which strongly resembled that of Eleusis, but sometimes with alternate names. Hekate was honoured at Samothrace as *Zerynthia* and was also associated with a cave in Zerynthos, on the east side of the island.

> *"Zerynthos, cave of the goddess to whom dogs are slain."* [149]

Olympias and Philip II, parents of Alexander the Great, met at their initiations at Samothrace, where she became his betrothed. Worship and celebrations at this sanctuary continued well into and beyond the Roman era. Nonnus wrote:

> *"Already the bird of morning was cutting the air with loud cries [in Samothrace]; already the helmeted bands of desert-haunting Korybantes were beating on their shields in the Knossian dance, and leaping with rhythmic steps, and the oxhides thudded under the blows of the iron as they whirled them about in rivalry, while the double pipe made music, and quickened the dancers with its rollicking tune in time to the bounding steps. Aye, and the trees whispered, the rocks boomed, the forests held jubilee with their intelligent movings and shakings, and the Dryades did sing. Packs of bears joined the dance, skipping and wheeling face to face; lions with a roar*

---

148 Ancient Greek Divination, Johnston, 2009.
149 Lycophron, Alexandra, 3rd century BCE, trans. Mair, 1921.

from emulous throats mimicked the triumphant cry of the
priests of the Kabeiroi, sane in their madness; the revelling
pipes rang out a tune in honour of Hekate, divine friend of
dogs, those single pipes, which the horn-polisher's art invented
in Kronos's days."[150]

The Sudas suggest that rituals were given to initiates at Samothrace which provided protection against particular types of danger. Among these was a ritual in which prayers would cause the feet of an attacker, presumably during warfare, to turn back. Likewise, the skills taught to initiates could cause storms to turn back, avert dangers on roads and also cause your enemy to hurt themselves as they approach, causing them to have to turn back.[151]

Worship at Samothrace went into decline after earthquakes in 200 CE, after which it was restored, but the cult went into decline with the rise of Christianity and activity officially ended in 400 CE. The temples fell after further earthquakes in around 600 CE.

HEKATE IN THESSALY

"The case for Enodia as a member of the Twelve Gods at
Pherai[152] is simple and straightforward. She replaces Artemis.
Enodia, although well-known throughout Thessaly, was
particularly venerated by the people of Pherai. She appears on
their coins, and is frequently called simply Pheraia, or the
Pheraian goddess, in literary sources. She is a combination of
Artemis and Hekate, with a dash of Alkestis thrown in."[153]

Enodia was worshipped as the city goddess of Pherai, a city in Thessaly, and was subsequently syncretised with Hekate, and became synonymous with her.

It is probable that Enodia is the source of Hekate's association with roads and crossroads, though they may have been conflated because they both already shared key attributes in common. Enodia certainly appears to be one of the primary sources for Hekate's association with witchcraft. Originally witchcraft would have been only a small part of the attributes associated with

---

150 Dionysiaca, Nonnus, 5th century CE, trans. Rouse, 1940.
151 See Sigma 79.
152 A city in ancient Thessaly.
153 The Altar of the Six Goddesses in Thessalian Pherai, Miller, 1974.

Hekate. It became more pronounced in later times and was frequently connected to the worship Hekate received in Thessaly.

> *'Of the famous witches in literature associated with Hekate, Erictho was a Thessalian witch, and Medea gathered her herbs there.'*[154]

41 - SILVER COIN MINTED IN PHERAE, THESSALY 369 -359 BCE SHOWING HEKATE-ENODIA WITH JEWELLERY, TORCH AND ON THE OBVERSE AN ARMED MAN ON HORSEBACK. PRIVATE COLLECTION OF A.S., WITH THANKS.

Thessaly was synonymous with magic to the extent that the term *Thessalian* was sometimes used to describe any type of magic by Roman poets[155] The small shrines Thessalian families used to set up opposite their homes for the sake of children may have had a tutelary and protective function. Similar practices are associated with the goddess Artemis, especially in the context of young girls, who were considered to be under her protection.

> *"The maiden daughter of Perseus, Brimo Trimorphos, shall make thee [Queen Hekabe] her attendant, terrifying with thy baying in the night all mortals who worship not with torches the images of Zerynthia [Hekate] queen of Strymon [in Thrace], appeasing the goddess of Pherai with sacrifice."*[156]

Also see: *Divine Mergers, Enodia.*

HEKATE OF THRACE

(present-day Bulgaria, parts of Greece & Turkey)

Orpheus the Thracian was one of the greatest mystics and spiritual teachers of the ancient world. He was the son of a Muse

---

154 Epodes, Horace, 30 BCE, trans. M Meyer.
155 Magic and Ritual in the Ancient World, Mirecki and Meyer, 2002
156 Lycophron, Alexandra, 3rd century BCE, trans. Mair, 1921.

and the King of Thrace, with some sources citing Apollo as his father. Through the work attributed to him, certain ideas and beliefs were transmitted as a living tradition for many centuries. Some of the work credited to Orpheus was likely the work of later authors, which none the less continued in the Orphic tradition spreading its philosophies through poetry. Orphic work informed many later philosophers and scholars, including Plato and Pythagoras. The Mysteries of Demeter and Persephone at Eleusis and that of Hekate at Aegina were all said to have been established by Orpheus. As previously discussed, the Thracian Bendis and Hekate were syncretised and widely believed to be the same goddess or equated based on the many qualities they have in common.

The cult of the goddess Phosphoros was well attested in the city of Kabyle[157] by the 3rd century BCE. Coins minted in the city show a female deity with torches and patera, symbols which were synonymous with the city in antiquity. [158] Phosphoros was also a name given to the Mother Goddess in Thrace[159] a role otherwise attributed to Bendis, or Bendis-Hekate in the region.

> "The presence of Phosphoros is also attested in Byzantion, where Bendis is usually identified either with Artemis or Hekate. On the other hand in Abdera, Bendis is associated with Hekate only. The reason for their association with Bendis is that the cults of Phosphoros and Hekate were accompanied by torch-lit night celebrations, similarly as in the case of Bendis in Athens. Additionally, the name Phosphoros means 'light-bringer' or 'torch-bearer' and is assigned to Artemis, Hekate and Eos. "[160]

Also see: *Divine Mergers, Bendis.*

The tombstone of Julia, daughter of a Nikias from Mesembria, dating to the second-century CE, provides a unique insight into how Hekate was viewed in the Black Sea region of Thrace during this period. The inscription expresses the idea of immortality

---

157 Thracian city, which was in what is now South-East Bulgaria.
158 Graeco-Latina Brunensia 18, 2013, 1 Petra Janouchová (Charles University, Prague) The Cult Of Bendis In Athens And Thrace
159 See Bilde 'Quantifying Black Sea Artemis' in From Artemis to Diana: The Goddess of Man and Beast, 2009
160, The Cult Of Bendis In Athens And Thrace, Janouchová, Graeco-Latina Brunensia 18, 2013.

through the act of becoming part of the goddess (apotheosis), merging with and becoming one with her upon death:

"I, the goddess Hecate, lie here, as you see. Earlier I was mortal, now, as a goddess, I am immortal and young forever."[161]

Mesembria was home to a temple of Demeter, at which images of Potnia Theron, as well as Artemis-Hekate, have been found. Bendis has also been equated to Hekate in the form she was worshipped at Neapolis and the Parthenos of the city there.

Also see: *Wandering Goddess, Hekate in Neapolis.*

HEKATE OF LYDIA

(Sart, near present-day Salihli, Turkey)

"Come, giant Hekate, Dione's guard, O Persia, Baubo Phroune, dart-shooter, Unconquered, Lydian, the one untamed..."[162]

Hekate was worshipped alongside Zeus at Sardis in Lydia, where she was depicted on coins during the first century CE. The Kingdom of Lydia was founded in around 1200 BCE and continued until 546 BCE when it became one of the most important cities of the Persian Empire. It became part of the *Roman Province of Asia* in 133 BCE.

The earliest known offerings resembling descriptions of Hekate suppers and dating to the sixth century BCE were found in Lydia, where they were buried outside the entranceway to homes. These offerings comprised clay vessels filled objects which typically included iron knives, jugs, pots and plates, together with the remains of puppy dogs. Several such burials have been found, but there is no indication as to why they were made or what their purpose was. Pausanias mentioned these sacrifices in Colophon, in Lydia, writing that:

"I know of no other Greeks ...who are accustomed to sacrifice puppies except the people of Kolophon; these too sacrifice a

161 Inscription, trans. Portefaix quoted from Wypustek's Images of eternal beauty in funerary verse inscriptions of the Hellenistic and Greco-Roman periods, 2013.
162 See PGM IV.2708-84, "Another love spell of attraction".

puppy, a black bitch, to Enodia [Hekate]. Both the sacrifice of the Kolophonians and that of the youths at Sparta are appointed to take place at night."[163]

42 - MASTUARA, LYDIA CIRCA 1ST CENTURY CE.
REVERSE - HEKATE TRIFORMIS, HOLDING HER WHIPS, DAGGERS AND TORCHES.
PRIVATE COLLECTION OF A.S. WITH THANKS.

Similar burials, dated centuries later, were found outside the gateway to the temple of Artemis in the same city, where the burials also included the remains of eggs. These offerings may have been apotropaic, and based on the context and available evidence it is possible that they were made for Hermes or Hekate, or both.

It is important to note that the puppy dog remains alone would not indicate Hekate, as dogs featured in many stories from the region. The name of an eighth-century BCE King of Lydia, Kandaulēs, can, for example, be translated as *dog-strangler*.

Also see: *Symbols of Her Mysteries, Dogs*

HEKATE IN BYZANTIUM

(also Constantinople, now Istanbul, Turkey)

It is probable that Hekate had an established presence in Byzantium from a time before the city was founded. Here Hekate was invoked by her title of *Phosphoros* by the local population for her help when Philip of Macedon (father of Alexander the Great) attacked the city in 340 BCE. Petridou summarises the account given by Hsych of Miletus:

---

163 Description of Greece, Pausanias, 2nd century CE, trans. Jones, 1918.

"Hecate, or so we are told, assisted them by sending clouds of fire in a moonless rainy night; thus, she made it possible for them to see clearly and fight back against their enemies. By some sort of divine instigation the dogs began barking[164], thus awakening the Byzantians and putting them on a war footing."[165]

There is a slightly alternative account of the attack, recorded by Eustathios. He wrote that Philip of Macedon's men had dug secret tunnels from where they were preparing a stealth attack. However, their plans were ruined when the goddess, as Phosphoros, created mysterious torchlight which illuminated the enemies. Philip and his men fled, and the locals subsequently called the place where this happened *Phosphorion*. Both versions attribute the successful defence of the city to the goddess as Phosphoros. In thanksgiving, a statue of Hekate, holding two torches, was erected in Byzantium soon after.

The support given by the goddess in battle brings to mind a line from Hesiod's *Theogony*:

"And when men arm themselves for the battle that destroys men, then the goddess is at hand to give victory and grant glory readily to whom she will." [166]

A torch race was held on the Bosphorus each year, in honour of a goddess which, in light of the above story, is likely to have been Phosphoros. Unfortunately, we have no evidence to clarify who the goddess the race was dedicated to was. Other than Phosphoros, it is possible that the race was instead held in honour of the Thracian Bendis, Ephesian Artemis or Hekate. All of which were also of course conflated with one another at times. Artemis and Hekate both share the title of Phosphoros. Bendis is never explicitly named in texts, but a torch race in her honour was held in Athens after her cult was introduced there in the fifth-century BCE. Likewise, torch-races took place in honour of Artemis.

There is also a theory that the name *Phosphoros* may have become linguistically jumbled due to a linguistic influence from

---

164 The barking of dogs have long been viewed as a sign that Hekate has arrived.
165 Divine Epiphany in Greek Literature and Culture, Petridot, 2016.
166 The Theogony, circa 8th or 7th century BCE, Hesiod, trans. Evelyn-White, 1914.

Thrace becoming *Bosphorus* in the process[167]. The Bosphorus is the narrow, natural strait connecting the Black Sea to the Sea of Marmara, separating the European side of Istanbul from the Asian side.

The goddess with two torches shown on coins of the time is unnamed. She is usually identified as Artemis but could equally represent Hekate.

43 - ARTEMIS-HEKATE AND CRESCENT WITH EIGHT-RAYED STAR ON THE BACK OF THIS BYZANTIUM COIN, THRACE. 1ST CENTURY BCE.

Star and Crescent

In Byzantium, the symbol of the upwards-pointing crescent moon and eight-rayed star (representing the sun) above it, was a symbol of Hekate, and sometimes Hekate-Artemis. The symbol may have indicated this goddess' connection with both the moon and the sun or a symbolic reference to Apollo (or Helios) as the god of the Sun.

The crescent and eight-rayed star were also sometimes used for other deities with a link to Persia and Anatolia. The crescent, with an eight-rayed star, was frequently used to depict the Babylonian goddess Ishtar and the moon god Sin.

44 – CONTEMPORARY FLAG OF TURKEY: CRESCENT AND STAR (WHITE ON RED)

Today a white crescent and five-pointed star feature prominently on the red flag of Turkey. There is no known

---

167 See Floss, *Ephesus After Antiquity: A Late Antique, Byzantine and Turkish City*, 1979.

historical connection, but the synchronicity of these two symbols used together, in the same region, thousands of years later is uncanny.

HEKATE AT DELPHI

Delphi was the home of arguably the most influential of the ancient oracles. The first known temple at Delphi was built in the seventh century BCE, and evidence suggests that the site was occupied, likely for religious use, from circa 1600 BCE. The deity of the Oracle of Delphi was Apollo, who took control of Delphi when he killed the Python of Delphi (a mythical serpent beast) for the Python's role in supporting the goddess Hera in her persecution of Leto, his mother.

45 – SCULPTURE OF THE OMPHALOS OF DELPHI WHICH CROWNED THE TOP OF THE 'DANCERS' COLUMN (RECONSTRUCTED). IN THE MUSEUM OF DELPHI, GREECE.

Evidence shows that the site was originally dedicated to the Earth Goddess Gaia, and later to her granddaughter Phoebe. Sometime during the Greek Dark Ages, Apollo, in turn, succeeded his grandmother, Phoebe, as the deity of the Delphic Oracle. Very little is written connecting Hekate to Delphi, but it would be an omission to ignore the so-called *Column of the Dancers*.

The Column of the Dancers is a colossal pillar which stood near the Temple of Apollo at Delphi. It was an ornate and highly symbolic monument topped with a statue of three women, on top of which was a tripod crowned with a replica of the omphalos stone. The three women, who appear identical, stood back to back around a central pillar in a posture which has been interpreted as dancing, but which could equally be indicative that they all once bore (unknown) objects in their hands.

The tripod was the seat of the priestess when she proclaimed the oracles of the god Apollo and was a significant symbol of Delphi. The omphalos was a conically shaped stone which was believed to be meteorite (*baetylic*) and similar-shaped stones were at the heart of the several cult centres in the Greek and Roman worlds. It represented the navel of the world in its centre. Like the tripod, the omphalos stone was synonymous with Delphi.

46 - THE 'DANCERS' OF DELPHI. IN THE MUSEUM OF DELPHI, GREECE.

The three female figures featured on the Column of the Dancers are nearly two meters high, and the monument when fully assembled stood at least 14 meters[168]. Considering the date given to the column of between 380 and 330 BCE, it was an enormous monument for its time. Its size alone would have given it prominence and importance at Delphi. For comparison, the columns of Apollo's temple were less than 12 meters in height,

---

168 This would be higher than four stories of a modern building.

which means that with its roof the column and the temple would have been of a similar height.

The notion that this column depicted anonymous dancing girls, or daughters of the first King of Attica, as suggested by some interpretations, seems unlikely. Alternative theories that the sculpture is meant to represent the *Graces* or *Charities* also does not fit with the posture and position of the three young women on the sculpture. Rykwert highlighted this and suggests that this image is not that of a group of unknown girls, but rather that it is more similar to depictions of Hekate:

> *"Some commentators wanted the women of the sculpture to be the Graces (who, however, usually turn toward each other), or the Charities. However, the back-to-back attitude is more characteristic of chthonic figures, as of the Hekate groups, for example."*[169]

In fact, the image strongly resembles Hekate. Three women, standing back to back, with their arms in positions which could indicate that they once held torches or other objects. They are each adorned with a polos, the headdress Hekate and other Anatolian goddesses are frequently depicted with. Although Hekate is more often shown with a longer dress, there are also numerous extant examples of Hekate with a shorter chiton.

The monument was a gift from Athens to Delphi, and in Athens we find Hekate being given the title of *On the Tower* by Pausanias describing the statue of Hekate which stood next to the temple of the Wingless Nike. There are also depictions of a Hekataia on pillars on coins from Lydia, and a depiction of Hekate on a pillar on a black-glaze ribbed vase dated 350-300 BCE now in the British Museum. This vase or *oenochoe* shows a single-bodied Hekate with two torches before an altar, behind which there is a pillar with a figure resembling a three-formed Hekate topping it. Hekate is also shown on a column in a painting found in the ruins of Pompei depicting the sacrifice of Iphigeneia.

Considering Hekate's association with Apollo's sister Artemis, her worship alongside Apollo at numerous locations, and her relationship with oracles, it should not be surprising to find her at

---

169 The Dancing Column: On Order in Architecture, Rykwert, 1998.

Delphi – indeed it should be expected. Hekate featured prominently at another celebrated Oracle of Apollo at Didyma, for example.

An oracle of the goddess Hekate in Abdera names Delphi in an oracle, saying that:

> *"The songs call (him) throughout fragrant Delos and around the high rocks of Parnassus the virgins of Delphi with bright headbands often set up a swift-footed chorus and sweetly sing with bronze voice."*[170]

The Pythia of Delphi fell silent circa 381 CE.

47 - REPLICA OMPHALOS. TEMPLE OF APOLLO, DELPHI, GREECE.

HEKATE OF THASOS

(Greek Island)

Hekate was worshipped on the island of Thasos at three significant gates, the *Maritime Gate*, the *Gate of Silenus* and the *Gate of Hermes*.[171] Wall decorations with depictions showing Hekate and Hermes which was discovered on Thasos were taken to the Louvre

---

170 Pindar's Paeans, Rutherford, 2001.
171 Restless Dead, Johnston, 1999.

museum in Paris during the late 1800's.[172]

Thasos was once part of Macedonia, and is in the Aegean Sea, not far from Samothrace.

HEKATE OF AEGINA

(Greek Island)

> *"Of the gods, the Aeginetans worship most Hecate, in whose honour every year they celebrate mystic rites which, they say, Orpheus the Thracian established among them. Within the enclosure is a temple; its wooden image is the work of Myron, and it has one face and one body."*[173]

Even though Pausanias wrote that the inhabitants of Aegina worshipped Hekate most, not much is known about her cult here.

The island was named as *Oenone* in antiquity, meaning the *Island of Wine* and was part of the Mycenaean world. This could indicate a connection to a vine cult, such as that of Dionysos. Oenone was also the first wife of Paris, who he left to pursue Helen of Troy. Her name can be translated as *wine woman*. She was the daughter of Queen Hekabe (*Hecuba*) and here the story goes into a strange and unexpected full circle. Hekabe was transformed, according to various ancient writers, into the attendant of Hekate or into a dog after she found out about the death of her husband and the fall of Troy. In some accounts, she committed suicide by hurling herself into the sea[174], and of course, the souls of suicide victims are amongst those said to be in Hekate's care. In other accounts, she is transformed into a dog, an animal closely associated with Hekate.

According to Lycophron[175] the transformed Hekabe spends her time frightening mortals who worship Hekate incorrectly. The correct way was thought to be with torches in Zerythia and sacrifices in Pherai. In Sicily, Odysseus is expected to make poured offerings on the shore to appease the three-necked goddess' anger, presumably for causing Hekabe's death or for his part in the fall of Troy. Hekabe was also the mother of Cassandra, the prophetess

172 Thasos: Cultural Crossroads in Archaeology, Pouilloux, 1955.
173 Description of Greece, Pausanias, 2nd century CE, trans. Jones, 1918.
174 Ex. Pseudo-Hyginus, Fabulae 111.
175 Lycophron, Alexandra, 3rd century BCE, trans. Mair, 1921.

who no-one would listen to, even though her prophecies were always highly accurate.

Minoan finds on Aegina go back to 2000 BCE and include the famous *Aegina Treasure* now in the British Museum, London. These include dozens of eight-petaled designs on gold, a male version of Potnia Theron and much more. A system of weights and measures was developed on Aegina, which subsequently became used throughout the Greek world. There is evidence that Hekate had a temple there, but the largest temple on the island was dedicated to Apollo.

There are also the remains of a temple dedicated to a goddess named as Aphaia, whose worship is only ever attested on Aegina with evidence suggesting it may date to at least 1400 BCE. It is probable that Aphaia was a local name or title for the Cretan virgin goddess Diktynna (also known as Britomaris), who was rescued by fishermen and taken to Aegina after she threw herself into the sea to avoid the advances of King Minos. Both Diktynna and Aphaia are equated to Artemis, and both are equated to Hekate. In some versions of the myth, Diktynna was a mortal who was so special to Artemis that the goddess decided to turn her into a goddess.

Aphaia's story has some interesting similarities to that of the Titan goddess Asteria (Hekate's mother in the *Theogony*) and other stories in which Artemis transforms women into the goddess Hekate. The remains of her temple can still be visited today, and was described by Pausanias as being on the mountain of the *Panhellenic Zeus*, where there was also a sanctuary to Zeus.

Aegina and Athens, which is only a short distance away by sea, were constantly at war with each other during the late fifth century BCE. Some of the disputes centred on cult images, which the Athenians threatened to carry away. We are told that when they approached the icons, the images fell to their knees and the Athenians fled empty-handed. Pausanias mentions that having seen the images he sacrificed to them as is customary at Eleusis, strongly suggesting a connection.

Campaigns by Christians in the fourth century CE succeeded in a crusade to destroy evidence of all the older religions on the island, including the Temple of Apollo. As a result of their efforts very little is known today of the religious history of the island, other than snippets passed down in literature, together with a few archaeological finds. Amongst the latter, there is an extraordinary votive relief dating to the late fifth century BCE from Aegina, which might have formed part of a ship model or depiction of an altar. The goddess who is thought to be Hekate is shown holding two torches and is depicted with animals, which includes a deer. It is believed that this goddess was worshipped locally by people who made their living at sea and could be Hekate, or Artemis, Diktynna or the local goddess Aphaia.

The Mysteries at Aegina were popular and continued to be sought out by citizens during the late Roman Era. In one example, Paulina, the wife of Praetextatus, wrote of her husband after his death that he was a pious initiate who internalised that which he found at the sacred rites, who learned many things and adored the Divine. Paulina's husband had introduced her to *'all the mysteries'* and in doing so *'exempted her from death's destiny'*. Named specifically are the Mysteries of Eleusis, Kybele, Mithras and that of Hekate at Aegina, where Paulina was a Hierophant.

> *"… her husband taught to her, the servant of Hecate, her "triple secrets" – whatever these secrets were, the Mysteries provided less "extraordinary experience" than soteriological hope and theological and philosophical knowledge."*[176]

It is possible to assume that the beliefs and customs at Aegina had something in common with those at other temples associated with the annual Mysteries said to be established by Orpheus, like those of Eleusis. The Mysteries of Aegina were renowned, as this early Christian writer indicates, and it is possible to conclude that they had an element of oathbound secrecy as we know so little about them today.

> *"For the mysteries of Mithras do not appear to be more famous among the Greeks than those of Eleusis, or than those in Aegina, where individuals are initiated in the rites of Hecate."*[177]

Aristophanes and others attributed healing powers to the

176 Greek Mysteries, Cosmopolous, 2005.
177 Chapter XXII, Ante-Nicene Fathers.

Korybantic rituals at Aegina.

HEKATE OF NEAPOLIS

(present-day West Bank, Palestine)

Neapolis, better known by its modern name Nablus, is on the West Bank of the Palestinian territories, about 50 kilometres from Jerusalem. It was appointed by a Roman Emperor in 72 CE and has been under the control of various empires and rulers.

A unique triangular diadem from the region depicts Kybele, with Hekate and Hermes on it. They are accompanied by other deities, including Zeus, Hera, Apollo, Artemis and Hephaistos, all of whom are shown as smaller than Kybele, Hekate and Hermes. Kybele is shown flanked by lions, and in a form resembling the local goddess Astarte, while Hekate and Hermes are shown in their Greco-Roman forms[178].

HEKATE OF KOS

(Greek Island)

Hekate was invoked as Soteira on Kos, and there is a strong possibility that she was included as one of the twelve gods[179] on the island. There are numerous inscriptions on the island attesting to her presence there.

With Machanonna, the son of Asclepius, Hekate is named on an altar dedicated to the Sun.

A curious inscription dated to between 300-100 BCE from the island of Kos, made by the Priests of Apollo at Halasarna, names the goddess as Hekate Stratia (war)[180]. It is likely that Hekate was worshipped alongside Apollo at this sanctuary:

> *"The new finds show that Apollon was worshipped in this sanctuary along with Hekate Stratia..."*[181]

Three of the inscriptions naming Hekate on Kos name her as

---

178 See Twelve Gods of Greece and Rome, Long, 1987.
179 See Twelve Gods of Greece and Rome, Long, 1987.
180 SEG 54-762-765. Kos (Halasarna).
181 Epigraphic Bulletin for Greek Religion, Chaniotis and Stavrianopoulou, 1990.

Hekate *Stratia*. This may be taken as a reference to a military group (army), or in its later Christian use to refer to a troop (host) of angels or possibly to a body of stars. No context for the inscription is given.

48 – AN IMAGINARY SCENE IN THE TEMPLE OF ASCLEPIUS IN KOS. PUBLISHED IN POPULAR SCIENCE, EDITED BY ARTHUR MEE, 1912-3

It has been suggested that a priesthood dedicated to Hekate, as a singular goddess, may have existed on Kos and as such epithets unique to the region may have developed, or it may have been specific to a smaller group of people. Considering the proximity of this Greek island to the mainland of Anatolia (Turkey) and Hekate's prevalence in that region, together with the evidence showing her presence on Kos, this would not seem altogether strange.

"There are three inscriptions made by a priest and hieropoioi of a particular god. Inscr. Cos 370 is a dedication to Hekate Stratia by Kleusthenes the son Heiron, the priest of Apollo, and five heiropoioi. The names of the individuals indicate that the priest and hieropoioi were all of the same family and thus that all the cult personnel probably served Apollo. Another dedication to Hekate Stratia by the priest Hekataios son of Hekatodoros and six hieropoioi was probably also a case of familial priesthood to one goddess: the names of the priest Hekateaios and his father are formed from the name of Hekate. The third dedication is probably a dedication by a priest and hieropoioi, but it is too fragmentary to helpful."[182]

Hippocrates of Kos, arguably the most celebrated physician of the ancient world, mentioned Hekate in his writings during the fifth century BCE. It is part of a discourse on how healers explain, in Hippocrates' opinion wrongly, various issues related to the Sacred Disease (i.e. mental illnesses). Nightmares in particular were attributed to Hekate by these individuals:

"If the patient is attended by fears, terrors, and madnesses in the night, jumps up out of his bed and flees outside, they call these the attacks of Hecate or the onslaughts of ghosts."[183]

An important feature of the Asklepion on Kos was its dream temple, where patients would sleep with the intention of being sent a dream vision regarding their ailments. Hekate's association with dreams was enduring. Much later Eusebius, recording Porphyry's writings in his *Praeparatio Evangelica*, tells us of Hekate that *"As ominous dreams thou dost to mortals send."*[184]

HEKATE OF ARGOS

"Over against the sanctuary of Eileithyia is a temple of Hekate ...."[185]

Hekate's temple at Argos stood, according to Pausanias, next to that of a sanctuary to the birth-goddess Eileithyia. This goddess is elsewhere equated to Hekate. Pausanias also mentioned two

---

182 he Hieropoioi on Kos, Smith, 1973
183 On the Sacred Disease, Hippocrates, 5th century BCE, trans. D. Ogden.
184 Praeparatio Evangelica, Eusebius, early 4th century CE, trans. Des Places.
185 Description of Greece, Pausanias, 2nd century CE, trans. Jones, 1918.

bronze statues of Hekate at the same location.

At Argos, Eileithyia is sometimes also equated to Hera or Artemis. Eileithyia with a quiver of arrows is depicted on the coins of Argos, which lends support to the idea that she may be Artemis here. However, the city gates of Argos were dedicated to the goddess as Eileithyia, a role more often associated with Hekate, illustrating again the tangled history of Artemis and Hekate.

The Suppliants, a fifth century BCE play by Aiskhylos, names Artemis-Hekate as the goddess who is entreated for both pregnancy and birth:

> *"And we pray that a succession of guardians of the land be born, and that Artemis Hecate watch over the child-bed of women."* [186]

HEKATE IN SICILY & SOUTH ITALY

The island of Sicily, as well as large parts of what is now Southern Italy, was a powerful and wealthy part of the Greek Empire and the influence of Hellenic religion on the region is still evident today. The Sicilian island Ortygia shares the same mythos as Delos, also claiming to be the birthplace of Apollo and Artemis, both of whom had temples there. In the Valley of the Temples, near Agrigento, the best-preserved examples of Doric Greek temples can still be seen standing today, built at a time when Agrigento was the jewel in the Greek Empire.

49 - TEMPLE REMAINS IN SELINUNTE.

Another smaller group of temples, equally impressive in size and its remarkable survival, are those of Selinunte, in the South

---

186 Aiskhylos, Suppliants, circa 5th century BCE, trans. Murray, 1958.

West of the island. Here Demeter, Persephone and Hekate – as well as Zeus - were worshipped. An ancient inscription found here appears to be a petition from a mother to Hekate for the sake of her child, reinforcing the idea that Hekate was worshipped, like Artemis, as a goddess associated with children.

Today in Syracuse the ruins of a temple of Demeter and Persephone can be seen through a metal fence, next to the *Santuario Madonna Delle Lacrime (The Sanctuary of the Madonna of the Tears)*. This church was built to house an icon made in the early 1950's and purchased for a newlywed couple, who hung it in their home. The icon wept for four days, causing quite a commotion. Then it stopped. It started again, when the wife was ill during pregnancy in the months that followed, and was attributed with healing her. Soon the icon was associated with around 300 miracles. The Church investigated, finding that more than 100 of the reported cases could be classed as miracles. The church of the Madonna of the Tears, completed in 1966, revealed in its construction the fifth-century Sanctuary of Demeter, which was excavated in the 1970's and 1980's.

50 - SANTUARIO MADONNA DELLE LACRIME AS SEEN THROUGH THE FENCE THROUGH WHICH SOME OF THE REMAINS OF THE SANCTUARY OF DEMETER AND PERSEPHONE IS VISIBLE.

Here it is impossible not to note the remarkable parallel between the story of the weeping Madonna and the goddess Demeter. Demeter was the mother who wept for her daughter when she was taken to be the wife of the god Hades. Her sorrow formed part of the Lesser Mysteries at Eleusis and elsewhere where it was celebrated.

The icon of the *Madonna Delle Lacrime* continues to draw many believers to it today.

Artemis as *Angelos* was honoured on Ortygia at the Fountain of the nymph Arethusa, just as Hekate as *Angelos* was elsewhere in Sicily.

> *"...Hekate with the epithet Angelos is known from a votive description from the Demeter Malophoros Sanctuary in Selinous, inviting a comparison, with Artemis Angelos in Syracuse. Indeed, Iphigeneia was honoured at Megara Nisaia as Hekate by the will of Artemis ... and Artemis and Hekate are divinities linked, for example at Syracuse and at Lipari."*[187]

Artemis was worshipped as Soteira at Syracuse, a title more often associated with Hekate, especially in Sicily and in the later Chaldean Oracles. Reachable from Syracuse via a small bridge today, Ortygia was home to three ancient temples, all of them of significant size, dedicated respectively to Artemis, Apollo and Athena.

Porphyry, who was known for his writings defending the older Pagan religious traditions during the third and fourth century CE, spent his life between Rome and Sicily, later retiring to Sicily. This was a time that Christianity was gaining prominence, and his works were so controversial that Christians sought out and burned his works for centuries afterwards, so much so that today only fragments of them remain, primarily preserved through other works.

Porphyry frequently mentioned Hekate in his work. One of the most interesting examples being his record of an Oracle of Hekate speaking in response to direct queries about Christianity and Jesus.

---

187 From Artemis to Diana: The Goddess of Man and Beast, Fischer-Hansen, 2009

*"And to those who ask why he [Jesus] was condemned to die,
the oracle of the goddess [Hekate] replied,*

*The body, indeed, is always exposed to torments, but the souls
of the pious abide in heaven.*

*And the soul you inquire about has been the fatal cause of
error to other souls which were not fated to receive the gifts of
the gods, and to have the knowledge of immortal Jove.*

*Such souls are therefore hated by the gods; for they who were
fated not to receive the gifts of the gods, and not to know God,
were fated to be involved in error by means of him you speak of.*

*He himself, however, was good, and heaven has been opened to
him as to other good men.*

*You are not, then, to speak evil of him, but to pity the folly of
men: and through him men's danger is imminent."*[188]

Long before Porphyry, the Sicilian-born Greek philosopher and root-cutter Empedocles spent time at Selinunte, as well as at many of the other temples in Sicily. Empedocles is credited as being responsible for the earliest doctrines of the four elements. He campaigned against animal sacrifices, worked with plants and roots and appears to have strong associations with the cult of Hekate during his life.

The story of Queen Hekabe, who according to some myths, became a dog attendant of Hekate after she committed suicide, is also linked to Sicily. In Lycophron her cenotaph is said to be at Pakhynos – the modern Capo Passero, in the southern part of the Syracuse province, Sicily.

In Southern Italy, several dedications name Hekate as one of a trio of goddesses: *Artemis-Hekate-Selene.* One such example from an underground temple sanctuary found in Lipari:

*"The altars bears an inscription dated early 3rd century, or at
least from before the destruction of Lipari in 252/1, a triple
dedication to Artemis - Hekate - Selene, where Artemis has
the role of Divinity of the Earth..."* [189]

---

188 Prophecy from Oracles, Porphyry, 3rd century CE, trans. J.R. King.
189 From Artemis to Diana: The Goddess of Man and Beast, Fischer-Hansen, 2009.

51 - HEKATE, WITH DEMETER AND PERSEPHONE,
IN AN EARLY 6TH CENTURY BCE RELIEF FROM A TEMPLE AT SELINUNTE.

HEKATE IN THE BOSPORAN KINGDOM

(present day Southern Russia)

The Bosporan Kingdom occupied an area which is now in Southern Russia. Their religion was probably a blend of indigenous Iranian and Greek ideas, with some Thracian influences and strongly focussed on the stellar aspects of the goddess Aphrodite. Evidence shows that Hekate's cult had a small but not insignificant presence in the Bosporan Kingdom.

"Hekate, ..., was worshipped in Panticapaeum in a small temple on the northern slope of the acropolis... Two three-faced hekataia have been discovered in the city..."[190]

An altar inscribed and dedicated to Hekate was also found here. The evidence further suggests that Hekate continued her affiliations with the Anatolian Great Goddess in this region. Hekate was worshipped here alongside Aphrodite, with the goddesses sometimes sharing a sanctuary.

"Since several figurines of dogs were discovered inside the Myrmecaeum ash altars, Hekate, the nocturnal leader of dogs..., may have had a share in the cult. Aphrodite and Hekate were probably joined by some other deities, but the existence of several cults in one sanctuary or their combination in a mixed cult was quite normal on the Bosporus".[191]

Other finds in the region show that Hekate was worshipped there alongside Hermes and Kybele. This recurrent connection between Kybele, Hermes and Hekate suggest that there may have been other Mystery cults in which Hermes and Hekate accompanied Kybele on a journey, perhaps one of katabasis, with similarities to that of Persephone at Eleusis.

It is also interesting to note that in the Theogony, Hekate when called upon with Hermes, is given a distinctively agricultural role:

"She is good in the byre with Hermes to increase the stock. The droves of kine and wide herds of goats and flocks of fleecy sheep, if she will, she increases from a few, or makes many to be less."[192]

HEKATE IN EGYPT

Alexandria, founded and named after Alexander the Great, flourished as one of the greatest cultural and spiritual centres of the world. It was celebrated as the home to the famous Library of Alexandria and as a melting pot of Hellenic Pagan, Jewish and Christian ideas.

---

190 The Supreme Gods of the Bosporan Kingdom: Celestial Aphrodite and the Most High God, Ustinova, 1999.
191 The Supreme Gods of the Bosporan Kingdom: Celestial Aphrodite and the Most High God, Ustinova, 1999.
192 The Theogony, circa 8th or 7th century BCE, Hesiod, trans. Evelyn-White, 1914.

52 - JUNIPER WOOD HEKATAIA, BELIEVED TO BE FROM ALEXANDRIA (EGYPT) DATED TO
APPROX. 304-60 BCE. A RARE SURVIVAL OF A WOODEN ICON.
IMAGE FROM METROPOLITAN MUSEUM OF ART, NEW YORK.

A defixiones entreating Hekate's help was found in Alexandria, believed to date to the 3rd century CE.

> *"..The precise purpose of the spell is unclear, although*
> *something to do with a love affair (homosexual) seems most*
> *likely."*[193]

The spell utilises many names and *voces magicae*, some of which are also found in the PGM. Hermes is also invoked in this spell

---

193 Curse Tablets and Binding Spells from the Ancient World, Gager,1992.

and Ereschigal, Kore and Persephone are all conflated with Hekate in it.

> *"Hekate, true Hekate,*
> *come and accomplish for me this very act!"* [194]

Hekate & Anubis

Hekate and Anubis are featured together on a third century CE jasper gemstone charm. It is an excellent example of the bringing together of elements from different religious traditions.

53 – A 19TH-CENTURY PLASTER CASTING OF A LATE 2ND OR EARLY 3RD CENTURY CE JASPER GEMSTONE CURRENTLY IN THE BERLIN, STAATLICHE MUSEEN ZU BERLIN, ÄGYPTISCHES COLLECTION. SIDE 1: AION, SIDE 2 ANUBIS AND HEKATE. IMAGES WITH THANKS FROM THE CORNELL UNIVERSITY LIBRARY.

The first side shows a lion-headed figure crowned with eight rays, facing right and holding a branch and wreath in his hands. This is almost certainly a depiction of the god Aion, god of unbounded time with a close association with the Mystery traditions. The inscription on this side of the gem combines elements of Judeo-Christian belief:

> *"Michael, the highest, Gabriel, the strongest"* [195]

The obverse shows a representation of the jackal-headed Egyptian god Anubis, holding a flail and possibly another wreath. He faces a three-formed Hekate, carrying whips, torches and daggers. Hekate and Anubis are being petitioned alongside Aion and the archangels Michael and Gabriel, providing an example of how the boundaries between religious traditions became blurred

---

194 Curse Tablets and Binding Spells from the Ancient World, Gager,1992.
195 See CBd, Collection of Classical Antiquities of the Museum of Fine Arts, Budapest

from a magical perspective.

This gemstone is not an isolated instance of Hekate and Anubis being petitioned together. The love spell recorded in PGM IV.1390-1495 requests help from among those who died a violent death, as well as invoking Hekate, Hermes, Kore, Pluto and Anubis. The same spell also employs the use of Hebrew divine names. Similarly, Hekate is called upon in conjunction with the archangel Michael in a *Spell to the Waning Moon*, PGM IV.2241-2358.

Another Roman period gemstone in the collection of the *Bibliothèque nationale Paris* also shows Hekate, with Anubis and two additional creatures. Hekate is shown as triformis with a tall torch (or sceptre) and snake, with a fire on an altar before her. Anubis appears to make a libation into the fire, and the two other characters stand behind him.

Also see: *Many Named Mother of the Gods, Divine Mergers, Isis*

54 - HEKATE, PLUTO AND ISIS. THIS IMPRESSION IS OF A YELLOW GLASS GEMSTONE.
IMAGE WITH THANKS FROM THE CORNELL UNIVERSITY LIBRARY.

THE CHALDEAN ORACLES

"Thereafter, when things are no longer visible, when the Vault of Heaven and the expanse of the universe have dissolved, when the stars have ceased to shine and the lamp of the moon is veiled, when the earth trembles and the lightning plays around

it, invoke not the visible phantom of Nature's soul, for thou must in no wise behold it until the body has been purified by the Holy ordeals. Enervators of souls, which they distract from sacred occupations, the dog-faced demons issue from the confines of matter and expose to mortal eyes the semblances of illusory bodies. Labour around the circles described by the rhombus of Hecate. Change thou nothing in the barbarous names of evocation, for they are pantheistic titles of God; they are magnetised by the devotion of the multitudes and their power is ineffable. When after all the phantoms thou shalt behold the shining of that incorporeal fire, that sacred fire the darts of which penetrate in every direction through the depths of the world - hearken to the words of the fire."[196]

Hekate is the foremost goddess of the *Chaldean Oracles*, a significant theurgic work which emphasises Hekate as being *Soteira* (*Saviour*) and as the benevolent source of souls and virtues. Hekate's place in the Chaldean Oracles has been the subject of many studies, primarily the books *Hekate Soteira* by Johnston and *The Goddess Hekate* by Ronan. In this section I provide only an introduction to Hekate's place in the Chaldean Oracles, readers seeking a more detailed study are directed to the aforementioned works.

"Hecate and Apollo are the central figures throughout, and the philosophical positions inside of the texts can nearly all be found within Greek Middle Platonism, of the sort which thrived at learning centres like Apamea."[197]

The Chaldean Oracles only survive as fragments, and much of it is incomplete, however Johnston writes that Hekate's name appears in 5 out of the 226 fragments. This is more than that of any other traditional deity. Johnston[198] further asserts that Hekate is referred to in at least 66 of the other fragments, 11 of which represent the words of the goddess herself.

"...the Mistress of Life and holds the plenitude of the full womb of the cosmos."[199]

The Oracles declare that Hekate is the Soul of Nature, and also

196 Chaldean Oracles, trans. Taylor, quoted from The History of Magic, Levi, 1860.
197 Birth of the Symbol,Struck, 2004.
198 Hekate Soteira, Johnston, 1990..
199 Fragment 96, Chaldean Oracles.

that she ensouls the light, fire, aether and the cosmos (world).

> *"For all around the hollows of the cartilage of Hekate's right*
> *flank, The abundant liquid of the Primal Soul gushes*
> *unceasingly, Completely ensouling the light, the fire, the aether*
> *and the Cosmoi."*[200]

In another fragment Hekate is given as the source of this liquid:

> *"In the left flank of Hekate resides the Source of Virtue,*
> *Which completely remains within, not sending forth its*
> *virginity."*[201]

The Oracles also emphasised that Hekate was the ruler of angels, a frequently overlooked role held by this goddess. The text described the three orders of angels (*'Angelos'* meaning *messenger*) who serve her and aids her followers. These are:

- *Iynges* - wrynecks after the bird
- *Synochesis* – connectors
- *Teletarchai* - rulers of initiation

These are the beings sent forth by Hekate when she is called upon for help according to the Oracles. The first order, the Iynges, shares its name with a magical device associated with Hekate and discussed in the chapter *Magic Wheels & Whirlings*. The Synochesis represent the point between things, such as the material and spiritual, the intelligible-intellective, they are a bridge on the liminal. The Teletarchai are the most important of these beings, representing the theurgic mysteries of the initiation rites.

Hekate was implored in spells to send the help of her angels, for example in PGM VII we find:

> *"...send forth your angel from among those who assist*
> *you".*[202]

This not an isolated example, in the PGM's *'Lunar Spell of Claudianus'*, Hekate is also asked to send forth her angels to assist the magician.

This hierarchy of spiritual beings, forming triads of angelic orders, subsequently influenced the work of Pseudo-Dionysus I in

---

200 Hekate Soteira, Johnston, 1990..
201 Fragment 52, quoted in Hekate Soteira, Johnston, 1990.
202 PGM VII.862-918, Betz, 1997.

the early sixth century CE. In his work *Celestial Hierarchy and Divine Names* he laid the basis for the hierarchy of angelic orders which has been used in Christianity ever since.

In *Living Theurgy* Kupperman provides some additional insight into Hekate's role in the Oracles, writing about the sub-lunar Demiurge:

> *"The virtue of Faith, Pistis, which has nothing to do with blind belief, is associated with the sub-lunar Demiurge. In the Oracles, this is represented by Hekate, Hades, and possibly Dionysos. Faith is represented by the rays of the visible sun in Iamblichean theology, and the crucified Christ in Christianity. Proclus sees it as the sole theurgic power through which union with the One occurs. Together, the Demiurges are the "Teletarchs of the mysteries," and are engaged in the most important parts of theurgic rites."*[203]

KING SOLOMON

Images of Hekate are frequently found on amulets and other charms. In some instances, her image or name is combined with that of Jewish divine names. An especially striking bronze amulet discovered in Southern Italy shows Hekate in triplicate form, holding her usual tools; and on the obverse side King Solomon with a wand and a container which might contain water. It might represent Solomon performing *hygromanteia,* the conjuring of a spirit into the water.

The figures are surrounded by a variety of symbols. Hekate appears with her usual tools, torches, daggers and whips. The caduceus appears on both sides of the disk. There are several eight-spoked wheels, and the eight-pointed symbol terminating in spheres are also shown.

Some of the symbols are in the Celestial script, discussed by Agrippa in his book III, see Fig.56.

---

203 See Living Theurgy, Kupperman, 2014

55 - METAL DISK FROM OSTIA. KING SOLOMON PERFORMING CONJURING (SIDE 1) AND HEKATE IN TRIPLE FORM. BOTH FIGURES ARE SURROUNDED BY SYMBOLS.

56 - CELESTIAL SCRIPT FROM AGRIPPA BOOK III.

BEYOND BORDERS

Even after the initial decline of the Hellenic and Roman pagan cults, and the rise of the new religion *Christianity,* Hekate maintained her position as an important goddess. She was able to adjust to the changing religious landscape, always finding a place in new and emerging philosophies. She must have had an enduring following who found ways of keeping her worship alive, and who continued to implore her in magical workings.

Religious propaganda will have us believe that after the rise of Christianity as the dominant state religion of Rome, the older gods and practices were simply forgotten. Some twentieth-century writers make it sound as if the old gods and their traditions were completely lost until being rediscovered and reintroduced by a civil servant in 1950's England. Such claims are evidently unsubstantiated, as both the gods and magic continued to feature in society throughout Europe.

The cults of some Pagan deities continued to thrive even when Christianity was increasingly gaining a foothold. It is possible that the qualities of particular goddesses made them indispensable, or that their cult offered something that Christianity, especially in its early form, was lacking. Goddesses, such as Artemis and Hekate, were linked to the fertility of the land, of animals and of humans. They were also believed to provide help with childbirth, healing and guidance on the journey towards the afterlife.

Christianity adopted symbols as well as natural resources, such as healing springs, into their religion and provided many of the old services through a new façade. It struggled to replace the qualities of the Great Mother goddesses, who continued to find expressions. It is interesting that the rise of the cult of the *Virgin Mary,* the mother of Jesus, started in what is now Syria. Mary was worshipped here as the Mother of God, arguably replacing (continuing?) what remained of the earlier Mother Goddess cult.

The gods, at least most of them, were never forgotten. The names of those who survived continued to be uttered, their images and symbols continued to inspire artists, poets and playwrights and their stories continued in folklore and myth, even if their temples fell silent. Knowledge of the gods survived through myths, which often turned the benevolent gods of nature into the demons of the newer religion, or children's fairy-tales.

Magic, like the gods, never went away either. It did what it always does, it took on the guise of the religion of its age, the techniques preserved in the pages of magical *grimoires* such as the popular *Key of Solomon.* The warnings designed to caution against the dangers of magic and the wickedness of the old gods served as inspiration for a few individuals, in each successive generation, to lift the veil and look beyond. And for many of us, Hekate lurked just on the other side, ready to inspire, and to traverse the oceans, air and land with those who knew her name, and also those who only knew her through visions and dreams.

Today Hekate continues to be invoked and supplicated for a variety of purposes around the world. Through the *Rite of Her Sacred*

Fires[204] which takes place at the Full Moon in May each year, it has become obvious that Hekate is still much venerated today. The rite brings together devotees from many different traditions in a simple ceremony in which a flame is lit for the goddess. Many thousands of people participate in this ritual, which has been offered on six continents, in around 30 languages, since 2010.

57 HAERESIS DEA - ANTON EISENHOIT – 1590
WITH ITS THREE HEADS – DRAGON, WOMAN AND BULL, THE EARS OF A DONKEY AND
PERSONIFYING 'HERESY' THIS IMAGE MAY HAVE BEEN INSPIRED BY HEKATE.

Here are some examples from literature, showing how Hekate was remembered, leading up to the twentieth-century:

- 10th century: Byzantine Suda

  "Some [say that she is] Artemis, others the moon, appearing in strange manifestations for those invoking curses. Her manifestations [are] humans with the heads of dragons, and of immense size, so that the sight stupefies those who see it."[205]

---

204 See www.hekatecovenant.com
205 Epsilon 364, Suda.

- <u>1582: Giordano Bruno in Incantations to Kirke</u>

  "I name you the one whom we call Hekate, Latona, Diana, Phœbe, Lucina, Trivia, Tergemina, and the threefold Goddess."

- <u>1585: The Flyting of Montgomery and Polwart (Scottish):</u>

  "On ane thre headit hekate in haist pair they cryit:"
  (On a three-headed Hekate in haste there they cried)

- <u>1595: Demonolatry by Remy</u>

  "Affecting the glory of such great majesty the demon, in the year 1121, appeared with three heads to a certain Premonstratensian canon and tried to persuade him that he was that threefold Deity (whereas in truth he was the Triform Hekate) in the contemplation of whom the canon so fixedly occupied his mind"

- <u>1600: Midsummer Night's Dream by Shakespeare</u>

  "Now it is the time of night
  That the graves all gaping wide,
  Every one lets forth his sprite,
  In the church-way paths to glide:
  And we fairies, that do run
  By the triple Hekate's team,
  From the presence of the sun,
  Following darkness like a dream,
  Now are frolic"

- <u>1604: Faustus by Marlowe</u>

  "Pluto's blue fire, and Hecat's tree,
  With magick spells so compass thee"

- <u>1634: Comus: A Masque by Milton</u>

  "He and his monstrous rout are heard to howl
  Like stabl'd wolves, or tigers at their prey,
  Doing abhorred rites to Hekate
  In their obscured haunts of inmost bow'rs."

- <u>1795 – A New and Complete Illustration of the Occult Sciences by Sibly:</u>

  "By the mysteries of the deep, by the flames of Banal, by the power of the east, and the silence of the night, by the holy rites of Hekate, I conjure and exorcise thee, thou distressed spirit"

- <u>1804 - A Dictionary of Polite Literature; or, Fabulous History of the Heathen Gods</u>

  "Tergemina, Triformis. Diana, so called on account of her triple character of Luna in heaven, Diana of earth, and Hecate in hell; though the actions for the first and last are ascribed to her under the second name."

- <u>1842: Immortalita, Gunderode</u>

  "Hekate goddess of midnight, discoverer of the future which yet sleeps in the bosom of chaos, mysterious Hekate! Appear."

- <u>1881: The Garden of Eros, Oscar Wilde</u>

  "Lo! while we spake the earth did turn away, Her visage from the God, and Hekate's boat; Rose silver-laden, till the jealous day Blew all its torches out:"

58 - COLLECTABLE GASOLINE CARD DEPICTING
"HECATE - GODDESS OF DARKNESS". 1890

- <u>1908: The Book of Witches, Hueffer</u>

> *'Originally an ancient Thracian divinity, she by degrees assumed the attributes of many, Atis, Cybele, Isis, and others ... Gradually she grew into the spectral originator of all those horrors with which darkness affects the imagination."*

- <u>1935 Mystical Qabalah, Dion Fortune:</u>

> *"To Yesod are assigned all the deities that have the moon in their symbolism: Luna herself; Hecate, with her dominion over evil magic and Diana, with her presidency over childbirth."* [206]

IAO, Adonai, Sabaoth

Hekate is also repeatedly implored for her assistance on amulets and defixiones in the fourth- and fifth-centuries. There are conspicuous examples of Hekate being called upon alongside, or even in some instances being conflated with the Gnostic *IAO*, a contraction of *IHVH*, the name of the Judaic God. In one example Hekate, by her name of Brimo, was merged with IAO, making *Brimiao.*

> *"I invoke you by the unconquerable god, Iao Barbathiao <u>Brimiao</u> Chermari."* [207]

In the same *voces magicae* (magical words) the Hebrew name *Adonai* (Lord) is also employed. This defixio, dating to the fifth century CE, was found in Upper Egypt in a sealed pot. It had been wrapped around two wax figures, holding them in an embrace, before it was placed into the pot. Similar spells were recorded in the *Picatrix.* This text, also known as *Ghāyat al-Ḥakīm,* is a collection of Arabic magical formulas and astrology dating to circa eleventh-century CE.

An image of Hekate and the name IAO Sabaoth was similarly used on a protection spell. Sabaoth is translated as *'Lord of Hosts'.*

> *"IAO Sabaoth protect".* [208]

---

206 Fortune in The Mystical Qabalah
207 Defixio from Assiut, Upper Egypt, C5th CE, trans. J. Gager.
208 Jewish Symbols in the Greco-Roman Period, Vol 2, Goodenough, 1953.

Gnosticism is a relatively modern term, derived from the Greek word for knowledge, to describe a variety of ancient beliefs and practices, including forms of early Christianity. Gnostics believe that the material world was created a by a *Demiurge*, and that the divine spark in each of us remains trapped until such time that we are able to liberate it through a divine experiential gnosis (knowledge) of it. There are some parallels with the Orphic concept of *Soma Sema*[209].

The Christian Gnostics made Hekate into one of their five *Archons*, allowing her to keep her three faces and giving her dominion over 27 demons. Their own goddess *Edem*, who is a form of *Sophia*, is depicted as half-human and half-serpent, and was likely derived from *Echidna* or *Isis-Hermouthis*. Edem created twelve angels, three of which were *Naas* (snakes) with connections to the tree in the garden of Eden.

Also see: *Symbols of the Goddess, Serpents or Snakes.*

Symbols associated with Hekate also appear in the fourth-century *Trimorphic Protennoia:*

> *"I am the movement that dwells in the All, she in whom the All takes its stand, the first-born among those who came to be, she who exists before the All. She is called by three names, although she dwells alone, since she is perfect."*[210]

Freedom and Liberty

The qualities of freedom and liberty fit well with the qualities which are embodied by Hekate, and maybe for this reason so many modern devotees wonder if the *Statue of Liberty* (New York, USA) and *Lady Freedom* (Atlanta, USA) depict Hekate. While there is no indication that these gigantic statues were intended to represent anything other than personified symbolic qualities, there are some striking similarities which are interesting to consider.

The goddess *Libertas* or *Liberty* is the personification of liberty and is shown with torches, shining light and showing the way to symbolic freedom. It is this image which inspired the creation of

---

209 Soma Sema was likely used as a chant, and is taken to mean that the body is the prison of the soul.
210 Trimorphic Protennoia, 4th century CE, trans. Turner.

the Statue of Liberty.

Dedicated in 1886 the Statue of Liberty in the harbour of New York has some apparent similarities to Hekate. In addition to the prominent symbol of the torch, the seven rays adorning Liberty is very similar to that found on images of Hekate, such as the Chairamonte Hekate, in the Vatican Museum (fig.59).

59 - HEKATE CHIARAMONTE, NOW IN THE VATICAN MUSEUM, ROME. THIS IS A TRIPLE STATUE, THE FACING SIDE SHOWS HEKATE CROWNED WITH SEVEN RAYS (FRONT ONE BROKEN) AND IS WEARING A PHRYGIAN CAP.

60 - THE STATUE OF LIBERTY, USA
LA LIBERTÉ ÉCLAIRANT LE MONDE – LIBERTY ENLIGHTENING THE WORLD

Miss Freedom (Originally *Lady Freedom*), which stands atop the Georgia State Capitol, in Atlanta, USA also bears a torch, with a sword in her other hand. This statue is crowned not with seven rays like that of the State of Liberty, but rather with a Phrygian cap – which one of the figures of the Chiaramonte Hekate statue is also wearing. The Phrygian cap, typically worn by Anatolian divinities, was sometimes confused with the *pileus*, a Roman hat which was placed on the heads of Roman slaves when they went with their owners before the magistrate to be declared free. The *pileus* was for this reason also known as the *liberty cap*.

61 - MISS FREEDOM, GEORGIA, USA.

As a curious aside, Zeus had a festival dedicated to him as *Eleuthera* (freedom). There are some interesting stories about slave women, pretending to be Free Women of the towns under attack. The women were being used (and according to accounts volunteered themselves for the role) to exhaust the enemy with intercourse the night before the battle. When victory was achieved, the festival *Eleuthera* was created to mark the victory.[211]

Significantly Artemis was worshipped as *Eleuthera* at Myra, Lycia. The temple there was dedicated to her under this name, and for a short time coins featuring Eleuthera were also issued.[212]

---

211 See Plutarch's Morals, vol. 5, trans. Goodwin.
212 See The Supreme Gods of the Bosporan Kingdom: Celestial Aphrodite and the Most High God, Ustinova, 1999.

The Body of the Goddess

"I come, a virgin of varied forms, wandering through the heavens, bull-faced, three-headed, ruthless, with golden arrows; chaste Phoebe bringing light to mortals, Eileithyia; bearing the three synthemata [sacred signs] of a triple nature. In the Aether I appear in fiery forms and in the air I sit in a silver chariot." [213]

Hekate is single-headed, double-headed, triple-headed and sometimes quadruple-headed. She comes with the faces of a young or adult female, but also with that of a bull, boar, cow, snake, dog, wolf, lion, dragon, goat and horse. She comes as a gentle and benevolent goddess, the saviour; and she also comes as a frightening goddess of the underworld, ruling over the souls of the restless dead. She comes known and unknown, seen and unseen, with the sound of baying hounds or the flickering of a flame marking her arrival.

"...because they did not understand the character of the goddess, or that she was the very "Deo," "Rhea," and "Demeter" so much honoured amongst them themselves." [214]

Hekate is often named as a *Triple Goddess*, and in this form, she is shown as three women, of the same age, usually standing side by side, or back to back – sometimes around a central pillar. In her triple form, Hekate is shown holding a variety of objects, which typically include at least two torches. However, Hekate is also

---

213 Chaldean Oracles, 2nd century CE, from Hekate Soteira, Johnston, 1990.
214 Oration Upon the Mother of the Gods, Julian the Apostate, 5th century CE, trans. Taylor, 1793.

recurrently depicted in a singular form, again holding objects associated with her. There are references in later texts to Hekate being four-headed, in the *Greek Magical Papyri* and *Liber De Mensibus*, as well as rare examples of what might be two-headed depictions. Her body is most often that of three women, of indeterminate age, standing around a central pillar; or of a single bodied woman standing, running/walking or seated. There are also examples of Hekate having a pillar-like body, decorated like that of Artemis of Ephesus as well as in the form of a herm.

> *"There are two examples of the Hekate herm with Charites dancing around it and one triangular draped herm without dancers which must be a Hekate although the heads are not preserved. There is also a head fragment, relatively large and well-preserved, that must be from a Hekate herm, probably of the sort with dancers."*[215]

Herms are more often thought of as being of the god Hermes, himself often associated with Hekate – especially in the cult of the Mother of the Gods, where Hekate and Hermes are often shown as chief attendants to Kybele. Hekate is also described as being a *theriocephalic* deity, that is with the body of a woman and the head(s) of different animals.

Shapeshifting?

The many forms assumed by this goddess hints that she might have shape-shifter qualities. Several of the other Hellenic deities appear to have the ability to transform their own shape, as well as that of mortals. Within the context of the traditions it would not be unusual, nor at all far-fetched.

Asteria practised shapeshifting to escape the embraces of Zeus, turning herself into a quail (bird) and floating island. In the same story, Zeus took on different forms in his pursuit of the goddess. The goddess Demeter turned Ascalabus[216] into a gecko after he laughed at her and mocked her during her search for her daughter Persephone. Demeter also turned herself into a mare to escape the

---

215 Archaic and Archaistic Sculpture, Harrison, 1965.
216 See Ovid, Metamorphoses 5.

advances of Poseidon[217], upon which the god of the sea transformed himself into a stallion in his pursuit of her. In other accounts of this union, it is said that Demeter took the form of one of the Erinyes during the affair. The result of the union between the shapeshifting Demeter and Poseidon was the birth of a goddess whose name is either not to be divulged to the uninitiated,[218] but which is sometimes given as Despoina,[219] or described as a horse. Despoina (Lady) is one of the many titles given to Hekate.

> *"This Despoine the Arkadians worship more than*
> *any other god, declaring that she is a daughter*
> *of Poseidon and Demeter..."*[220]

Artemis changed Actaeon into a stag, before setting his own hunting dogs on him after he spied on her and her nymphs whilst they were bathing. In one account, Hekate herself may have been the result of Artemis changing the mortal maiden Iphigeneia into Hekate. Kirke, sometimes named as being a daughter of Hekate, turned Odysseus and his men into pigs.

62 KIRKE TURNS ODYSSEUS AND HIS MEN INTO PIGS.
ANTONIO TEMPESTA, 16-17TH CENTURY.

---

217 Description of Greece, Pausanias, 2nd century CE, trans. Jones, 1918.
218 Description of Greece, Pausanias, 2nd century CE, trans. Jones, 1918.
219 Callimachus, Fragment 207.
220 Description of Greece, Pausanias, 2nd century CE, trans. Jones, 1918.

Iphigeneia's Transformation

"Now I have heard another account of Iphigenia that is given by Arkadians and I know that Hesiod, in his poem A Catalogue of Women, says that Iphigenia did not die, but by the will of Artemis became Hekate."[221]

63 - PAINTING SHOWING A SCENE FROM THE SACRIFICE OF IPHIGENEIA'S SACRIFICE FOUND AT THE HOUSE OF THE TRAGIC POET IN THE BURIED REMAINS OF THE ROMAN CITY OF POMPEII. NOW IN THE ARCHAEOLOGICAL MUSEUM NAPLES. ARTEMIS (TOP LEFT) IS BRINGING A DEER TO SACRIFICE IN PLACE OF IPHIGENEIA. THERE IS A SMALL IMAGE OF A SINGLE-BODIED TORCH-BEARING HEKATE FLANKED BY TWO DOGS ON THE PILLAR TO THE LEFT BEHIND THE GIRL'S MOURNING FATHER.

Iphigeneia was frequently incorporated into the cult of Hekate and she may have apotheosised into the goddess Hekate. There are a number of possibilities.

"According to the Hesiodic Catalogue of Women, "Iphimede", after her rescue by Artemis from the sacrificial altar, was made an immortal attendant of the goddess and is worshipped under her name, Artemis, with the epithet ein(h)odia, "in the road". Since this epithet was properly applied to Hecate as guardian of

---

221 Description of Greece, Pausanias, 2nd century CE, trans. Jones, 1918.

144

*crossroads, Stesichorus and others assumed that Hesiod meant
to identify Iphigeneia/Iphimedeia with Hecate; the frequent
confusion of Artemis with Hecate undoubtedly helped to
confirm this identification for all time. On the other hand, the
possibility should not be overlooked that the poet of the
Catalogue did really mean Enodia to signify the traditional
goddess of crossroads - that he knew, in other words, an old
tradition which actually identified Iphimedeia with Hecate."*[222]

Iphigeneia was also said to be transformed into the birth
goddess Eileithyia, who in turn was thought to be Hekate.

*"Over against the sanctuary of Eilethyia is a temple of Hekate
[probably identified here as the apotheosised Iphigeneia], and
the image is a work of Skopas (Scopas). This one is of stone,
while the bronze images opposite, also of Hekate, were made
respectively by Polykleitos (Polycleitus) and his brother
Naukydes (Naucydes)."*[223]

Icons

Icons are used as both symbolic representations of the deity,
and as vessels for the deity to manifest through. They may take the
form of statues (ranging from small to gigantic), pictures or
symbolic objects. The interaction of devotees with the icons of
their deities often follow particular patterns. Select offerings are
typically made at a specific time of the day or phase of the moon
while following a precise ritual methodology through which it is
hoped that the efficiency of the offering will be maximised. These
components ritualised devotional practice for devotees, creating
expressive and meaningful experiences.

Devotees interact with icons of deities in diverse ways and
images are often treated as if the deity it represents presides within
it. This is especially true of images which have been consecrated
and blessed, and on which invocations have been performed to call
the deity into the image (ensouling) or which has a long history of
use, where the icon is believed to have otherworldly powers of their
own. Devotees may prostrate themselves before images, touch,
kiss, wash, anoint, dress, or otherwise make offerings of food or

---

222 Hecate: Greek or 'Anatolian?, Berg, 1974.
223 Description of Greece, Pausanias, 2nd century CE, trans. Jones, 1918.

drinks to the deity. Icons are often created to very exacting standards, preserving the symbols and characteristics of the deity from one generation to the next.

Porphyry recorded an example of offerings being made to statues of Hekate and Hermes. He accentuates the timing (New Moon) during which the rite should be done, together with details of how the icon should be treated (adoring and crowning it) and also names the offerings which were made (frankincense, wafers, cakes):

> *"...he diligently sacrificed to them at proper times in every month at the new moon, crowning and adorning the statues of Hermes and Hecate, and the other sacred images which were left to us by our ancestors, and that he also honoured the Gods with frankincense, and sacred wafers and cakes."*[224]

Johnston[225] says that *Theopompos* also recorded that images of Hekate and Hermes were washed and crowned as part of new moon rituals. Washing the statues of the deities worshipped in the home, as well as in the temples, formed a regular part of devotional practice as it kept the images clean from dust and debris.

In another of his works Porphyry expressed some of the reasons behind the creation of religious statues:

> *"... they moulded their gods in human form because the deity is rational, and made these beautiful, because in those is pure and perfect beauty; and in varieties of shape and age, of sitting and standing, and drapery; and some of them male, and some female, virgins, and youths, or married, to represent their diversity."*[226]

The goddess Hekate was honoured at the gateway of the famous oracle temple of Apollo at Miletos with poured offerings of wine. Here the Molpoi (priests) also employed the use of gulloi stones which they carried in procession and on which offerings were made to the goddess. One stone was placed at the shrine of Hekate by the gate, and the other upon the threshold of her temple.

> *"Just outside the gate of Miletos on the Sacred Way there was*

---

224 On Abstinence, Porphyry, 3rd century CE, trans. T. Taylor.
225 Johnston, Hekate Soteira, 1990.
226 On Images, Porphyry, 3rd century CE, trans. Gifford.

> *a shrine of Hekate, where the Molpoi, beginning their march to*
> *Didyma, deposited a gyllos and made a libation of unmixed*
> *wine (akretos). In her we may see Hekate Propylaia: she is*
> *called Hekate Before the Gates"*[227].

The gulloi stones may have been meteoric, such as the baetyls used in some other regional cults, or may have been symbolic representations of a deity.[228] A cubic altar stone also stood at Apollo's temple in Delos, his place of birth according to legend and closely linked to Asteria, the mother of Hekate. Cubic altars can also be found in the context of Hittite religious rites.

Also see: *The Wandering Goddess, Hekate at Didyma and Miletos.*

Icons of Hekate were made from a wide range of different materials, including stone (including crystals), metal, wood and clay. An example from the fourth century CE showing how an icon of Hekate should be constructed survives in the writings of Eusebius. He recorded instructions, which he proposes was given by the goddess (presumably in an oracle), on how to create an icon:

> *"'That they themselves suggested how even their statues ought to*
> *be made, and of what kind of material, shall be shown by the*
> *response of Hecate in the following form: "My image purify, as*
> *I shall show: Of wild rue form the frame, and deck it o'er with*
> *lizards such as run about the house; These mix with resin,*
> *myrrh, and frankincense, Pound all together in the open air*
> *under the crescent moon, and add this vow." 'Then she set forth*
> *the vow, and showed how many lizards must be taken: "Take*
> *lizards many as my many forms, and do all this with care. My*
> *spacious house with branches of self-planted laurel form. Then*
> *to my image offer many a prayer, And in thy sleep thou shalt*
> *behold me nigh."*
> *'And again in another place she described an image of herself of*
> *this same kind.'"*[229]

While this is a graphic and compelling description, it is necessary to consider it with caution. Eusebius was a dedicated Christian Bishop and theologian of the time, and as such his accounts of other religions may have expressed a bias. Agrippa repeated Eusebius' instructions in his own work, Occult

227 Didyma: Apollo's Oracle, Cult, and Companions, Fontenrose, 1988.
228 Understanding Greek Religion, Larson, 2016.
229 Praeparatio Evangelica, Eusebius, early 4th century CE, trans. Des Places.

Philosophy, Book III one-thousand-one-hundred-years later which perpetuated this particular instruction.

64 - COIN REVERSE SHOWING HEKATE RIDING ON
A LION TYPE CREATURE WITH AN UNUSUAL TAIL (CANINE?) FROM CARIA,
EARLY FIRST CENTURY CE.

SINGLE-BODIED

*"Then to my image offer many a prayer,
And in thy sleep thou shalt behold me nigh."*[230]

The earliest known images of Hekate, dating to the 8th century BCE, show her as single-bodied seated and enthroned, in a manner usually associated with the goddesses Demeter and Kybele. The evidence suggests that the earlier forms of Hekate, before the fourth century, all showed her as single-bodied.

In Eleusis Hekate is most often depicted as single-bodied, holding torches or other objects associated with the Mysteries. Here a single-bodied figure of a female in a position which implies movement known as *The Running Maiden* was found believed to date to 460-480 BCE. Edwards[231] and other scholars have interpreted this image as representing Hekate, probably in her role as companion to Persephone.

---

230 Praeparatio Evangelica, Eusebius, early 4th century CE, trans. Des Places.
231 The Running Maiden from Eleusis and the Early Classical Image of Hekate, Edwards, 1986

148

Medallions and reliefs depicting Hekate accompanying the Phrygian goddess Kybele also show Hekate as being single-bodied. In these instances Hekate is most often depicted alongside the god Hermes, accompanying, or standing with Kybele. Likewise, coins from across a broad geographic region and spanning many centuries show her with one body.

Images of Hekate in triple-form became popular from the fourth century onwards, but single bodied depictions of the goddess continued to be used. For example Hekate is depicted as single-bodied on a coin dating to early first century CE, showing her riding a lionesque creature with a veil arching over her, reminiscent of earlier depictions of the lunar goddess Selene.

TRIPLE-BODIED

Pausanias, the travel writer, tells us that the first triplicate image of Hekate may have been a statue which stood next to the temple of the Wingless Nike (Victory) at the Parthenon in Athens. This portrayal named as *Hekate on the Tower* was, according to Pausanias, created by the sculptor Alkamenes in the fourth-century BCE. Later in the same century, the city of Athens presented Delphi with an impressive 14-meter high column depicting three females standing back to back around a column known today as the *Column of the Dancers*.

Also see: *The Wandering Goddess, Hekate at Delphi.*

Triplicate depictions of Hekate gained in popularity from this time on and triplicity became synonymous with her. However, as stated above, single images of Hekate also continued to be used.

There is no evidence for triplicate images of Hekate prior to the fourth century BCE, so Pausanias' account of the first triple image dating to this period is likely correct. However, it is also possible that Alkamenes in creating that statue was continuing in a tradition for which we lack evidence. Alternatively, it is plausible that Hekate at this time became syncretised with another unknown goddess, or triplicate group such as the Erinyes.

Creating three-formed icons of Hekate also fits perfectly with the goddess' association with roads and crossroads. Depictions of

149

Hekate gazing into three directions have a natural apotropaic symbolism and emphasises the goddess' role as a protectress. Three-formed representations may, therefore, have been a natural development, especially if this function increased in popularity at the time.

65 - ROMAN INTAGLIO OF A HECATAION.
WITH KIND PERMISSION, ANDRES MATA PRIVATE COLLECTION, NEW YORK

The Gnostics continued the tradition of depicting Hekate as three-formed when they incorporated her as one of the five evil Archons. In the 3rd or 4th century CE *Pistis Sophia* we find Hekate described:

*"The third order is called Triple-faced Hekatē, and there are
under her authority seven-and-twenty [arch]demons, and it is
they which enter into men and seduce them to perjuries and lies
and to covet that which doth not belong to them."*[232]

66 – ANIMAL-HEADED HEKATE AND THE GODDESS DIANA, BY W. HOLLAR, 17TH CENTURY CE.

THERIOCEPHALIC HEKATE

*"But Hecate, when invoked by the names of a bull,
a dog, and a lioness, is more propitious."*[233]

The goddess Hekate is most frequently portrayed as having the
head (or heads) of a woman, but on occasion, she is also described
or presented as theriocephalic. These depictions show the goddess
with the body of a woman but the head of an animal, hinting
perhaps ancient primordial origins. The animal-headed Hekate is
wild and irrepressible, possibly even dangerous, and undoubtedly
otherworldly and powerful.

*"With her came one who takes on various shapes, having three
heads, a deadly monster you do not wish to know: Hecate of
Tartarus. From her left shoulder leapt a horse with a long*

---

232 Pistis Sophia, Mead, 1921.
233 On Abstinence, Porphyry, 3rd century CE, trans. Taylor.

*mane. On her right shoulder there could be seen a dog with a
maddened face. The middle head had the shape of a lion of wild
form.*"[234]

In the Orphic Argonautica Hekate is described as having the
heads of a horse, dog and lion. Here she is also described as having
the ability to take on various shapes, with the animal-headed
Hekate referred to specifically as being of Tartarus and as being a
deadly monster. This emphasises the primordial, wild and
dangerous side of the goddess, especially as she may appear to
those who upset the natural balance or otherwise offend her.

67 – DETAIL OF HEKATE IN CARTARI, SHOWING THE GODDESS
WITH THE HEADS OF A HORSE, PIG AND DOG.

Theriocephalic images believed to date to as early as 30 000
BCE have been found, with the earliest being the lion-headed
Löwenmensch (lion-person) figurine found in Germany. This icon
shows a human body with the head of a European cave lion. The
Egyptian pantheon had several animal-headed deities, including the
lion-headed Sekhmet who resembles the *Löwenmensch* figurine as
being a female with the head of a lion. Other examples include the
jackal-headed god Anubis and the cow-headed goddess Hathor.
Several other world pantheons also feature deities with the heads
of animals and humanoid bodies. Here it is worth noting that

---

234 The Orphic Argonautica, Colavita, 2011.

according to Duquesne:

> "...*in ancient Egypt, the tendency to represent gods as animals
> increased over time, contradicting the cliche that indigenous
> religions 'develop towards the worship of a single god in human
> form.*" [235]

The same appears to be true of Hekate. Descriptions and depictions of Hekate with the heads of different animals appear to be later additions to her cult, which may have been through influences from Egypt or from elsewhere in Asia.

Hekate is not unique in Greek mythology and religion in having been given animal heads, but it is more usual for a deity to have one or two animals linked to them, rather than several as is the case with Hekate. The heads of the animals she is depicted with also appear to be interchangeable, with the most popular being the head of a bull/cow (sometimes just the horns), pig or boar, dog, dragon, goat, horse, and serpent[236]. The PGM features several invocations where the goddess is specifically evoked with the heads of animals, for example:

> "... *Come to me, horned-faced, light-bringer,
> Bull-shaped, horse-faced goddess, who howls doglike;
> Come here, she-wolf, and come here now, Mistress...*"[237]

Evidence for the reason Hekate is given a zoomorphic form and why the particular animals' heads are given to her is lacking.

It is possible to speculate that these depictions reveal a shamanic-like ecstatic tradition (such as that of Dionysos) being associated with her cult. Rarely spoken about, but hidden in plain sight, there is also the shapeshifting aspect to Hekate previously discussed. While literary evidence for this is lacking, it would explain the varied forms that Hekate manifests in – whether animal or human-headed. Alternatively, the different animal heads might represent different goddess cults which were assimilated into that of Hekate at various times and places.

---

235 Anubis, Upwawet, and Other Deities: Personal Worship and Official Religion ...,
DuQuesne, 2007.
236 See Hekate: Liminal Rites, d'Este & Rankine, 2009
237 PGM IV:2547-2550, Betz, 1997.

THE INVISIBLE GODDESS

Also see: *The Wandering Goddess, Hekate of Rhodes.*

The multiplicity of forms claimed by Hekate in antiquity include that of invisibility, that is, no form at all. Examples of this can be seen in the cult of the empty throne at Rhodes and Chalke, where Hekate was worshipped alongside the god Zeus. The thrones add an unusual level of intrigue and challenge in the context of trying to understand Hekate through iconography, as it renders her as invisible or otherwise absent. Anatolian, and perhaps Sumerian, influence may also provide an explanation for the incidences where Hekate was worshipped, alongside Zeus, on an empty throne:

> *"Anatolian influence is seen too in traces of the cult of the empty throne, which is Sumerian in origin, found at Rhodes and Chalke... In the rocks of Chalke, an empty throne is carved out, with a dedication to Zeus and Hekate. A Rhodian rock inscription, over a similar throne, invokes Hekate (as 'hiera soteira euekoos phosphorus Enodia[238]'). Of clear Minoan origin is the title Zeus Kronides Anax, accompanied by the motif of the double-axe, at Rhodes."[239]*

68 - THE THRONES OF ZEUS AND HEKATE, CHORIO, HALKI (MONOLITHOS, GREECE). LOCATED NEAR THE MEDIEVAL CASTLE OF THE KNIGHTS OF ST.JOHN. IMAGE: FOTOLIA

238 Hiera "Holy"; Soteira "Saviour"; Eukoos "utterances"; Phosphoros "Light Bringer" and Enodia "of the Road". Soteira, Phosphoros and Enodia are all titles of Hekate.
239 The Dorian Aegean, Craik, 1980.

69 - THRONE ROOM IN THE PALACE OF KNOSSOS, CRETE.
DATED TO CIRCA 1450-1400 BCE.

There are also examples from Phoenicia in which empty thrones were used in ceremonies honouring the gods, possibly again with stones being used to represent the deities.

> *"...in Phoenicia, the "empty throne" is a familiar object of devotion from the eighth century until the Roman period. Othmar Keel notes the remarkable spread of such aniconic cults among the Uratean, Anatolian, Irania, and Old Arabic peripheral cultures during the second and first millennia. In Phoenicia, the deity is conceived of as truly present not only on the throne but also through the placement of sacred stones upon the throne..."*[240]

There is no clear dating for the thrones on Rhodes or Chalke, both may have been in use for several centuries, and may well be remnants from a much older cult to the Magna Mater or an earlier cult to Hekate and Zeus.

The Throne Room in Knossos is believed to be an early example of the Cult of the Empty Throne, one of many examples of ancient cultures employing this practice, discussed by Agamben:

---

240 Theological Dictionary of the Old Testament, Botterweck & Ringgren, 1995

"The adoration of an empty throne has ancient roots and can be found in the Upanishads. In Mycenaean Greece, the throne discovered in the so-called Throne Room in Knossos is, according to the archaeologists, an object of worship and not a seat designed to be used. The bas-relief in the Medici Villa in Rome, which represents the empty throne from the front and surmounted by a crown surrounded by towers, appear to testify to a cult of the throne in the rites of the Magna Mater."[241]

As an aside, it is interesting to note here that the goddess Isis is depicted with a throne headdress. She is also represented by a throne hieroglyph and the name *Isis* translates as *throne*. Egyptian culture had a significant influence on that of Phoenicia, and of course, Hekate and Isis were later conflated. In ceremonies in which Isis and Osiris were honoured, thrones were sometimes used.

The empty thrones may have had sacred rocks, maybe of meteoric origin, or other symbols placed on them. It is also possible that they were used as seats for initiates or priesthood embodying the deities, perhaps as oracles. The implication being the deities manifested during the ceremonies, either through the stones, in invisible form or in another unknown way.

70 - AT THE TEMPLE OF HEKATE IN LAGINA, THE DECORATION ON THE TOP RIGHT OF THIS PHOTO IS A LABRYS, THE DOUBLE-AXE FREQUENTLY ASSOCIATED WITH ZEUS, WHO WAS ALSO WORSHIPPED ALONGSIDE HEKATE IN CARIA.

---

241 The Omnibus, Agamben, 2017.

Interesting religious counterparts centred around empty thrones can be found in contemporary indigenous tribal traditions in India today. In the state of Orisha, there are instances of tribal cults where male and female deities are worshipped as having invisible forms, seated on otherwise empty thrones or swings[242]. The Buddha was also worshipped as an empty seat, in an attempt to avoid making icons of him. The tradition and symbol of the empty throne continued into the Christian world where the empty throne became a symbol of the Son of God, in the form of the *hetoimasia* (prepared throne).

In the examples where Hekate and Zeus are honoured together on empty thrones, it is interesting to consider the relationship this implies they may have been understood to have. Remembering, in particular, Hesiod (700 BCE) writing that Zeus honoured Hekate *"above all"*, and the placement of Zeus and Hekate in the Chaldean hierarchy (circa 200 CE) as the father and mother.

THE ROCK GODDESS

As noted above, the cult of the empty throne was sometimes connected to the use of sacred stones representing deities. These stones were frequently revered cult objects, and held to represent or otherwise house the deity. Baetylic (meteoric) stones were central to the cult of Artemis of Ephesus, as well as that of the Delphic Oracle Apollo (the omphalos) and it is probable that the black stones described in the worship of Hekate would have been baetyls. These stones are highly symbolic as they are literally a star stone fallen from the sky to earth, symbolising therefore both the earth and the heavens.

In Thera, Artemidorus created a throne for Hekate Phosphoros on which he placed a black stone to represent her[243]. The cubic stones placed at the start and end of the Sacred Way by the shrine of Hekate in Didyma, likewise may also have been thought to possess unique qualities[244].

---

242 A collection of examples can be viewed on display at the Museum of Tribal Arts and Artefacts, Bhubaneswar, India (2015/2016)
243 Artemidorus the oneiromancer, a dream interpreter, circa 237 BCE.
244 See Johnston, Hekate Soteira, 1990.

Magnetite was also associated with Hekate and employed in the use of charms. It is black in colour and would have been considered to possess special magical qualities if it was magnetised.

Also see: *The Wandering Goddess, Hekate at Didyma and Miletos,* and *Hekate in Thera.*

GODDESS OF LIGHT

Hekate manifested as a column of light after being petitioned by Thrasybulus for help in his escape, guiding him to safety.

Also see: *Symbols of Her Mysteries, Torches*

She manifested as mysterious torch light on the Bosporus in Byzantium when the city was under attack from Phillip II of Macedonia.

Also see: *The Wandering Goddess, Byzantium*

MAIDEN MOTHER CRONE?

'The Persephone Painter's bell krater gives us a clue to the deeper meaning of the image [Running Maiden of Eleusis]. Persephone is represented as a bride, richly crowned and draped, a young woman at the height of her beauty and sexuality. Hekate is characterized as a younger girl by her open peplos. Demeter is a matron, the archetypal mother. The three together constitute the three ages of woman, a notion that connotes not only fertility, but also the order of life as established by Zeus.''[245]

Hekate is a *Maiden Goddess* and sometimes a *Mother Goddess* and based on evidence left behind by observers and devotees, this is how she was thought of until the twentieth-century, when she also became described also as a *Crone Goddess.* This idea would have been foreign to her ancient devotees, but continues to be perpetuated by a handful of teachers and authors today, sometimes with an apparent disconnect to her history and how this concept

---

245 The Running Maiden from Eleusis and the Early Classical Image of Hekate, Edwards, 1986

developed.

It is evident that Hekate manifested in different forms at different times and places throughout history, so it is entirely possible that she is able to reveal herself in new manifestations to devotees today. It can be challenging and sometimes emotional to put aside the conditioning and presumptions passed on to us by our teachers, however doing so can often open up much wider and often more interesting perspectives.

Understanding where ideas originate can often shed light, illuminating pathways to deeper understandings.

What is the Maiden, Mother and Crone?

The Maiden, Mother and Crone (MMC) construct proposes that the feminine divine is singular, manifesting in many different forms (or *aspects*). Adherents of this construct usually believe that *'all Goddesses are one Goddess'* and that *The* Goddess manifests with three faces, representing the three phases they feel epitomise the life of a woman: Maiden, Mother and Crone. The three stages are each given attributes and used to refer both to the aspects of *The* Goddess and used as archetypes in ritual for women to connect with both their feminity and the Divine.

MMC can provide powerful and emotional symbolic models to explore in ceremonies, especially rites of passage linked to menarche, marriage, birthing, and menopause. However, while it is undoubtedly empowering for some women, the MMC is restrictive and painful for others.

Not all women have a choice in experiencing the MMC phases of life in straightforward and predictable ways, and for them, the MMC can be uncomfortable and problematic. This includes women who have been unable to fulfil their desire to have a child, women who had their maidenhood taken from them by force, women who decided to not have children (for whatever reason) and women who experience menopause early. MMC excludes these, and some other women.

Origins: Jane Ellen Harrison

One of the suggested originators of the idea of the MMC is the Cambridge classicist Jane Ellen Harrison. Her work *Prolegomena to the Study of Greek Religion* (1903) is often cited as the first example of Maiden, Mother and Other (unnamed) Goddess. However, studying her book makes it clear that her work has not always been read in the right context, as she makes an apparent distinction between the Maiden and Mother on the one hand and the triple Maiden (which would include Hekate) on the other. Harrison writes that:

> *"Once the triple form established, it is noticeable that in Greek mythology the three figures are always regarded as maiden*
>
> *Goddesses, not as mothers. They may have taken their rise in the Mother and the Maid, but the Mother falls utterly away."*

Harrison goes on to give some examples of the triple Maiden, not mentioning Hekate, but emphasising the occurrence of the phenomenon, commenting that:

> *"The Charities, the Moirae [Fates], the Horae, are all essentially maidens."*

Origins: Aleister Crowley

The earliest mention I have been able to find of Hekate with attributes that fit the archetype of the Crone, is in the works of the controversial magician and occult writer, Aleister Crowley. In his poem *Orpheus*, published in volume 3 of his Collected Works (1907), he published an invocation of Hekate beginning:

> *"O triple form of darkness! Sombre splendour! Thou moon unseen of men! Thou huntress dread! Thou crowned demon of the crownless dead!"*

In the same invocation, he calls upon her as:

> *"Hecate, veiled with a shining veil, Utterly frail"*

Here the use of frail might indicate that Crowley associated physical age to Hekate. It could equally be a reference to the last phase of the moon.

Ten years later, in his novel *Moonchild* (1917) Crowley declares of the triple lunar Goddess that:

> "... *thirdly, she is Hekate, a thing altogether of Hell, barren, hideous and malicious, the queen of death and evil witchcraft ... Hekate is the* **crone,** *the woman past all hope of motherhood, her soul black with envy and hatred of happier mortals."*

This is the first reference to Hekate as an old woman or Crone.

Origins: Robert Graves

Robert Graves is the likely source which popularised the concept of Hekate as a Crone in his *The Greek Myths*, where he wrote that:

> "*Core, Persephone, and Hecate were, clearly, the Goddess Triad as Maiden, Nymph, and* **Crone**, *at a time when only women practised the mysteries of agriculture. Core stands for the green corn, Persephone for the ripe ear, and Hecate for the harvested corn - the 'carline wife' of the English countryside. But Demeter was the goddess' general title, and Persephone's name has been given to Core, which confuses the story."* [246]

Graves played with the construct, sometimes interchanging mother with nymph, for example:

> *"The moon's three phases of new, full, and old recalled the matriarch's three phases of maiden, nymph (nubile woman), and crone."* [247]

The author, who was a poet, apparently did not apparently intend for his work to be taken as historical fact, rather as his poetic take on Greek myth. Due to the popularity of his work, which is beautifully written, the creative aspects of it is often overlooked by readers who believe it to be an accurate historical record – which it clearly is not.

Origins: MMC Conclusion

Crowley and Graves, as well as those who subsequently

---

246 The Greek Myths, Graves, 1957.
247 The Greek Myths, Graves, 1957.

perpetuated this idea, evoked the witch stereotype when they were describing Hekate. They encouraged their readers to believe that witches were old women with crooked noses, living on the edges of society. Stories which are usually told to scare children, and probably hoodwink some of the uneducated.

Like Edwards,[248] I believe that it is possible to group deities together to represent the different ages of a woman. If this is done, Hekate would comfortably fit into both the maiden and mother positions. This would depend on the supporting cast she was given from among the other immortal goddesses. If you take the attributes she was given over the last nearly three thousand years into consideration, it is seriously doubtful that she would comfortably fit in the role of Crone.

Using the goddesses of the Eleusinian Mysteries, we might conclude that:

- **Maiden**: Hekate, she supports Demeter, and she becomes the guide (preceder and follower) to Persephone. Like Persephone, Hekate is referred to as Kore (Virgin).
- **Mother**: Persephone in the original mythos of Eleusis becomes the bride/mother to Hades, she loses her innocence and becomes Queen. When she returns to the earth she brings with her the tide of Spring, new life is born, and the crops flourish.
- **Crone**: Demeter transitions from being the Mother (her name means Earth Mother, from *Ge Meter*) and becomes the mother of the goddess who transitions to adulthood. She is the grain mother, but in the absence of her daughter life withers and the crops fail. She brings winter and barrenness to the earth.

The ancient and immortal gods are **all** old, without exception.

They are ancient, and both age and ageing are simply not relevant to them in the same way that it is for us as humans. Deities with long and complicated millennia of acknowledgement and who

248 The Running Maiden from Eleusis and the Early Classical Image of Hekate, Edwards, 1986.

are as pervading as Hekate will not fit into a human model. Age, as linked to the phases of life, is an immaterial element through which to understand an eternal ageless ancient deity. The bodies and bones of Hekate's ancient devotees are nothing more than dust now, absorbed back into the body of Nature, and yet she endures.

Also see: *The Wandering Goddess: Hekate at Eleusis.*

71 - TRIPLE HEKATE STATUE, STANDING BACK TO BACK, ENCIRCLED BY THREE FEMALE
FIGURES, POSSIBLY NYMPHS. IN THE LOUVRE, PARIS. THE INSCRIPTION INDICATES THAT THIS
DATES FROM EITHER 188BCE OR 389BCE AND IS FROM FLAVIUS GERONTIOS GIVING THANKS
TO HEKATE. FROM THE GREATER SYRIA / PHOENICIA.

Symbols of Her Mysteries

"But, again, the moon is Hecate, the symbol of her varying phases and of her power dependent on the phases. Wherefore her power appears in three forms, having as symbol of the new moon the figure in the white robe and golden sandals, and torches lighted: the basket, which she bears when she has mounted high, is the symbol of the cultivation of the crops, which she makes to grow up according to the increase of her light: and again the symbol of the full moon is the goddess of the brazen sandals."[249]

Previous generations of devotees, magical practitioners, believers and chroniclers, recorded images and ideas associated with the goddess Hekate, providing us with insights into the symbols and objects related to her. Examples of these symbols survive through to the present day in literature, art, votive offerings and other depictions of Hekate, providing unique insights through which we can connect both with the goddess and her ancient followers. Unfortunately, the symbols are not accompanied by neat and unambiguous explanations giving information on their purpose and meaning, leaving interpretation to us.

One of the many problems when attempting to interpret symbols is that they have to be understood in the context of the time and place they originated; as well as living and evolving symbols which may have gained, and continue to gain, additional levels of meaning. Symbols can, with time become more than just the thing they were intended to represent, as each person

---

249 On Images, Porphyry, 3rd century CE, trans. Gifford.

encountering the symbol evokes it and in doing so adds something of their own lifeforce and understanding into the symbol. As such, especially in a religious context, symbols can become living entities in their own right.

The objects listed here are not the only objects Hekate is shown or described as holding. As a multifaceted goddess with such a long history of worship, it would not be possible to compile a complete list of all the symbols and objects ever associated with her. This list covers the symbols most frequently related to her and instances where the symbolic association is noteworthy.

TORCHES

> *'The torches carried by the maiden at the Mother's side are the attributes of several goddesses, but primarily Hekate.'*[250]

Torches are synonymous with Hekate, and she is sometimes shown with just one, frequently with two, and on a few occasions in her triple form with up to six torches, one for each arm. When she is depicted in single form with two torches, there are instances, usually associated with death-related customs, where she is shown holding one torch up to the heavens and the other down to the earth, or both torches downwards.

Hekate is not the only goddess to be shown holding torches. Notably, Demeter, Persephone and Artemis are all also depicted with torches. More often these goddesses are shown with a single torch, but on occasion, they do wield two torches making an identification based on the torches very challenging. This even more so when considering the close relationships and other points of commonality between these goddesses in different contexts.

> *"And where did you cut the pine for torches, lit by what flame? It was on Mysian Olympus, you breathed into the torches the unquenchable light of fire"*[251]

Hekate leads the way with her torches aloft in her capacity as the *preceder* and *follower*[252] of Persephone on her yearly journey from the realm of the living on Earth above to the world of the dead,

---

250 The Mother of the Gods and a Hellenistic Bronze Matrix, Reeder, 1987
251 Callimachus, Hymn 3 to Artemis.
252 See Homeric Hymn to Demeter.

below. From the world of her mother the Grain Goddess Demeter to that of her husband, Hades. These journeys were part of the public mysteries celebrated at Eleusis, which Clement of Alexandria wrote about, echoing the story told in the *Homeric Hymn*:

> *"Deo [Demeter] and Kore became [the personages of] a mystic drama, and Eleusis with its dadouchos [torch-bearers, a title of Hekate] celebrates the wandering, the abduction, and the sorrow."*[253]

72 – STATUE, BELIEVED TO BE ARTEMIS, HOLDING TWO TORCHES, FROM THE RUINS OF GOLGOI, CYPRUS. THIS IMAGE COULD REPRESENT HEKATE OR ARTEMIS EQUALLY. 300-100 BCE. METROPOLITAN MUSEUM OF ART, NEW YORK.

When wielding two torches Hekate is frequently shown as leading others, or standing in doorways to sanctuaries. This suggests that Hekate, and by extension her priestesses, were responsible for leading or guiding candidates on their journey towards initiation. The role of psychopomp is a reflection of Hekate's role towards Persephone, guiding her throughout her

---

253 Clement of Alexander, Protrepticus, 2nd century CE, trans. H.R. Willoughby.

yearly journeys.

"Hekate's role in the story of Persephone is that of an escort across a very important boundary; in later literature, as mistress of souls, she regularly guided the dead back and forth across this same line."[254]

Initiation often marks a new beginning, a symbolic death and rebirth during which the initiate is transformed through the experience and the new knowledge or insight they gain in the process. Hekate's presence in this role would highlight her existing connection to the cycle of birth and death. The fire of her torches can be understood to represent life. In its wider context of Greek thought her torches may also represent wisdom and knowledge which is gained through the process of initiation.

Depictions of the Eleusinian Mysteries also show a male torchbearer, Iakchos. He also wields two torches and he also shows the way in what appears to be a similar role to that held by Hekate.

"Best known for his torch-bearing role in the nocturnal rites of Eleusis, Iakchos was the chthonic guide and dadouchos (Hierophant) to the initiates of the mysteries: the 'light-bringing star' who led souls down into the underworld by the light of his burning torches. During the Eleusinian initiations, a blazing statue of Iakchos led participants into the temple or Hall of Mysteries at which time all lights would be extinguished, and the initiate plunged into darkness simulating the journey beyond death and entry into the subterranean realms."[255]

Fire can also be used both as a weapon and for protection. In the war against the Titans Hekate is shown using her torches as an effective weapon of war. In accounts of the Gigantomanthia Hekate fights on the side of Zeus against the Giants. Depictions on reliefs and vases celebrating the victory of the Olympian Zeus over the Titans shows Hekate using her torches as weapons, killing the giant Klytios. Zeus emerges triumphant and banishes the Titans to Tartarus, having avenged the misdeeds of his father the Titan leader Kronos.

---

254 Hekate Soteira, Johnston, 1990.
255 Dionysos: Exciter to Frenzy, Bramshaw, 2013.

73 - HEKATE WIELDING A "DOUBLE" TORCH SOMETIMES ASSOCIATED WITH THE ELEUSINIAN MYSTERIES. DETAIL FROM AN APULIAN VESSEL, CIRCA 400 BCE, IN THE BRITISH MUSEUM.

74 - DEPICTION OF CANDIDATES FOR INITIATION ARRIVING AT ELEUSIS. DEMETER AND PERSEPHONE SEATED ON THE RIGHT, AND HEKATE LEADING THE WAY WITH HER TORCHES. ELEUSIS, GREECE.

The torch when wielded by one of the three Erinyes, the three female spirits who punish transgressions against the natural order and balance of things, was a tool for torture and punishment. In this context, the torch is dangerous but also an instrument that is used to help restore balance to a situation, and possibly to purify.

Hekate, specifically as *Phosphoros*, was invoked for help in battle. The example of Phosphoros being petitioned in Byzantium where Hekate was called upon for protection against Philip II's invasion was discussed previously in the chapter *The Wandering Goddess*,

Hekate in Byzantium. In this example the goddess provided a warning in the form of dogs barking, and assistance in the form of mysterious light just when it was needed most.

In another recorded example, Thrasybulus petitioned Phosphoros to help with his escape in 404 BCE, a journey closely linked to the restoration of democracy in Athens. In this instance the goddess was said to have manifested as a column of mysterious and illuminating fire which guided Thrasybulus safely to freedom. The light vanished when he reached Munychia[256], and he subsequently erected a shrine to the goddess there in thanksgiving.

In both examples above, the goddess was petitioned for help and provided it in the form of light, which protected and guided those who called upon her. These are practical and manifest uses of both fire and light throughout history, continuing today. We feel safe when we can see where we are going and when we can see what is ahead.

Hekate's association with torches and light is continuous. Many centuries after the instances above, she was frequently invoked in the PGM with reference to her torches. For example:

> *"Come, giant Hekate, Dione's guard,*
> *O Persia, Baubo Phroune, dart-shooter, Unconquered,*
> *Lydian, the one untamed,*
> *Sired nobly, torch-bearing, guide,*
> *who bends down…"*[257]

Hekate's torches are equated to the light of the Moon (and the stars) in an undated scholion, which juxtaposes Hekate as being the light in the dark, with Apollo being the light in the day in his role as God of the Sun. It is also possible to equate Hekate's torches to the morning and evening stars (Venus), the light of this planet is the first and last in the morning and evening skies.

On occasion, Hekate is shown holding two torches down to the earth, sometimes extinguished. Light can be taken to represent knowledge and wisdom, but also life itself. The downwards pointing torches may be understood to represent the transition of life into the afterlife at death.

---

256 Kastella Piraeus, Greece.
257 See Betz, PGM IV. 2708-84, 1997.

The seventh century BCE Spartan lyric poet Alkman mentioned a group of torch-bearing nymphs who were companions to Hekate.[258]

DAGGERS

> "On the mountain Berecynthus[259] there is said to be a stone called "Dagger." If anyone finds it when the mysteries of Hecate are being celebrated, he becomes mad, as Eudoxus says."[260]

Daggers can arouse complex emotions in modern devotees of the goddess, because of their perceived association with violence. However, daggers are also used to cut, carve and create, and are a valued practical tool for humans. Daggers were also among the sacrificial objects associated with animal sacrifice.

In the hands of Hekate, the dagger (or sometimes the sword) might be considered in the context of her association with the cycles of life, death and rebirth. The dagger could be taken as symbolising the goddess' ability to end a life and to assist in giving life, by cutting the umbilical cord at birth.

The Erinyes are shown holding a dagger, which they use to torture those who upset the natural balance of things. This may indicate that the dagger, like the torch, is a tool used to induce a primordial fear aimed at achieving spiritual purification. Like the blade of a physician a dagger may be used to cut away that which is infected and is no longer required, facilitating a necessary sacrifice to ensure that the future is better than the present.

Daggers can be taken to represent both life and death, as well as being a symbol of power. It was used by Emperors of the Roman Empire to symbolise their position of power, and continues to be used to represent personal power in some ceremonial magic traditions today.

Hekate is usually shown as holding two daggers in triple depictions, where the other arms are generally shown with torches and whips. On occasion single-bodied depictions show her holding

258 Fragment 63, Alkman, C7th BCE.
259 In Phrygia, associated with the cult of Kybele.
260 Aristotle, de Mirabilibus Auscultationibus

one dagger, with another tool in her other hand.

WHIPS

Hekate bears the epithet *Mastigophorous* (whip-bearer) as a reference to the whips she is frequently portrayed with. The whip has a long history of use in many different religious customs, and it is possible that the purpose of the whip(s) of Hekate can be found in looking at some of these examples, as unfortunately information on Hekate's association with whips is negligible.

Like the torches and daggers she is shown with, the whip is also associated with the Erinyes, who sometimes use snakes as whips, in their efforts to restore natural balance. In this context, the whip is a symbol of power and dominion, a tool which – like the dagger and torch, connects to a primordial fear. This fear can be used to control and also tame, both wild animals and people. Whips are used to control domesticated animals, including horses and bulls, both of which are associated with Hekate. In the Argonautica, we find that Medea is specifically mentioned as taking up the whip. She first purified herself seven times and called on the goddess as Brimo, before taking control of the chariot:

> *"And she herself took the reins and in her right hand the well-fashioned whip, and drove through the city; and the rest, the handmaids, laid their hands on the chariot behind and ran along the broad highway; and they kilted up their light robes above their white knees."*[261]

Hekate is called upon as the bearer of the whip in defixio spells. On a lead tablet dating to circa third century CE found near Carthage in North Africa, she is invoked alongside a number of other deities. The purpose of the spell was to prevent a rival circus from winning races on a specified date. The spell curses both the charioteers and their horses and among the deities invoked we find Hekate who is named as scourge-bearing:

> *"… throughout the earth, by the names of triple-form Hekate, the tremor-bearing, <u>scourge-bearing</u>, torch-carrying, golden-slippered-blood-sucking-netherworldly and horse riding one. I*

---

261 Argonautica, Apollonius Rhodius, 3rd century BCE, trans. Seaton, 1912.

*utter to you the true name that shakes Tartarus, earth, the
deeps and heaven…"* [262]

The priests of the Phrygian goddess Kybele, the *Galli* (Eunuch priests) practised self-flagellation until blood flowed from their bodies to show their total dedication to the goddess. In particular, this was done on the *Dies Sanguinis* (the day of blood) on the 24th of March each year. This festival formed part of a longer period of celebrations dedicated to Kybele between the 15th and 27th of March, which may have been linked to the Spring Equinox. This Near-Eastern ritual act continued to be practised into the Roman period until it was outlawed after the rise of Christianity.

When celebrated in honour of Kybele it is likely that it was done to show that the men, as devotees of the Great Mother, were willing to share in her suffering following the death of her beloved Attis. The same festival was also linked to the act of self-castration practised by this priesthood which formed part of their initiation as Galli, a likely identification with Attis.

The whip may also symbolise blood sacrifice, and be part of Hekate's iconography due to her conflation with Artemis. Whips are linked to Artemis through the ritual flogging or *diamastigosis*, which happened at the altar of Artemis Orthia. Young men would be flogged until the altar of the goddess was smeared with blood. It was both a test of endurance and an attempt at demonstrating worthiness to enter into manhood and become warriors. This particular ceremony originated from the discovery of an image of Artemis Orthia which had previously been lost, but possibly for a good reason. It is said that the Spartan warriors Astrabakos and Alopekos who found the statue went insane after doing so. To propitiate Artemis, a temple was set up for her around the statue. Unfortunately, during the sacrifice a group of Limnatians, Kynosourians and Mesoans got into an argument. The argument turned violent and many were killed at the altar of the goddess during the resulting fight. The goddess Artemis was furious with the disrespect shown by those involved and punished the survivors by sending out a disease which killed them all.

The Spartans in desperation to appease Artemis turned to an

---

262 Curse Tablets and Binding Spells from the Ancient World, Gager, 1992.

Oracle for help. They were told that the only way to win back the favour of the goddess was by staining her altar with human blood, this resulted in human sacrifices at her altar with the human offering chosen by lot. These sacrifices were replaced with a ceremony in which the young men were whipped as part of a rite of passage into manhood, providing a plentiful supply of human blood for the altar of the goddess in the process.[263] An interesting feature of this ceremony was the priestess who held the image of the goddess aloft during the scourging. She would chastise the adult men if the statue became heavy as this was interpreted as a sign that they were not scourging a particular boy hard enough, because of the high rank held by the young man or because he was considered particularly handsome.

This is not an isolated example of scourging at the altars of Artemis. In another example, which Xenophon[264] wrote about, two groups of young men would fight over cheese which was placed on the altar of Artemis. The first group defended the cheese with whips, and the second group tried to steal it. In the process much blood would be spilt on the goddess' altar, an act which was believed to appease the goddess for another year.

The goddesses Kybele, Artemis and Hekate were all closely linked throughout their respective histories, conflated and believed to share attributes in common. As such the possibility is there that Hekate's association with the scourge draws on similar ideas to that described in the examples above with Kybele and Artemis, and involved some form of flagellation as part of sacrifice and devotion to the goddess. It is interesting to note that in both instances, it is the male devotees who undertake the flagellation.

The whip also had a unique use in the cult of the Grain Goddess Demeter, where it was used as a tool to separate the wheat from the chaff. Here the whip is an agricultural tool with an important function in the grain cycle. The same technique of threshing the wheat is still used in rural communities in developing countries today.

---

263 Pausanias 3.16.7.
264 Lakedaimonion Politeia 2.9.

KEYS

"Persian, unconquerable huntress hail!
The world's key-bearer never doom'd to fail."[265]

Hekate is given the title of *Kleidouchos* (key-bearer), a term specifically associated with her at her temple in Lagina. Here key-bearing processions or *Kleidos Pompe* were held down a Sacred Way between the temple and the nearby city of Stratonicea. As previously discussed, the purpose of the ceremonial key is not entirely clear, however exploring the ideas associated with keys provide some clues.

Also see: *The Wandering Goddess, Hekate at Lagina and Stratonicea.*

In addition to being connected with keys, Hekate was also linked to doorways, gateways and entranceways. These are liminal points through which a person passes from inside to outside, and also the point where one is most likely to use a key. As such the key symbolises the permission to move from one place to the other. Moreover, the person who holds the key to a particular door or gate can usually be assumed to be the person in charge or at the very least a person with some accountability for what lies beyond. It is curious to note that the key in the procession at Lagina was carried by a child, rather than by someone of high rank.

Future excavations at Lagina may reveal additional information, but until then it is only possible to speculate. It is likely that the key carried in the procession served a particular local purpose, which may not be related to the use of the key the goddess wields, though this would seem unlikely. The key may have been the key to the city, to the temple or perhaps a distinct religious space; or conceivably it was purely symbolic.

Hekate's keys are said to be the keys that open the gates to Hades, as Johnston puts it this *"agrees with her duties as the guide of disembodied souls".* [266] It is also referred to in the PGM as respectively the keys that open the *"bars of Cerberus"*[267] and the key of *"she who rules Tartaros"* or the *"Lady of Tartaros"*[268].

---

265 Orphic Hymns, trans. Taylor, 1792.
266 Also see Johnston, Hekate Soteira, 1990.
267 Greek Magical Papyri in translation, PGM IV.2292, Betz, 1997.
268 Greek Magical Papyri in translation, PGM IV.2335 and LXX.10, Betz, 1997.

Numerous ancient cosmologies teach that the world is separated into *Heaven*, *Earth* and the *Underworld*. To pass between these three realms, it is necessary to go through gateways between them, and it is for this reason that Hekate's association with gateways and keys makes her such an essential ally for magicians. Indispensable to those who want to gain divine revelations by accessing the realms beyond to obtain access to the souls of the dead - a journey which necessitates passing through the gates between the world of the living and that of the dead.

Keys also symbolise freedom, the ability to choose whether to enter a space and when to leave. Keys are also a form of protection, by locking an area you prevent others who do not hold the keys from entering.

Keys symbolise transition, moving from one place to another across a liminal point. Today this continues as a recognisable symbol in western countries marking the change between childhood to adulthood, and symbolic keys are given to represent this transition.

SPEARS

> *"O Lord Helios and Sacred Fire*
> *The spear of Hekate of the Crossroads*
> *Which she bears as she travels Olympus"*[269]

Sophocles emphasises that the spear is sometimes Hekate bears when she travels Olympus, the realm of the Olympian gods. The association of Hekate with spears is attested in both literature and depictions showing her with one or sometimes, two, spears. This is a likely result of the syncreticising of the Thracian goddess Bendis and Hekate, as Bendis is described as having spears. Mishev highlights this, writing that:

> *"In the incantation the dual nature of the Goddess is named*
> *through the white and black. She is made closer to the image of*
> *Bendis, who was called δίλογχος – 'the one with the double*
> *spear', explained by the lexicographers by the meaning that the*

---

269 The Root-Cutters, Sophocles, C5th BCE, trans. Z. Yardley.

Goddess accepts honour both from earth and sky."[270]

The spear in this context is therefore best understood as representing Hekate's association with Olympus, and her connection to both the earth and the heavens, as mentioned in the *Theogony*.

SERPENTS OR SNAKES

"the snake-girdled the three-headed,"[271]
and "the She-serpent, and the snake-girdled: others calling her
on account of her appearance girt in serpent coils."[272]

Serpents are undeniably significant symbols of Hekate. At different times she is shown or described as wielding serpents, having serpent hair, possessing snake-like arms or legs or as having serpents coiled around her arms or body. Ogden highlights some of the connections Hekate has with snakes in the following quote:

"...an Aristophanes fragment speaks of 'Hecate of the earth
(Chthonia) rolling coils of snakes' whilst a Sophocles fragment
describes her as 'garlanded with oak and the twisted coils of
savage drakontes'. Aristophanes' words suggest an anguipede,
like the Hecate of the lekythos. Sophocles' combination of
serpent and plant is also generally suggestive of that image with
its associated branching Erinyes, whilst his specification of
drakontes in the hair assimilates Hecate to images of the
Erinyes of the estheton-lekythos types."[273]

As with the torch, dagger and whip, there is an iconographic link to the Erinyes, who sometimes wielded serpents as whips. This adds an additional layer of terror when they fulfil their function of torturing those who have contravened the natural order. The torture continues until they are able to purify themselves from the miasma caused by their wrongdoings.

In the following description Eusebius, quoting Porphyry, provides a description of how a Hekate statue should be formed. It is claimed that these instructions originated from the goddess

---

270 Mishev, G, in Thracian Magic, 2012.
271 Chaldean Oracles, C2nd CE, trans. S. Ronan.
272 Chaldean Oracles, C2nd CE, trans. S. Ronan.
273 Drakon: Dragon Myth and Serpent Cult in the Greek and Roman Worlds, Ogden, 2013.

herself, calling (amongst other things) for snakes to adorn her waist:

> *"White robes, and feet with golden sandals bound.*
> *Around the waist long snakes run to and fro,*
> *Gliding o'er all with undefiled track,*
> *And from the head down even to the feet*
> *Wrapping me fairly round with spiral coils."*[274]

The Greek Magical Papyri also highlights Hekate's continued association with serpents, and provides some very vivid descriptions, for example in the *Prayer to Selene for any spell*, in which Hekate and Selene are equated we find:

> *"Of fearful serpents on your brow..."* [275]

> *"With pois'nous rows of serpents down the back..."*[276]

> *"And you keep Kerberos in chains, with scales*
> *Of serpents are you dark, O you with hair,*
> *Of Serpents, serpent-girded..."*[277]

And earlier by Sophocles, in the Root-Cutters as:

> *"She who is crowned with oak-leaves*
> *and the coils of wild serpents."*[278]

Dionysos was also crowned with serpents, as Bramshaw notes:

> *"...the unborn child in Semele's womb survived the lightning -*
> *for cooling ivy vines wrapped around him and protected him*
> *from the heat that had killed his mother. Zeus then quickly*
> *transferred the unborn child into his thigh; a temporary womb*
> *which would bring the baby to term. Zeus later gave birth to*
> *Dionysos - the bull-horned and serpent-crowned child - at*
> *Phoinie, on Mount Nÿsa. And so the Second Incarnation of*
> *Dionysos – Dionysos Bromios, or the Olympian Dionysos –*
> *was born..."*[279]

In addition to Dionysos, Hekate is depicted in assembly with other serpent deities, among them the gods *Aion, Asclepius, Hermes, Serapis* and *Chnoubis*. The Maenads who had such a crucial role in

---

274 Praeparatio Evangelica, Eusebius, early C4th CE, trans. Des Places.
275 See PGM IV.2785-2890, "Prayer to Selene for Any Spell". Trans. Betz, 1996.
276 See PGM IV.2785-2890, "Prayer to Selene for Any Spell". Trans. Betz, 1996.
277 See PGM IV.2785-2890, "Prayer to Selene for Any Spell". Trans. Betz, 1996.
278 Sophocles' description in his play The Root-Cutters.
279 Dionysos: Exciter to Frenzy, Bramshaw, 2013.

the Mysteries associated with Dionysos are also described as having wild snakes in their hair:

> *"The Fates made him perfect ... the god with ox's horns,*
> *crowned with wreaths of snakes – that's why the Maenads*
> *twist in their hair wild snakes they capture.'*[280]

These descriptions are reminiscent of the Gorgon Medusa, who like Hekate held an apotropaic function. Interestingly, Medusa was one of three Gorgon sisters, all of which had serpent hair and evil-averting functions and are likely to have had their origins in ancient beliefs of the feminine divine from a time before the Greek Dark Ages.

A defixio from Athens dated to the first century CE shows a three-formed Hekate, with six arms, bearing torches in the upper pair of arms, with the lower pair being serpentine.[281] Ogden highlights an example of Hekate being depicted with a serpent tail as feet, and notes that:

> *"...a striking image of ca.470BCE, actually is the earliest*
> *positively identifiable image of the goddess to survive, represents*
> *her as an anguipede, her serpent tail making one large coil*
> *behind her clothed humanoid form, with a pair of dogs*
> *emerging as far as their forelegs from the lower part of her*
> *humanoid frontage."*[282]

Earlier images of Hekate do exist, but this particular image is definitely an early example of the goddess with attributes making her distinguishable. The idea that Hekate is part serpent also appears in the work of Lucian (125–180 CE):

> *"And the magician in his Philopseudes brings up Hekate from*
> *below in the form of a woman, half a furlong high, snake-footed*
> *and with snakes in her hair and on her shoulders, with a torch*
> *in her left hand and a sword in her right; while Selene comes*
> *down from the sky in the shapes of a woman, an ox, and a*
> *dog; we may suppose the latter form to have been assumed out*
> *of compliment to the other goddess."*[283]

---

280 The Bacchae, 129-135, Euripides, c 400BCE, trans. Ian Johnston
281 Athenian Defixio, first century CE.
282 Dragons, Serpents, and Slayers in the Classical and Early Christian Worlds, Ogden, 2013.
283 The Cults of the Greek States, Farnell, 1896-1909.

Ogden goes on to note the similarity between this image and that of the Sicilian Skyla, who is sometimes named as Hekate's daughter. Here it is also interesting to note the striking similarity and shared symbols Hekate has with *Shamaran*, the Queen of Serpents who is still popular in Turkey today, especially in Kurdish contexts, and in the region which was once Anatolia.

75 - SHAMARAN, QUEEN OF SERPENTS AND GUARDIAN OF WISDOM

76 - QADESH STELE, IN THE EGYPTIAN MUSEUM IN TURIN.
STANDING ON A LION, WITH THREE LOTUS FLOWERS, A SPEAR AND SNAKE.

Snakes are a common theme in religious iconography, and Hekate's own relationship with snakes are mirrored in depictions of other deities. For example, the Canaanite wisdom and mother goddess *Asherah* was known as the *Lady of the Serpent* (*dāt batni*). Images of the Egyptian goddess *Qudshu* (or *Qadesh*), who was associated with Asherah, frequently depict her as holding serpents. Qudshu is also linked to lions, serpents, lotuses and spears.

Deities or spirits who are invoked for magic and spells are habitually accompanied by snakes. The Buddhist Vajrapāni, the thunder-bolt wielding Buddha, is depicted as wearing snakes on his arms and ankles.[284] Likewise, the goddess Isis who has the title of Mistress of Magic is recurrently associated with snakes, for example:

> *"Isis is portrayed as a Healing Goddess on a number of Alexandrian coins and also on an engraved carnelian gemstone. On her head she wears the modius (a cup used to measure corn) and holds an erect snake. In front of her is a globe and a flaming altar."*[285]

The god of healing, Asclepius, and the god Hermes, the messenger god of Olympus, are both shown with snakes, which also feature on the staffs of both gods. Asclepius has a single serpent wrapped around his staff, which is a symbol of healing. Hermes has the Caduceus, a staff wrapped with two serpents, which is rich in symbolism, primarily associated with polarity, ideas associated with kundalini energy and also later with alchemy and healing. Hygeia, worshipped alongside Asclepius, was also shown with snakes, sometimes wrapped around her. Hekate had a noteworthy presence on Kos, where she may have been worshipped there as one of the Twelve Gods[286].

Also see: *The Wandering Goddess, Hekate of Kos*

---

284 The Gods of Northern Buddhism: Their History and Iconography, Getty, 2009
285 Isis: Eternal Goddess of Egypt and Rome, Jackson, 2016
286 The Twelve Gods of Greece and Rome, Long, 1987.

77 – HEKATE, WITH TWO TORCHES, STANDING BEHIND SEATED DEMETER, WITH ASCLEPIUS AND SONS OF DOCTORS AND OTHERS WHICH WERE BEING HONOURED WITH THIS RELIEF BY ATHENS. THIS IS A RARE DEPICTION OF ASCLEPIUS IN AN ELEUSIAN SETTING.
LATE 4TH CENTURY BCE.
WELLCOME LIBRARY.

PATERA & OFFERING VESSELS

"For to this day, whenever anyone of men on earth offers rich sacrifices and prays for favour according to custom, he calls upon Hekate. Great honour comes full easily to him whose prayers the goddess receives favourably, and she bestows wealth upon him; for the power surely is with her."[287] *"And propitiate only-begotten Hecate, daughter of Perses, pouring from a goblet the hive-stored labour of bees."*[288]

The Theogony, like other subsequent texts, highlights the importance of sacrifices to the goddess. These offerings were ritualised with the use of special offering vessels, including the patera and jug.

Hekate is shown holding a patera (offering or libation bowl) on coins from Stratonicea , Caria, the city nearest the famous temple of Lagina in ancient Anatolia. In this example Hekate is usually shown as single-bodied, with a dog by her side, holding a torch in

---

287 The Theogony, circa 8th or 7th century BCE, Hesiod, trans. Evelyn-White, 1914.
288 Apollonius Rhodius, Argonautica

her left hand, with the patera in her right, pouring it to the ground.

Hekate is also sometimes shown holding a jug, most often an oenochoe or amphora, as depicted on carved relief of Hekate found at Aegina.

78 - DETAIL FROM A COIN FROM STRATONICEA

Offerings made to the chthonic gods and the dead were usually made straight into the ground. The Greeks often libated wine mixed with water (as this was the customary way to drink it), as well as unmixed wine, oil and honey. The Romans did the same, but also sometimes offered perfumes.

79 - ILLUSTRATION OF THE HEKATE RELIEF OF AEGINA

This description of a poured offering of wine is from Virgil's *Aeneid* where the sibyl Deiphobe sacrifices to Hekate and invokes her to guide the heroes of the story:

> *"The priestess pours the wine betwixt their horns;*
> *Then cuts the curling hair; that first oblation burns,*
> *Invoking Hecate hither to repair:*
> *A powerful name in hell and upper air."*[289]

Deiphobe was a priestess of both Hekate and Apollo and a Cumaean Sibyl. Like Medea and Kirke she was semi-divine, being named as the daughter of the prophetic sea-god *Glaucus*.

Another example can be found in the *Orphic Argonautica* Orpheus makes a libation of water around a triangular altar pit which was previously dug, and then invokes the goddess:

> *"I poured water and made a libation around the pit..."*[290]

In the Orphic *Derweni Papyrus* libations of wine are made to the three Erinyes, but rather than being poured the wine is offered in small drops. This may indicate that it was sprinkled (asperges), or that it was offered drop by drop.

> *"...sacrifices of wine in small drops..."*[291]

BASKETS

Eusebius describes her, in her association with the Moon, as holding a basket:

> *"...and torches lighted: the basket, which she bears when she has mounted high, is the symbol of the cultivation of the crops."*[292]

This is a likely reference to Hekate as the Moon Goddess, and the close association of agriculture and the lunar cycle she had. The basket is also a symbol frequently associated with the fertility of the land, a natural association for a tool which is used to hold the fruits of a harvest.

289 Aeneid, Virgil, late C1st BCE, trans. Dryden.
290 *Orpheus. Hymns. Argonautica*, Batakliev, 1989 quoted in Thracian Magic, Mishev, 2012.
291 Hellenic orphic sources, Aleksieva, 2004 in Thracian Magic, Mishev, 2012.
292 On Images, Porphyry, C3rd CE, trans. Taylor.

The Mysteries of Dionysos also involved the use of a basket, which was used to present the sacred mask:

> *"The Orphics also spoke of a figwood mask, which was given to the goddess Hipta (or Rhea) the nurse of Dionysos. She placed it in a winnowing basket for safety, around which a snake entwined. The fig was also associated with the Eleusinian tales of Kore, who was snatched by Hades and taken down into the subterranean depths to become his queen, as Persephone."*[293]

In the Mysteries at Eleusis, a basket was also used to hold sacred objects, and as a symbol is associated with both Demeter and Persephone.

It was a common household object and as such it is not surprising to find that it features in the stories of many of the deities of Greece and the nearby regions. It is however interesting to note, in this context, that in both the Mysteries of Eleusis and those of Dionysos a basket was used to hold something sacred, which was revealed to initiates.

DOGS

> *'On her right shoulder there could be seen a dog with a maddened face."*[294]

In addition to the description of Hekate as having the head of a dog with a maddened face in the *Orphic Argonautica*, the goddess' association with dogs is well-attested. She has dogs as companions, and as heralds, they are said to be sacred to her and sometimes presented to her as ritual offerings. The most infamous association today is the idea that black dogs (or puppies) were sacrificed to Hekate at the crossroads. This is sometimes used as a generic, but misguided, indicator that ritual remains uncovered had an association with Hekate. Dogs were also sacrificed to other deities, as well as for the purpose of scape-goating and purification rituals.

> *"A baying of hounds was heard through the half-light: the goddess was coming, Hecate."*[295]

293 Bramshaw, Dionysos: Exciter to Frenzy, 2013
294 The Orphic Argonautica, Colavita, 2011
295 Aeneid, Virgil, late C1st BCE, trans. J. Dryden.

The sound of dogs barking is often given as an announcement of Hekate's presence. It can be found in a variety of legends associated with Hekate, such as the story of how Phosphoros came to the aid of the Byzantines when they were under attack by Philip II discussed earlier in this volume. Listening for the sound of baying dogs is still considered a useful sign when invoking the goddess's help.

The dog as the companion to Hekate might be linked to the tale of Queen Hekabe, the wife of King Priam of Troy. After the city of Troy was defeated, Queen Hekabe was taken by Odysseus as his captive. On the voyage back to Greece, Hekabe saw her son Polydor's corpse on a beach. He had been murdered by the Thracian king Polymestor, who had been looking after him with an amply- sized treasure he coveted. Enraged, Hekabe killed the king and was attacked and stoned by the locals. The gods stepped in and transformed Hekabe into a black dog, after which she became the companion of Hekate. Ovid also equated queen Hekabe to the dog star, Sirius. In Lycophron's *Alexandra*, Hekabe's cenotaph is said to be at *Pakhynos* – the modern Capo Passero, Sicily.

The dogs who were shown accompanying Hekate have sometimes been thought to represent the spirits of the restless dead travelling with the goddess. However, as Johnston wrote:

> *"…its docile appearance and its accompaniment of a Hecate who looks completely friendly in many pieces of ancient art suggest that its original signification was positive and thus likelier to have arisen from the dog's connection with birth than the dog's demonic associations."* [296]

Plutarch equates Diana with Hekate, and further links the dog to Hekate while discussing the Egyptian gods and religion.

> *"For the Grecians both speak and think aright in these matters, when they tell us that the pigeon is sacred to Venus, the serpent to Minerva, the raven to Apollo, and the dog to Diana, as Euripides somewhere speaks: Into a bitch transformed you shall be, And be the image of bright Hecate."* [297]

---

296 Restless Dead, Johnston, 1999.
297 Plutarch, Plutarch's Morals, vol. 5, trans. Goodwin, 1878.

The Thracians offered black dogs in sacrifice to their goddess Bendis, who was syncretised with Hekate. It is possible that the story of Hekabe is a representation of that assimilation:

> *"The maiden daughter of Perseus, Brimo Trimorphos, shall make thee [Queen Hekabe] her attendant, terrifying with thy baying in the night all mortals who worship not with torches the images of Zerynthia [Hekate] queen of Strymon [in Thrace], appeasing the goddess of Pherai with sacrifice. And the island spur of Pakhynos shall hold thine awful cenotaph, piled by the hands of thy master [Odysseus], prompted by dreams when thou hast gotten the rites of death in front of the streams of Heloros. He shall pour on the shore offerings for thee, unhappy one, fearing the anger of the three-necked goddess, for that he shall hurl the first stone at thy stoning and begin the dark sacrifice to Hades."[298]*

In his work *Moralia* Plutarch wrote that the dog sacrifice made to Hekate was for members of a household, drawing comparisons to the goddesses Geneta and Eilioneia (Eileithyia). Question 52 in which he discusses dogs is quoted below in full for convenience.

> *"Question 52. Why do they sacrifice a dog to Mana Geneta, and pray that no home-born should become good?*
>
> *Solution.*
>
> *Is the reason that Geneta is a deity that is employed about the generation and purgation of corruptible things? For this word signifies a certain flux (i.e. Mana from manare) and generation, or a flowing generation; for as the Greeks do sacrifice a dog to Hecate, so do the Romans to Geneta on the behalf of the natives of the house. Moreover, Socrates saith that the Argives do sacrifice a dog to Eilioneia (Lucina) to procure a facility of delivery. But what if the prayer be not made for men, but for dogs puppied at home, that none of them should be good; for dogs ought to be currish and fierce? Or is it that they that are deceased are pleasantly called good; and hence, speaking mystically in their prayer, they signify their desire that no home-born should die? Neither ought this to seem strange; for Aristotle says that it is written in the treaty of the Arcadians with the Lacedaemonians that none of the Tegeates*

---

298 Lycophron, Alexandra, 3rd century BCE, trans. Mair, 1921.

> *should be "made good" on account of aid rendered to the party*
> *of the Lacedaemonians, i.e. that none should be slain."*[299]

Geneta or *Manis Geneta*, is only mentioned by Plutarch and Pliny, and might be a title of a goddess as not much else is known. She is historically linked to both Eileithyia and Hekate, possibly as a birth goddess presiding over the decision on whether a new-born child lives or dies. Dogs were thought to have less painful labours, and as such dogs may have been sacrificed to these goddesses to ensure safety and reduce pain in childbirth. This point is made several centuries later by the sixth-century CE Greek chronicler Hesychius of Miletus who also recorded that Genetyllis was associated with Hekate. He emphasised this connection by writing that the dog sacrifice was made to Genetyllis to ensure a comfortable, peaceful and natural childbirth.

It is thought that the association of dog sacrifices with Hekate is due to a foreign (i.e. non-Greek) influence on her cult. In addition to the Lydians, Hittites also sacrificed puppies in ritual, and often in association with the goddess *Gula*, who was associated with healing.

Also see: *The Wandering Goddess, Hekate of Lydia.*

> *"We may assert therefore that, outside of offerings, puppies were among the animals most often used in ritual. Their function in these, as we have seen, was to prevent impurity or to purify. The killing of puppies in these rituals was not done for the benefit of the gods, but as an essential part of the processes of prevention and purification…"*[300]

Aristophanes names Hekate as one of a trio of goddesses, with Artemis and Diktynna, the Cretan Goddess of the Hunt. In the *Frogs*, Diktynna is given a pack of hunting hounds. Artemis was also said to have a pack of hunting dogs, and Hekate is frequently accompanied by dogs. This shared connection with dogs may have contributed to the three goddesses being equated, or point to a shared origin.

> *"O Artemis, thou maid divine, Diktynna, huntress, fair to see, O bring that keen-nosed pack of thine, and hunt through*

---

299 Plutarch, Plutarch's Morals, vol. 5, trans. Goodwin.
300 The Puppy in Hittite Ritual, Collins, 1990.

all the house with me. O Hecate, with flaming brands.[301]

The story of Diktynna (Britomaris, Aphea) has fascinating parallels to others linked to Hekate. She was worshipped initially on Crete, as a goddess of hunters and fishermen, before becoming assimilated into the cult of Artemis.

Also see: *The Wandering Goddess, Hekate of Aegina.*

The Greek Magical Papyri links Hekate to wolves, the wild cousin of the dog.

> *"Your ankle is wolf-shaped, fierce dogs are dear to you,*
> *wherefore they call you / Hekate, Many-named, Mene..."*[302]

Artemis' mother the goddess Leto, the sister of Asteria, travels in the form of a she-wolf. Mishev explains in *Thracian Magic:*

> *"In the guise of a she-wolf the Goddess Leto goes from the lands of the Hyperboreans to Lykia, which until then has another name, and because wolves greet her there, she renames the land Lykia (Antonius Liberalis, Metamorphoses 35). Porphyry writes that in the language of the mysteries Artemis is called she-wolf λύκαινα. The name of the Thracian heroine Harpalyke ('Αρπαλυκη) is derived etymologically with the meaning "predatory she-wolf". It is not uncommon for the Goddess to take the guise of a she-wolf or to have wolf traits – ankle of a wolf or an image of a dog (which appears as its substitute). The Trojan queen Hecuba turns into a bitch attendant of the "ruling over the Strymon kingdom Zerynthian goddess", and her tomb is called "the sign of the dog" (κυνος σημα). The role of the wolf, respectively the dog, as a mediator of the Goddess and her image, is also reflected in the legend of the saving of Byzantium (which is an old Thracian settlement) because of the barking of dogs, and therefore the worship of the Goddess there as torchbearer. In ancient magic, the Goddess is called as wolf taming..."*[303]

The wolf is sacred to both of Leto's children. The temple of Apollo at Delphi had a statue of a wolf. Here at his most celebrated temple, there were stories of the god sending his wolf to hunt a thief who successfully stole gold from his temple. Apollo could

---

301 Aristophanes, Frogs 1358.
302 PGM IV.2785-2870, Betz, 1996.
303 Thracian Magic, Mishev, 2012.

also manifest in wolf shape, and was known as the Wolf God.

In the 1960's archaeologists unearthed thirty clay vessels with food which were buried as part of rituals which may have been with the purpose of warding off evil or natural disaster. These offerings of ritualised dinners have been dated to circa 500 BCE. Similar burials, in the same region, were uncovered in 2013 containing eggshells which have been dated to around 1 BCE.

These burials contained the remains of dogs, bronze tools and coins. They differ significantly from those mentioned by Aristophanes as they were buried, and therefore the poor would not have been able to take the food to eat. Furthermore, these offerings are only attested through archaeology, and as such we do not know the context or whether offerings were also left above ground at the time. There is no evidence linking Hekate to the offerings found at Lydia, however we know that Hekate, as well as Zeus, was worshipped in this region, as evidenced through inscriptions, statues and coins.

Plutarch also discusses the reason why priests were forbidden to avoid dogs and goats, not touching or naming them saying that while dogs were less smelly than goats, dogs were not permitted on the high streets of Athens, nor on the island of Delos[304]. He says that dogs are quarrelsome creatures and that they are expelled out of sanctuaries and sacred temples for this reason, allowing suppliants safe refuge – implying that it would not be so if they had to pass a dog at the doorway.

> *"Neither did the ancients at all repute this creature clean; for he is offered in sacrifice to none of the celestial Gods, but being sent to Hecate, an infernal Goddess, at the three cross-ways for a supper, takes a share in averting calamities and in expiations. In Lacedaemon they cut puppies in pieces to Mars, that most cruel God. In Boeotia public expiation is made by passing between the parts of a dog divided in twain. But the Romans sacrifice a dog in the cleansing month, on the festival which they call Lupercalia. Hence it was not without cause, to prohibit them whose charge it was to worship the highest and*

---

304 This is interesting as previous names for Delos included *Cynethus* (dog).

*holiest God from making a dog familiar and customed to
them."*[305]

Less known was the Greek belief in the *Kynokephaloi*, a tribe of
dog-headed people they thought lived in India and Africa. Hesiod
apparently believed in a similar tribe of dog-headed people, the
Hemicynes (half-dog people) which is reminiscent of the later images
of Hekate where she is given the body of a human and the head of
a dog.

*"No one would accuse Hesiod of ignorance though he speaks of
the Hemicynes... "*[306]

The Roman equivalent of the Erinyes, the *Furina*, had dogs
sacrificed to them. The Furina additionally took on the form of
dogs to hunt and torture criminals who acted in contravention of
natural balance. The deities Demeter and Hades were also said to
sometimes take the shape of a dog.

Likewise, the Roman Lares, ancestral spirits of the home, were
believed to sometimes take on the form of a dog or a man dressed
as a dog. The much later St. Christopher, called upon frequently
for protection while travelling, would also be depicted as having
the head of a dog.

The Chaldean Oracles mentions dogs, associating them with
Physis (Nature) which it presents as an aspect of Hekate.

BULLS & COWS

*"...the head of a bull, which snorts like some bellowing spirit,
is raised towards the sphere of air..."*[307]

The bull was a symbol of the Moon Goddess Selene, who was
extensively assimilated into the cults of Hekate and Artemis. In the
Greek Magical Papyri Hekate is frequently equated with Selene,
and their names are used interchangeably. Selene is depicted in
iconography as riding a bull, or as on a chariot pulled by two bulls.

*"Take a lodestone and on it have carved / a three-faced
Hekate. And let the middle face be that of a maiden wearing*

305 Plutarch, Plutarch's Morals, vol. 5, trans. Goodwin.
306 Fragment 44, Catalogues of Women.
307 De Mensibus, Lydus, C6th CE, trans. Wunsch.

horns, and the left face that of a dog, and the one on the right that of a goat.[308]

Hekate is recurrently described as being bull-headed or bull-horned, as well as possessing other attributes associated with the bull. In examples from PGM IV we find her referred to repeatedly as having the face and eyes of a bull, as well having the shape of a bull. For example:

"O Night-bellower, Lover of solitude, Bull-faced and Bull-headed One" and *"bull-eyed, horned, mother of all things."*[309]

Bulls were also depicted alongside Hekate on a gemstone, showing the goddess with three heads, and with a lower body similar to that of Artemis at Ephesus. One example shows an ironstone amulet[310], depicting a cow-headed goddess, wearing a long dress and holding two torches. The stone has unidentified *voces magicae* around the edges, and it would be interesting to know if the stone was magnetised.

Hekate is additionally associated with the Apis bull, who is shown on Tessera coins from Memphis, Egypt, showing Isis-Hekate with three heads on the other side. The Apis bull was where he was mixed with other gods becoming Serapis, and the companion to Isis, as well as having connections to Hekate.

Numerous terracotta icons have been found depicting a female divinity crowned with both the moon and small discreet cow horns. These are often identified as Isis-Demeter, as Io-Isis or as Selene. However, the iconography of the Moon, cow horns could equally indicate Hekate. Moreover, many of these icons are also crowned with a polos, shown wearing a veil and holding a single torch. Io was the beloved of Zeus who was, according to myth, turned into a cow and subsequently revered in human form. Isis assumed the cow horns of the goddess Hathor, and was also syncretised with Hekate, as Isis-Hekate as discussed earlier in this book.

Considering Hekate's oceanic associations and connections to Poseidon, it is interesting to note that this Sea God is sometimes

---

308 PGM IV.2880-84, trans. Betz, 1996.
309 PGM IV.2785-2870, trans. Betz, 1996.
310 In the Kelsey Museum of Archaeology.

named as *The Bull of the Sea.*

The Khalkotauroi, King Aeetes' (father of Medea) colossal bulls, had hoofs of bronze and breathed fire. These otherworldly bulls were gifted to Aeetes by the Smith God Hephaestus. In the story of Jason's quest for the Golden Fleece, he has to yoke the bulls and use them to plough a field as part of the challenge set by the King. Jason does so with the help of Medea.

Another interesting connection between Hekate and bulls can be found in Antoninus Liberalis' version of Iphigeneia's transformation. In this version, when the King places his daughter on the altar as a sacrifice to Artemis, the goddess replaces the girl with a bull. She then takes the girl to the Sea of Pontos, where Iphigeneia becomes the founder of the Taurean tribe, in memory of the bull.[311] Later this led to the founding of Artemis' famous sanctuary at Brauron, when Iphigeneia and her brother, Orestes take with them a cult statue from Tauros to Brauron. In other versions of the story, Iphigeneia is transformed into the goddess Hekate. Pausanias recorded that *Theseus* founded a temple to *Artemis Soteira* after he had slain the Minotaur.

The bull was very important in Crete, which is interesting in the light of the numerous tentative Minoan influences on the cult of Hekate.

Also see: *The Wandering Goddess, Minoan Crete.*

Likewise, the god Dionysos, whose cult intersects with that of Hekate at various points, was also worshipped as a bull-faced deity.

> *"Dionysos I call loud-sounding and divine, inspiring God, a two-fold shape is thine; thy various names and attributes I sing, O' firstborn, thrice begotten, Bacchaean King. Rural, ineffable, two-formed, obscure, two-horned, ivy-crowned, and Euion pure. Bull faced and martial, bearer of the vine...[312]*

This is further emphasised in the Dionysiaca, where the transformation of Dionysos is highlighted.

> *"Semele was kept for a more brilliant union, for already Zeus ruling on high intended to make a new Dionysos grow up, a*

---

311 Antoninus Liberalis, Metamorphoses, 27.
312 Orphic Hymn 53 to Amphietus quoted by Bramshaw in Dionysos: Exciter to Frenzy, 2013.

bullshaped copy of the older Dionysos…" [313]

Magicians in the Balkans have long claimed the ability to draw down the moon. This practice as also associated with the Witches of Thessaly, who were thought to invoke Hekate in their potent magical rites. Curiously, Mishev notes that the moon was sometimes thought of like a cow in this context:

> *"Drawing the power of the moon, the sun or the stars in traditional Bulgarian belief is done most often as the celestial body takes the image of a cow and it is milked by the magician, and the milk is the essence of its power."* [314]

HORSES

> *"From her left shoulder leapt a horse with a long mane."* [315]

Hekate is described with the head of a horse in the *Orphic Argonautica*, a belief which can also be found in other texts and depictions of the goddess. In the PGM *Spell of Attraction*[316] Hekate is described as a *"horse-faced goddess"*. The horse was also one of the animals named in the list of Hekate symbols used in the prayer provided in PGM VII.756-94.

Hekate is also otherwise associated with horses, and in particular as being able to grant favours to those who work with racehorses.

> *"… she is good to stand by horsemen, whom she will…"* [317]

The PGM provides one example of a spell where the goddess is entreated for her help in restraining the horse of the opposition in a race[318]. This is a theme that can also be found in surviving examples of defixiones curse tablets. The idea that she is able to support the winning side in games can be found in the Theogony:

> *"Good is she also when men contend at the games, for there too the goddess is with them and profits them: and he who by might and strength gets the victory wins the rich prize easily with joy,*

---

313 Dionysiaca, Nonnus, 5th century CE, trans. Rouse, 1940.
314 Mishev in Thracian Magic: Past and Present, 2012
315 The Orphic Argonautica, Colavita, 2011.
316 PGM IV.2441-2621, Betz, 1996.
317 The Theogony, circa 8th or 7th century BCE, Hesiod, trans. Evelyn-White, 1914.
318 PGM III.1-164, Betz, 1996.

and brings glory to his parents."[319]

John Lydus' *Liber De Mensibus* provides an elemental description of forms in which Hekate might appear. The horse here is linked to the element of fire:

'For the fire-breathing head of a horse is clearly raised towards the sphere of fire'[320]

This is not just the head of a horse, but precisely that of a fire-breathing horse. In Greek mythology, the god Ares possess four such horses, the *Hippo Areioi*: Phlogeus, Phobos, Konabos and Aithon. They draw the chariot of the God of War, and are the offspring of the Anemoi Boreas, the North Wind, with one of the three Erinyes. It is interesting to note that Boreas is a cousin to Hekate in mythology. And as previously discussed, the Erinyes may have been the source for some of the symbolic tools carried by Hekate, the torches, whips (snakes) and daggers. Ares is also named as a brother to the goddess Eileithyia, the goddess of childbirth equated with Artemis, Hera and Hekate.

When Hippo, Queen of the Amazons, refused to perform the annual dance at Ephesus, Artemis transformed her into a horse.[321]

The goddess Selene, who is syncretised with Hekate was invoked as *"Lover of Horses"* in the Orphic Hymn 8, *To the Moon, Selene*, where she is also named as bull-horned.

"Hear, Goddess queen, diffusing silver light, bull-horn'd and wand'ring thro' the gloom of Night.

...

Lover of horses, splendid, queen of Night, all-seeing pow'r bedeck'd with starry light."[322]

LIONS

"The middle head had the shape of a lion of wild form."[323]

Hekate is described in the *Orphic Argonautica* as being three-headed, with the middle head being that of a wild lion. She is also

---

319 The Theogony, circa 8th or 7th century BCE, Hesiod, trans. Evelyn-White, 1914.
320 Chaldean Oracles, C2nd CE, trans. S. Ronan, 1989.
321 Callimachus Hymn 3 to Artemis.
322 Orphic Hymns, trans. Taylor, 1792.
323 The Orphic Argonautica, Colavita, 2011

depicted with a lion either side of her on a coin from Lydia, dated to circa 69-79 CE. In the Chaldean Oracles Hekate is described as being *"lion-possessing"*,[324] and significantly, *"If you call upon Me often you will perceive everything in lion-form."*[325] In the *'Prayer to Selene for any Spell'* from the PGM, lions are given a protective function, *"you stand protected by two rampant lions"*.[326]

A depiction of a three-formed Hekate standing on the back of a lion can be found on a black haematite gemstone in the *Kunsthistorisches* (Art History) Museum collection in Vienna. This amulet dates to circa 200-300 CE and has an image of Aphrodite on the reverse.

Goddesses are frequently depicted as flanked by lions in imagery from the Near and Middle East, as evident in the iconography of goddesses such as Inanna, Astarte and Kybele. Likewise, Artemis is also sometimes flanked by big cats. Hekate's association with lions could therefore be interpreted as pointing to Eastern origins, or as being a remnant of the influence of a tradition from that region on her worship.

80 - BRONZE STATUE OF KYBELE HOLDING A CYMBAL, ON A CHARIOT DRAWN BY TWO LIONS. LATE 2ND CENTURY CE, ROMAN. IN METROPOLITAN MUSEUM, NEW YORK.

---

324 Chaldean Oracles, C2nd CE, trans. S. Ronan.
325 Chaldean Oracles, C2nd CE, trans. S. Ronan.
326 PGM IV.2811-12, trans. Krause.

SANDALS

The footwear of the Goddess of the Crossroads is not discussed that much in modern literature. Porphyry names Hekate as being *"the goddess of the brazen sandals"*[327]. The term brazen was used for both bronze and brass, so brazen does not automatically mean brass. Likewise, Eusebius records an oracle of Hekate, where she describes herself as having golden sandals:

> *"Hecate also speaks of herself thus:*
> *'Do all anon: a statue too therein;*
> *My form - Demeter bright with autumn fruits,*
> *White robes, and feet with golden sandals bound."*[328]

Bronze sandals are also mentioned in the PGM[329] and on a second/third century CE Egyptian lead tablet as part of a sequence of Hekate symbols.

The Greek Platonic fourth-century BCE philosopher *Heraclides of Pontus*, in his lost dialogue was the first person to report the allegorical legend of Empedocles' death by jumping into the volcano Mount Etna, leaving only a bronze sandal floating on the lava to show his passing. There are many interesting parallels recorded in the life of Empedocles suggestive of connections to the cult of Hekate, especially in his homeland, Sicily in *Magna Graecia*.

PILLARS, TREES & HEKATE'S POLOS

Hekate, when shown in her triplicate form, is most frequently depicted as standing around a pillar, with her back to it. On other occasions, she is shown standing on a pillar or column. Far from being just a coincidental decoration, the pillar appears in the context of depictions of Hekate so frequently that it undeniably has a symbolic meaning which points to historical influences. When worn by Hekate it sometimes terminates in, or is decorated with a crescent moon.

---

327 On Images, Porphyry, C3rd CE, trans. Gifford.
328 Praeparatio Evangelica, Eusebius, early C4th CE, trans. Des Places.
329 PGM IV.2334-38, Supplementum Magicum 49, trans R.G. Edmonds III.

81 - DETAIL FROM A DRAWING BY COSWAY OF A TRIPLE IMAGE OF HEKATE FROM THE BRITISH MUSEUM COLLECTION SHOWING HEKATE WITH A POLOS HEADPIECE.

The word polos is taken to mean axis or pole and is believed to have originated as a tree, which became stylised and simplified with time. Depictions of divinities in the style of Artemis of Ephesus with a pole-like body represents another probable survival of the pole symbolism found in earlier mythologies. The goddesses Artemis, Aphrodite, Hekate and Hera are all on occasion depicted with this type of body which is indicative of the eastern influences on their cults.

The pole as a symbol associated with the Divine Feminine has a long and rich history in the Near East. It is this region which is also the most likely place of origin for the polos as worn by Hekate which as a headdress was given to significant mother goddesses from the Anatolia region. Those depicted with a polos, both divine and mortal, were usually authoritative female rulers. The polos is a divine headdress.

The polos is somewhat similar in appearance to the *modius* and *kalathos* headdresses also worn by Hekate. They are all cylindrical, but the polos is shorter and slightly tapered outwards at the top as shown in the illustration above. Other than surviving in artwork and sculpture, no known ceremonial example of this headdress is known to have survived. This has led to speculation that it was made from wood or possibly woven from another natural material which has long since decomposed.

The Biblical Goddess *Asherah* is possibly the best-known goddess to be associated with the worship of poles. References to her can be found throughout the *Torah* or *Old Testament* of the Bible, where she is equated to a pole.

> *"they set up for themselves pillars and sacred poles [Asherim]*
> *on every high hill and under every green tree; there they made*
> *offerings on all the high places"*[330]

The Wisdom Goddess as Asherah was worshipped both as a symbolic (and sometimes ornately carved) sacred pole and as a living tree (sometimes named as a *tree of life*). In *Proverbs 3:18* this Tree of Life is referenced, highlighting and preserving the importance of this goddess:

> *"She is a tree of life to those who lay hold of her".*

Like her later Greek counterparts, Asherah's symbols included lions and serpents. She is also shown seated on a lion throne, much like that of Kybele, or as standing on the back of a lion; and is called *dāt batni*[331] which means *Lady of the Serpents*. Inscriptions to Asherah with Yahweh dating back to the eight-century BCE shows that she was his likely consort, much in the way that Hera, and sometimes Hekate, is depicted with Zeus. Asherah was later replaced by the *Shekinah*.

A possible connection between the goddesses Artemis and Asherah through the Greek Spartan *Ortheia*, and the persistent connection between Artemis and Hekate, makes for another interesting possibility. This is discussed in *The Cosmic Shekinah*, which I co-authored with David Rankine (2010):

> *"...Carter has argued convincingly that the Greek Spartan*
> *goddess Ortheia, who was subsumed into the maiden huntress*
> *goddess Artemis around the fifth century BCE, was originally*
> *derived from Asherah.*[332] *Her argument is based on a number*
> *of factors, including the hundreds of terracotta masks found at*
> *the temple of Ortheia, which are unique in such quantities to*
> *the whole of Greece. The name Ortheia, meaning 'upright' or*
> *'standing' is taken from the story of how a lost wooden cult*
> *statue was found amongst trees by two Spartan men who*
> *subsequently went mad. Carter makes the connection between*
> *this wooden statue, which would preside over rites, and the*
> *carved poles (Asherim) used in the worship of Asherah. All of*
> *these elements, like the masks and poles could have been*
> *brought by the Phoenicians from the Middle East to Greece,*

330 2 Kings 17:10-11, 7th century BCE.
331 Canaanite Myth and Hebrew Epic, Cross, 1997.
332 The Masks of Ortheia, Carter, 1987.

and this is a plausible possibility for the origins of
Ortheia...."[333]

The Spartan goddess Ortheia may equally have been a form of Hekate. Ortheia was linked to the cult of the birth-goddess Eleithya, who in turn was thought to be Hekate or Artemis.

MODIUS

The modius headpiece which Hekate is frequently depicted with was named after jars used to measure dry products, and in particular grain. It symbolises fruitfulness in the wearer, and when worn by Hekate it could be understood to be a reference to her involvement in the agricultural cycle.

The modius is specifically associated with the deities of the Eleusinian mysteries and the subsequent derivatives of the tradition in the Roman Empire.

Serapis, who is linked to Hekate through her conflation with Isis, is also sometimes shown wearing the modius.

82 - DETAIL FROM A 1ST CENTURY HEKATE ICON SHOWING THE MODIUS ON THE HEAD OF THE GODDESS.

---

333 The Cosmic Shekinah, Rankine & d'Este, Avalonia, 2010.

KALATHOS

With similarities to both the polos and modius in appearance, the kalathos was a basket headdress which Hekate was sometimes depicted with. It to some extent resembles a top hat.

> *"Baskets in the shape of a kalathos adorned altars too. Although these were seldom filled with wool, such baskets are mostly interpreted as symbols for the Eleusian cult and for the cult of Ceres."*[334]

It was primarily a container used for storing wool, but also for food and flowers. Worn as a headdress it represents fertility. It was used in the late Roman period to signify marriage. It continued on as a symbol in Christianity and can be found in Apocryphal images of the Annunciation, next to the Virgin Mary.

83 - CARVING OF HEKATE TRIFORMIS WITH HER TOOLS AND TWO DOGS ON WHITE CHALCEDONY. EACH OF THE THREE HEADS IS CROWNED WITH A KALATHOS. NATIONAL MUSEUM OF ANTIQUITIES, LEIDEN.

---

334 Greek and Roman Textiles and Dress: An Interdisciplinary Anthology, Harlow & Nosch, 2014

The kalathos was also linked to Hekate in Caria, where she was frequently depicted as wearing it. One such example is this silver coin dated to 81 BCE showing the laurel-crowned head of Zeus, with Hekate on the obverse wearing a kalathos, with a torch and patera.

84 - SILVER COIN, 81BCE FROM STRATONICEA, SHOWING ZEUS AND HEKATE.
FROM ZEUS: A STUDY IN ANCIENT RELIGION. VOLUME 2, PART 1., COOK, CAMBRIDGE, 1925

PHRYGIAN CAP

The Phrygian cap is a pointy hat-like cap with the point flopping over. It is believed to be derived from *Attis*, beloved of the goddess Kybele, and hence called Phrygian. Attis, whose cult dates to at least 1250 BCE, according to legend castrated himself. This gave rise to the practice of self-castration by the Galli, the priesthood of Kybele. These men castrated themselves in public as part of their initiation and dedication to the Great Mother. Attis' mythology is closely linked to the cycle of life, death and resurrection, and through that to the seasonal agricultural cycle.

Hekate is depicted with this cap on statues and reliefs, though it is rarer than depictions showing her with a polos or modius. Depictions of Hekate with a Phrygian cap most likely indicate her conflation and relationship with Kybele.

The Thracian goddess Bendis, the Persian god Mithras and the Thracian mystic poet Orpheus are all also shown wearing this particular cap on their heads.

AGRENON

Hekate is sometimes shown with a veil-like fabric net draped over her, the agrenon. It was worn by seers, oracles and bacchanals and was made from fine wool.

Some translations of the Homeric Hymns translate the text describing Hekate as having a glistening veil, for example:

> *"...Hecate of the glistening veil, who-from her cave-heard, and so did Lord Helios the glorious son of Hyperion..."*[335]

Hekate is also described with a veil in the Orphic Hymns:

> *"Sepulchral, in a saffron veil array'd,*
> *leas'd with dark ghosts that wander thro' the shade..."*[336]

This is a symbol associating Hekate specifically with the bacchantes, but also with oracles and seers. However, it has also been interpreted as being a tool she uses to create the phases of the moon and in which she covers herself during an eclipse.

The earlier moon goddess Selene, was also depicted with a veil.

Also see: *Body of the Goddess, Single Bodied*

OAK LEAVES

> *"She who is crowned with oak-leaves ..."*[337]

In addition to Hekate being described by Sophocles as being crowned with oak leaves, according to the Argonautica, there was also an oak tree at the centre of Hekate's garden. The practice of garlanding statues of deities was prevalent in Greece, and it is possible that the reference to Hekate as being crowned with oak leaves was a description of this devotional practice. The oak was also sacred to the Thracian goddess Bendis, as well as Artemis, and in both instances the icons of the respective goddesses would have been wreathed in this way. One depiction on a silver coin (191 BCE), believed to represent the goddess as Artemis, shows the goddess holding torches crowned with a wreath of oak.

The polos or pole of Hekate discussed in the previous section may have been represented initially by a tree. Although there is no indication that this was a reference to an oak tree, it is believed that it originated with a tree and as such the oak tree may be a candidate.

Another possibility is that Hekate's association with the oak

---

335 Sources for the Study of Greek Religion: Corrected Edition, Rice & Stambaugh, 2012
336 Orphic Hymns, trans. Taylor, 1792.
337 Sophocles' description in his play The Root- Cutters.

originates through her lasting relationship with the god Zeus. The oak was associated with Zeus, and his most famous oracle was at Dodona (Epirus, North-West Greece) was notable for its grove of oak trees.

Oak trees held a significant place in the cult of the Roman Diana, especially when she appeared in her triple form. As with Artemis, Hekate's relationship with Diana is a very close one, and overlaps in significant ways.

Magnificent oak leaf crowns crafted from gold have been found in ancient Thracian and Hellenic tombs belonging to Kings. This includes a superb example which belonged to Philip II, father of Alexander the Great.

POPPIES

> *"… and from the poppy her productiveness, and the multitude of the souls who find an abode in her as in a city, for the poppy is an emblem of a city…"*[338]

It is tempting to focus on the narcotic and potentially lethal qualities of the poppy, but this is not the meaning Porphyry ascribed to it in his work. He highlights the symbolism of productiveness, evident in the sheer number of seeds one poppy pod contains. He also likens the poppy to a city, being home to countless numbers of people, and uses this as a symbol for the goddess. While the sleep and euphoria-inducing qualities of this plant have also been known about for a long time, the idea that the poppy is a symbol of fecundity is an ancient one, especially in Anatolian folklore.

> *"It has to be noted that the plant has always been referred to as a symbol of fertility in Anatolian folklore. Needless to say, the countless seeds contained in the poppy pod make it an ideal symbol of birth"*[339]

Ronan also highlights this in a discussion about the parallels between the goddesses Hekate and Atagatis, when he quotes from Cornutus' *Theologiae Graecae compendium*:

---

338 On Images, Porphyry, C3rd CE, trans. Gifford.
339 Friedland, Food and Morality: Proceedings of the Oxford Symposium on Food and Cookery, 2008

"They also gave her a poppy-head,
symbolising that she was the cause of the production of life."[340]

Porphyry also mentioned the poppy as a symbol of Hestia, Demeter and Rhea. This provides further symbolic parallels between Hekate, Demeter and Rhea, and emphasises that the poppy was viewed as a symbol of fertility.

"Demeter in other respects is the same as Rhea, but differs in
the fact that she gives birth to Kore by Zeus, that is, she
produces the shoot from the seeds of plants. And on this
account her statue is crowned with ears of corn, and poppies are
set round her as a symbol of productiveness." [341]

The idea that it represents a city is also interesting. The detailed crowns worn by the Ephesian Artemis and Kybele show city walls and other features of culture. These were not merely rural goddesses, they were goddesses whose rulership underpinned civilisation itself.

Also see: *The Wandering Goddess, Hekate at Eleusis.*

85 - CITY WALLS DECORATE THE TOP OF THE EPHESIAN ARTEMIS' HEADPIECE.

340 Ronan, The Goddess Hekate, 1992
341 On Images, Porphyry, C3rd CE, trans. Gifford.

RAYS

The most famous statue of the goddess Hekate crowned with rays is perhaps the *Chiaramonte Hekate* in the Vatican collection, Rome. These rays may be taken to indicate Hekate's association with the Moon as a luminary, shining forth light in the darkness. It could however, also indicate a solar connection, which is hinted at through Hekate's association with Apollo and Helios.

86 - Detail of the Chiaramonte Hekate, showing 7 rays.
In the Vatican Museum, Rome.

87 - Detail from a statuette of Apollo or Helios, with typical solar rays. 300-200 BCE, Etruscan in Hellenic Style. In the Metropolitan Museum of Art, NY.

Where depictions show seven rays, it may be symbolic of a connection to the seven wandering stars (Sun, Mercury, Venus, Moon, Mars, Saturn and Jupiter). Seven may also be linked to the seven vowels used in magical incantations. These were used for both the seven wandering stars, and associated with the Iynx in the Chaldean Oracles.

It is interesting here to note that Hekate is shown with an aureole on an Apulian red-figure krater vase, dated to circa 350 BCE. The painting shows Hekate, with Hermes, accompanying Persephone and Hades, during Persephone's return journey.

STARS OR WHEELS: 4- AND 8-RAYED

Circles with both four-fold and eight-fold divisions can be found associated with Hekate.

The symbol can be found carved by pilgrims into the marble steps and pediment of the Temple of Hekate in Lagina. When these carvings were made is not clear, but there are dozens of examples of this symbol carved into the monument, so it must have been important in some way. Numerous other symbols are also found carved into the stones, many of which suggest magical practices. While not as prolific as at Lagina, I have also noticed this symbol (and others) crudely carved at Eleusis, and at other temple sites.

It is unfortunately not clear when these carvings were made, by whom or why. The further scheduled archaeological work at Lagina will hopefully shine a further light in due course.

88 - FOUR SPOKED WHEELS CARVED BY PILGRIMS ON THE STEPS OF THE TEMPLE OF HEKATE AT LAGINA WHERE THERE ARE DOZENS OF SUCH CARVINGS. 2015.

⊕ Equal-armed crosses in circles appear on images showing the Eleusinian deities. This includes Hekate, and the so-called Eleusinian torch which is topped by an equal-armed cross.

⊕ It has been suggested that the four-fold symbolism is indicative of the division of the year into four seasons. However, in the context of Eleusis this would seem inappropriate, as here the cycle is specifically divided into three. Persephone spends one-third of the year in Hades as Queen, and the rest with her mother Demeter upon the Earth.

⊕ Suggestions that the symbol represents millstones (because of the grain connection at Eleusis) are unsubstantiated, as saddle querns were used to grind flour until the late Hellenistic period. These bear no resemblance to the symbol.

⊕ The circled cross is also sometimes known as the Greek Cross, and although it has ancient origins and applications, was also used by the later Christians.

⊕ This symbol appears in the PGM CXXIIIa-f, in a spell where Brimo (Hekate) is called upon in a love charm. The accompanying invocation recalls qualities associated with Hekate too. It also appears in the next charm for childbearing, where Brimo is once again implored, as well as in a spell to cause one to speak while sleeping found in PGM VII.411-16. It might be worth noting here that Brimo had a close connection with the Mysteries at Eleusis.

⊕ Four-spoked designs could also symbolise the Iynx or magic wheel.

Also see: *Symbols of Her Mysteries, Magic Wheels & Whirlings.*

⊕ This symbol today is used to represent the element, as well as the planet, Earth in astrology and Western esoteric symbolism.

⊕ This is also the symbol for the letter representing the sound 'ka' in Linear B, the Mycenaean language and script which was an earlier form of Greek. Linear B disappeared after the cultural breakdown known as the *Bronze Age Collapse*, which took place suddenly and violently in the region circa 1200-1150BCE.

⊖ The symbol can be found on a stone matrix dating to the Minoan period and found in Sitia. Researchers claim that it is part of the world's oldest computer, and that it was used to calculate the solstices and equinoxes, also that it can be used as both a sundial and to calculate latitudes. It may have been used for navigation. If there is a connection, this may support the idea that it was a symbol of the four-fold division of the year.

⊖ It is also associated with Nemesis, the Greek Goddess of Divine Justice. An example on a yellow jasper gemstone depicts Hekate as the primary deity, with a smaller Hermes to her left and Nemesis to her right and is dated to the late second century CE. The symbol can be found at the feet of Nemesis.

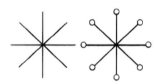

Eight-rayed stars have a long history of being associated with solar deities, which are commonly depicted with them. Although Hekate is today considered to be a lunar deity, earlier sources make no mention of Hekate's association with the Moon. Her later relationship with the Moon is primarily because of syncretisation with Moon goddesses, such as Selene.

Artemis also was associated with lunar symbols until much later, and indeed shares many solar qualities in common with her brother Apollo. Artemis' bow was described as golden, as were her arrows, and she rode through the sky in a golden chariot. Likewise, Artemis is associated with solar animals, such as the lion. As Apollo's association with the sun expanded in the late Hellenistic period, so Artemis became increasingly associated with the Moon – in so doing the twins, in part, replaced the older Helios (Sun) and Selene (Moon). Hekate also replaced Selene, and in many instances, was paired with Apollo in the context of Moon and Sun, rather than Artemis.

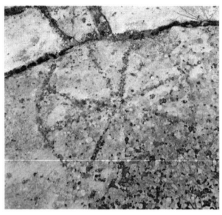

89 - EXAMPLE OF AN EIGHT-RAYED STAR, WITH A CIRCLE IN THE CENTRE, ENCLOSED IN A CIRCLE CARVED ONTO THE STEPS BY PILGRIMS AT THE TEMPLE OF HEKATE, LAGINA.

The above example of an eight-rayed star on the pediment of the Temple of Hekate in Lagina is of unknown date. Eight-rayed motifs also appear on other depictions of Hekate, sometimes carved onto the polos on her head, or otherwise around the image of the goddess on carved reliefs and gemstone intaglios and charms. Sometimes instead of being enclosed in a circle, the lines each terminate in a small circle. There are also depictions showing Hekate with the eight-rayed star on her headdress or body, such as a triple bronze believed to be from Aegina, now in the Boston Museum of Fine Arts.

The journey of the Sun marks the yearly cycle, and like the four-rayed cross, this symbol may represent the annual cycle of seasons. The equinoxes and solstices being the equal-armed part of the design, and the cross-quarter lines being the intervals between, such a calendar has long been used beneficially in agriculture. An eight-fold *Wheel of the Year* was created in the 1950's by Gerald Gardner to illustrate a yearly cycle of religious festivals. The set of eight Pagan festivals or *sabbats* on this Wheel are Halloween, Winter Solstice, Candlemas, Spring Equinox, Beltane, Midsummer, Lammas, and the Autumn Equinox. The festivals are about six weeks apart and mark points in the position of the Sun and the agricultural year. The Wheel of the Year also marks a cycle of ascent and descent for the deities of Gardner's Wicca, which echoes ideas of katabasis found in the Mysteries.

Eight-pointed stars are also found in association with the

Mesopotamian goddess Ishtar (Inanna), and four-rayed stars were shown with Ba'al, her counterpart. The 6000-year-old cave mural, the *Star of Ghassul*, which was found in the Jordan Valley, features an eight-rayed star, with further geometric designs towards its centre.

Eight-rayed stars are also found in the PGM where they are used as part of spells and charms.

This ✳ is used in PGM VII:795-845 as a symbol for Capricorn in the context of a Pythagorean Dream Oracle and dream divination. It also appears in a charm to restrain anger (PGM X.24-35), in another charm to suppress or silence (PGM VII396-404), and in PGM XLIX, a charm with the name Aion and a group of other kharaktêres. An educated guess then might be that it represents Capricorn, or a spirit associated with Capricorn. This symbol also appears below the hand of Hekate on a silver lamella, featuring Hekate and Anguipes[342].

In later texts, this ✳ symbol is also sometimes given as a symbol of Christ, especially in the Gnostic tradition.

90 - OBSIDIAN GEMSTONE, FIRST CENTURY CE. SIDE 1: THREE FORMED HEKATE, WITH HAPOCRATES AND CHNOUBIS. SIDE 2: OUROBOROS CIRCLE ENCIRCLING 7 STARS.

✳ This symbol is sometimes stylised to ✳ and appears on numerous charms and gemstone charms featuring Hekate. For example, there are seven such eight-rayed stars on the reverse of an obsidian charm featuring Harpocrates, Hecate, Chnoubis and Ouroboros (Fig.90, above).

---

342 See the Campbell Bonner Magical Gems Database.

On another, circa third-century CE charm made from green and red jasper[343], Hekate is shown with six such stars, three each side of her, and with the inscription on the back, four more such stars. Occasionally seven-rayed versions of this symbol are also used on images featuring Hekate, which may echo the possible symbolism for the seven-rayed headdress discussed in the section above, linking Hekate to the seven wandering stars, seven vowels and seven levels of the Chaldean Oracle Hierarchy (seven heavens).

✳A bronze Hekataia statue, 18 cm high, believed to be from Aegina, now in the Boston Museum of Fine Arts, shows each of the three goddess images wearing a polos with an eight-pointed star, with each line ending in a circle. This possibly denotes Hekate's association with the starry heavens.

THE MOON

> *"…subject to apparent wanings and waxings and transformations, some call her an earth-like star, others a star-like earth, and others the domain of Hecate, who belongs both to the earth and to the heavens."* [344]

Hekate was not initially thought of as a Moon Goddess, but as her cult spread throughout the Greek, Greco-Egyptian and Roman empires she gained lunar attributes. In his work *On Images*, Porphyry wrote of Hekate as being associated with the phases of the triple moon, which may have been the template for the idea of the twentieth-century *Witches' Triple Goddess*.

> *"But, again, the moon is Hecate, the symbol of her varying phases and of her power dependent on the phases. Wherefore her power appears in three forms, having as symbol of the new moon the figure in the white robe and golden sandals, and torches lighted: the basket, which she bears when she has mounted high, is the symbol of the cultivation of the crops, which she makes to grow up according to the increase of her light: and again the symbol of the full moon is the goddess of the brazen sandals."* [345]

---

343 British Museum Collection, OA.9522
344 See Plutarch, Moralia Vol.IV, trans. Babbitt
345 On Images, Porphyry, C3rd CE, trans. Taylor.

91 – HEKATE CROWNED WITH AN UPWARDS-POINTING LUNAR CRESCENT

Eusebius, again quoting Porphyry, wrote in the *Praeparatio Evangelica*, giving instruction for the creation of an icon of the goddess, which is made at the new moon:

> *"Pound all together in the open air*
> *Under the crescent moon, and add this vow."*[346]

The twelfth-century Byzantine poet John Tzetzes identified Selene, Artemis and Hekate as the three forms of Hekate.[347] In doing so, he was continuing an ancient tradition, as evidenced in the papyri texts. Hekate-Selene was the most prominent goddess in the PGM, balancing the solar Apollo-Helios as the most prominent god.

One of the earliest known literary references to Hekate being lunar can be found in the first-century CE Roman philosopher Seneca's play *Medea*. It expresses the syncretisation between Hekate and Selene, who was portrayed as riding a chariot through the night sky:

> *"I see Trivia's swift gliding car, not as when, radiant, with full*
> *face, she drives the livelong night."*[348]

These examples highlight that Hekate's association with the Moon linked her with all the phases of the Moon, and in particular that of the full Moon. Rituals were also performed to her on the last and first day of the lunar month, which includes the Hekate Suppers which are discussed in a later chapter. There is no reason to believe that the use of the lunar crescent in ancient iconography

---

346 Praeparatio Evangelica, Eusebius, early C4th CE, trans. Des Places.
347 Scholiast on Alexandria of Lycophron, C12th CE.
348 Medea, Seneca, C1st CE, trans. Miller.

indicated a new, waxing or waning moon as it might do in modern calendars. Instead, it should be taken to represent the Moon as a whole. It is however possible that the upwards pointing horns of the lunar crescent on the Goddess' brow may have additional symbolism.

When observed in the night-sky the crescent moon appears as a banana shape, pointing to the left or right, depending on whether it is waxing or waning. It does also appear, depending on the time of the year and latitude, to be leaning with points upwards (like a U) or downwards. If the perfectly upwards pointing crescent is to be taken to be more specific than a general symbol for the Moon, it could then indicate a precise time of the year and region at which the Moon can be observed like this.

The upwards-pointing crescent may also be a stylised version of bullhorns, which often have a lunar crescent shape. Hekate is, as previously discussed, described as being bull-horned.

Also see: *Symbols of Her Mysteries, Bulls & Cows*

Ideas linking Artemis to the moon can be found some centuries earlier. For example, in his third century BCE *Hymn 3 to Artemis* the Greek poet Callimachus places a silver (rather than the previously gold) bow in Artemis' hand. This could be taken as a symbol of the waxing or waning moon:

> *"And how many times, Goddess,*
> *did you test your silver bow?"*[349]

By the second century BCE, the references to Artemis as a lunar goddess were more substantial.[350] So, while evidence is lacking in extant literature of Hekate having earlier lunar associations, it is possible to postulate that she may have had previous lunar connections through her conflation with both Artemis and Selene.

---

349 Hymn 3 to Artemis, Callimachus, C3rd BCE, trans. F.J. Nisetich
350 For example in fragments of the writings of the Stoic philosophers Apollodorus and Diogenes.

92 - DETAIL FROM THE RELIEF OF MITHRAS FROM HEDDERHEIM, TAKEN FROM THE 1918 A
NEW MITHRAIC RELIEF FROM SYRIA BY FROTHINGHAM.
MITHRAS HERE IS SHOWN WITH THE BULL, WEARING THE PHRYGIAN CAP.

RIBBONS

Hekate is shown with ribbons on a coin from Lydia dated to the late first century CE. It is possible that other depictions where she is assumed to be holding a snake or whip-like object might also be ribbons.

Like today, in antiquity ribbons were used to tie things, including hair and dresses. There is no indication as to the reason Hekate is shown with ribbons, but it is most likely that it was due to her association with the dead.

> "The commonest way of decorating the tomb was by winding a broad, flat sash or ribbon around the shaft of the stele and then tying it into a knot or bow with the loose ends hanging down. Such ribbons (called taeniae) were provided with terminal strings which also hang loose."[351]

POMEGRANATES

Although it is rare, there are extant icons of Hekate where she is shown holding a fruit, presumed to be a pomegranate. While it is likely that this highlights either Hekate's connection with Persephone or her conflation with the Queen of Hades, it is also conceivable that Hekate is shown holding the pomegranate to show her own special involvement with the Mysteries of Demeter and Persephone.

---

351 Gardland, The Greek Way of Death, 2001

93 - DETAIL FROM A HEKATE STATUE, SHOWING THE FRUIT THE GODDESS HOLDS.
IMAGE FROM THE NATIONAL MUSEUM OF ANTIQUITIES, LEIDEN.

In the legend of Persephone's abduction the pomegranate has an intrinsical and unique place as a symbol. When Persephone makes the decision to consume a few seeds of pomegranate she is offered by Hades, she seals her fate. She becomes the wife and Queen of Hades, fated to remain in his domain. It is only through (divine) intervention, and the subsequent yearly journeys on which Hekate accompanies Persephone, facilitating her ascent and descent, that Demeter allows life to return to the land. This is the story of the seasons, the grain cycle and the transformation of a Virgin Goddess into a Queen – as well as being a story of lust or love, the loss of innocence and the simultaneous coming into power of a woman, depending on your interpretation.

Images of Hekate holding a pomegranate are a reminder of her intimate and often overlooked, maybe in part secretive (and if so, deliberately obscured), association with the mysteries of Demeter and her daughter.

Also see: *The Wandering Goddess, Hekate at Eleusis.*

The cycle of Persephone's descent and her ascent can also be understood through the cycles of life and death. It is said that initiation into the Mysteries provided the initiate with a different understanding of death, knowledge which took away the fear of death. For this reason the pomegranate is closely associated with the cycles of death and rebirth. Persephone consumed it knowing that by doing so she would bind herself to Hades and his domain.

In this context the pomegranate also becomes a symbol of free will - loss of innocence, by choice.

The pomegranate is also a symbol of abundance and fertility, with its many seeds representing the many possibilities of life.

RED MULLET FISH

Triglê (Red Mullet, a type of fish) was offered to Hekate, and said to be sacred to her based on the principle that it reminded worshippers of qualities associated with her. For example:

> *"Apollodorus also, in his treatise On the Gods, says that the Triglê is sacrificed to Hecate because of the associations in the name; for the goddess is triform. But Melanthius, in his work On the Eleusinian Mysteries, includes the sprat with the Triglê because Hecate is a sea-goddess also."* [352]

Red Mullet is believed to spawn three times a year which is the reason it is believed to have *tri* or *three* in its name. This provides a sympathetic correspondence to Hekate as the three-formed goddess.

> *"The Triglê, on account of the syllable in its name which is common to the epithets of Hecate, is dedicated to her. For she is the goddess of the three ways and looks three ways, and they offer her meals on the thirtieth days."* [353]

Likewise, it may provide a link to fertility in the sea, highlighting Hekate's association with the ocean and with fishermen. This idea can also be found in the Theogony, where we are told:

> *"...and to those whose business is in the grey discomfortable sea, and who pray to Hecate and the loud-crashing Earth-Shaker, easily the glorious goddess gives great catch, and easily she takes it away as soon as seen, if so she will..."* [354]

Red Mullet also produces a magical display of colour change as the fish dies which may have added to its association with Hekate. In his *Natural Questions* Seneca describes the death of a red mullet saying that there is nothing more beautiful. This may have been the

---

352 The Deipnosophistae of Athenaeus, Loeb Classical Library edition, 1929
353 The Deipnosophistae of Athenaeus, Loeb Classical Library edition, 1929.
354 The Theogony, circa 8th or 7th century BCE, Hesiod, trans. Evelyn-White, 1914.

reason that the fish was sometimes brought to die on the table as part of the spectacle of feasts (outside of the context of sacrifice) before being cooked. It is said that as it dies it turns a bright red, before changing colour again settling into paler hues.

It was a very expensive fish and considered a delicacy. Mosaics depicting red mullet can be found preserved at Pompeii.

CAKES

Different types of cakes and bread were offered to Hekate, these likely varied according to regional customs and availability.

Sweet cakes or balls were offered to Hekate in devotional ceremonies. These cakes were likely made from barley sweetened with honey and it is most often the women of the household who are recorded as making offerings of such cakes. It may have been made by boiling finely ground flour with honey. Sweet balls made from barley are specifically mentioned as being offered to Hekate at Miletos.

As a curious aside, honey cakes were also given by new arrivals to Hades to Cerberus, the three-headed hound of Hades. Cerberus guarded the gateway and he was more likely to be friendly to those who gifted him such cakes.

Another type of cake, amphiphon, is named as being offered to Hekate at full moon, and possibly new moon, ceremonies. Amphiphon can be translated as *light-about*, or *shining of both sides*, an appropriate name for this flat cheesecake which was surrounded by small torches.[355] These cakes were offered to Artemis-Hekate at Mounykhia, a full moon festival on the 16th Mounykhion[356] at Piraeus. Likewise, in Philemon's *The Beggar-Woman* the main character, named as the *Woman from Rhodes*, addresses the goddess Artemis saying:

> *"Mistress Artemis, I bear to you,*
> *O Lady, this amphiphon and libation"*[357]

---

355 The Deipnosophists, Athanaeus, C3rd CE.
356 April/May.
357 Woman and Girls in Ancient Greek Religion, Dillon, 2003.

PAEANS – SONGS FOR THE GODDESS

In addition to food-related sacrifices, songs and music were considered among the essential devotional offerings to Hekate.

The singing of hymns was a significant part of celebrations at the sanctuary of Hekate in the city of Stratonicea , connected to Hekate's temple at Lagina with a Sacred Road. According to Graf the sanctuary to Hekate was neglected at one time because of the reluctance of fathers to dispatch their sons for the job of offering songs to the Goddess. In response the secretary of the assembly, Sosandros, led the meeting with a decree. He himself was a former High Priest, married to a Priestess, and from a family of priests of the *Imperial Cult*, who was both experienced and dedicated to his duties.

> *"The assembly also decreed that thirty noble boys should walk
> every day to the bouleuterion, 'clad in white, wreathed, and
> carrying in their hand boughs,' to sing a hymn for the two main
> city divinities, Zeus Panamoros and Hekate, whose
> intervention more than two centuries earlier had saved the city
> from the marauding troops of Caesar's former lieutenant
> Labienus and who thus deserved all possible honours."* [358]

Songs were also sung for Hekate at the gateway shrine she had in Didyma.

In Aristophanes' *The Frogs* the singing of dithyrambs, the wild choral singing associated with Dionysian rites, are referenced in association with Hekate, with a warning against those who do not take due care to honour and respect the mysteries.

> *"…Or persuades anyone to send supplies to the enemies' ships,
> Or defiles Hecate's shrine, while singing dithyrambs,
> Or any politician who bites off the pay of the poets
> For being ridiculed in the ancestral rites of Dionysus.
> All these I warn, and twice I warn, and thrice I warn again,
> stand aside from our mystical dances; but as for you: arouse the
> song and the night-long dances, that belong to our festival
> here.."* [359]

---

358 Roman Festivals in the Greek East: From the Early Empire to the Middle Byzantine Era, Graf, 2015.
359 The Frogs by Aristophanes, 405 BCE, Trans. Dillon, 1995.

This mention to defiling Hekate's shrine is a reference to the unfortunate Athenian poet Cinesias, who defecated over statues of Hekate during a choral performance. Cinesias was repeatedly mocked for the incident in literature and society, for what was likely an embarrassing accident. Lysias wrote a speech in which it is made abundantly clear that Cinesias had offended the gods with his behaviour and as such would be punished unceasingly for it – even to the extent that his enemies would rather see him live with the sufferings, than see him die.

THE FOUR ELEMENTS: AIR, FIRE, WATER & EARTH

> *"The number and the nature of those things,*
> *Called elements, what Fire, Earth, Air forth brings;*
> *From whence the heavens their beginnings had;*
> *Whence tide, whence rainbow in gay colours clad,*
> *What makes the clouds that gathered are, and black,*
> *To send forth lightning, and a thundering crack;*
> *What doth the nightly flames, and comets make;*
> *What makes the Earth to swell, and then to quake:*
> *What is the seed of metals, and of gold*
> *What virtues, wealth, doth Nature's coffer hold..."*[360]

Hekate's association with the elements can be found in Hesiod's *Theogony*:

> *"The son of Cronos*[361] *did her no wrong nor took anything*
> *away of all that was her portion among the former Titan gods:*
> *but she holds, as the division was at the first from the*
> *beginning, privilege both in earth, and in heaven,*
> *and in sea"*[362]

Here Hekate's dominion over a portion of the earth (earth), heaven (air), and sea (water) is emphasised. Hekate is also depicted with torches (fire) and other sources of light throughout her history, from very early on. Hesiod's work is not the only to hint at elemental associations. In the later PGM texts we find Hekate described as being four-faced. For example, in a *Spell of Attraction*

---

360 Three Books of Occult Philosophy, Book I, Ch. 2, Agrippa.
361 i.e. Zeus.
362 The Theogony, circa 8th or 7th century BCE, Hesiod, trans. Evelyn-White, 1914.

we are reminded of Hekate's associations with the heavens and fire, and other specifically four-fold attributes are highlighted:

> "Star-coursing, heavenly, torch-bearer, fire-breather, woman
> four-faced, four-named, four-roads' mistress."[363]

There are also other allusions to the four elements indirectly associated with Hekate and her magic, for example in the Argonautica in a discussion about the young Medea we find:

> "There is a maiden, nurtured in the halls of Aeetes, whom the
> goddess Hecate taught to handle magic herbs with exceeding
> skill all that the land and flowing waters produce. With them
> is quenched the blast of unwearied flame, and at once she stays
> the course of rivers as they rush roaring on, and checks the stars
> and the paths of the sacred moon."[364]

All four elements are specifically highlighted here. The magic herbs (earth), flowing waters (water), flame (fire) and the stars and moon (air).

Empedocles (c.495-c.435 BCE), a philosopher from Magna Grecia, is credited with inventing the classical doctrine of the four elements. In his work *Tetrasomia (Doctrine of the Four Elements)* he shared his vision that the four elements were both physical manifest realities and spiritual essences.

> "Now hear the fourfold Roots of everything:
> Enlivening Hera, Aidoneus, bright Zeus,
> And Nestis, moistening mortal springs with tears."[365]

Empedocles' life was filled with circumstantial connections to Hekate. In one account, by *Diodorus of Ephesus*, we are told that Empedocles ordered and paid for two rivers to be diverted so that it could purify a third river which he (rightly) believed to because of a plague, thereby stopping it successfully. The rivers were in Selinus (Sicily), the location of temples of Demeter, Persephone and Hekate.

Hekate continued to be associated with the four elements, and by the sixth-century CE, in *Liber De Mesibus* by John Lydus, the connection is indeed made very clear:

---

363 PGM IV.2559-60, trans. E.N. O'Neill.
364 Argonautica, Apollonius Rhodius, 3rd century BCE, trans. Seaton, 1912.
365 Tetrasomia, Empedocles, 5th century BCE.

"From whence they [the Chaldean tradition] hand down the mystical doctrine concerning the four elements and four-headed Hekate. For the fire-breathing head of a horse is clearly raised towards the sphere of fire, and the head of a bull, which snorts like some bellowing spirit, is raised towards the sphere of air; and the head of a hydra as being of a sharp and unstable nature is raised towards the sphere of water, and that of a dog as having a punishing and avenging nature is raised towards the sphere of earth." [366]

The four elements, their attributes, history and uses will be covered in more detail in *Volume II of Circle for Hekate*.

ROADS AND CROSSROADS

"The Greeks, Romans and many other ancient civilizations regarded both natural and man-made liminal points of all kinds - doors, gates, rivers and frontiers, as well as crossroads - as uncertain places, requiring special rituals." [367]

As a three-formed goddess Hekate has a natural place at three-way crossroads, where shrines to her were often erected. Hekate Triformis makes the perfect protectress, able to see all that is coming simultaneously. Ovid highlights this connection:

"You see Hecate's faces turned in three directions, To guard the crossroads branching several ways" [368]

Katharmata, Katharsia, Oxuthumia

Three types of offerings were left at the crossroads for Hekate (and other crossroad gods and spirits), all of which were ritualised but for different purposes. These were:

- *katharmata* ('offscourings')
- *katharsia* ('cleansings')
- *oxuthumia* ('sharp anger').

In addition to the above, offerings linked to specific spells may have been made at crossroads, as well as the Hekate Suppers

---

366 De Mensibus, Lydus, 6th century CE, trans. Wunsch.
367 Crossroads, Johnston, 1991.
368 Fasti, Ovid, 8 CE, trans. A.S. Kline.

(*deipna*) and possibly other devotional offerings. Not all offerings at the crossroads to Hekate would have been a Hekate Supper and though it is possible that katharmata, katharsia or oxuthumia formed part of deipna offerings, evidence to support this is lacking.

The first of these, *Katharmata*, was the offering of portions of the sacrifice not used in the ceremony, this included waste blood and water. The fifth-century BCE Athenian poet Eupolis mentioned in one of the few remaining fragments of his work that these offscourings were burned.[369]

This term was also sometimes applied to people, specifically those used as scapegoats and sacrificed when serious natural disasters indicated to worshippers that a deity needed to be propitiated, for example drought or plague.

The second kind (*katharsia*) was the actual remains of sacrifices, such as eggs and the bodies of dogs. The first-century CE Roman historian Plutarch mentioned this in *Roman Questions* when he wrote *"dogs are carried out to Hecate with the other katharsia"*[370] and also *"When it [the dog] is sent to crossroads as a supper for the earth-goddess Hecate, it has its due portion among sacrifices that avert and expiate evil."*[371] We know animal sacrifices to chthonic deities were usually black, and that black dogs were sacrificed to her.

The third kind (*oxuthumia*) was a baked clay censer used to fumigate the house for protection, and then taken and left at the crossroads. It could also describe the household cleansings (sweepings) which were taken and burned on the censer, as referenced by Electra in Aeschylus' *The Choephori*:

> *"Or shall I pour this draught for Earth to drink,*
> *Sans word or reverence, as my sire was slain,*
> *And homeward pass with unreverted eyes,*
> *Casting the bowl away, as one who flings*
> *The household cleansings to the common road?"*[372]

By determining the purpose of the ritual at the crossroads, we can better understand the interactions between deities and spirits associated with the crossroads, the variety of rituals done at the

---

369 Fragment 120, Eupolis, 5th century BCE, trans. R. Parker.
370 Roman Questions, Plutarch, late 1st century CE, trans. R. Parker.
371 Roman Questions, Plutarch, late 1st century CE, trans. R. Parker
372 The Choephori, Aeschylus, 450 BCE, trans. Anon.

crossroads and the offerings, which undoubtedly serve very diverse purposes. Johnston proposes that this can be clarified by distinguishing between two different types of crossroad rituals, rituals for protection and rituals that are exploitive.[373] I would add a two more, rituals of devotion and rituals of purification.

Hekate was not the only deity to be honoured at the crossroads, gods such as Hermes and Apollo were also honoured with roadside shrines, as were the dead.

Triekostia: Thirtieth Day Rites

The triekostia, rituals on the thirtieth day of the month, i.e. the last day of a lunar month (dark moon) were dedicated to the dead. It included taking the sweepings and dirt from the house to a grave or crossroads and was followed by leaving food offerings. Celebrations sometimes took place for two or three days and were widespread. It is likely that Hekate featured in some of these rites, even if not exclusively.

Solon's law, in the sixth-century BCE, amongst other things, banned the triekostia. These practices were mostly done by the women of the house to ward off evil spirits. It was also done after deaths in the household, and immediately after the funerals were held, to purify the house from the spirit of the deceased. It is likely that Solon's law was an attempt at replacing superstitious practices with more hygienic ones, but based on the continuous popularity of these rites, Solon's attempt clearly failed. Nevertheless, it provides us with a unique record of the practices and their purpose during this period.

Hekate Suppers

> *"Plutarch says that these suppers were intended for Hekate and also for… the gods who averted evil."*[374]

The Hekate *Deipna* (Suppers) left for Hekate at crossroads at the dark moon is perhaps the most frequently spoken of ritual offerings associated with Hekate, and maybe the most speculated

---

373 Crossroads, Johnston, 1991.
374 Crossroads, Johnston, 1991.

about. As discussed in the previous section, not all offerings made to Hekate at crossroads were necessarily Hekate Suppers, and not all offerings at crossroads were for Hekate. The reasons for offerings at crossroads were manifold.

The writings of the satirist Aristophanes' suggest that there may, perhaps, have been a charitable motivation to the suppers:

> *"Ask Hekate whether it is better to be rich or starving; she will tell you that the rich send her a meal every month and that the poor make it disappear before it is even served."*[375]

These words are echoed down the centuries, and in the Byzantine Suda more than fourteen centuries later we find:

> *"From her one may learn whether it is better to be rich or to go hungry. For she says that those who have and who are wealthy should send her a dinner each month, but that the poor among mankind should snatch it before they put it down.' For it was customary for the rich to offer loaves and other things to Hekate each month, and for the poor to take from them."*[376]

Considering the importance given to the Hekate Suppers it is perhaps surprising that not much more is known. The available information (Aristophanes and the Suda) has been interpreted as the equivalent of a modern-day charitable offering: food left by the wealthy, in the name of Hekate, which was taken and eaten by the poor. If Aristophanes was referencing a practice of offerings left out in the name of Hekate for the underprivileged at the crossroads, then these offerings could be considered a type of early charity. They then become the equivalent of the road-side kitchens created by members of other faiths, including Buddhists, Christians and Hindus to help travellers passing through, as well as the poor.

There is also an echo of the equality meals offered in the cult of Zeus Panamoros, where Hekate was worshipped alongside Zeus in Caria, Anatolia. No mention of a crossroads is made, but food was offered on tables and rich and poor, regardless of social or cultural status, were invited to eat together.

---

375 Plutus, Aristophanes, 380 BCE, trans. anon.
376 Suda, Epsilon 363, 10th century CE, trans. W. Hutton.

FIG. 163.

94 - FROM THE EVIL EYE, ELWORTHY 1895

THE DEAD

*"But either thou art frightened of a spectre beheld in sleep and
hast joined the revel-rout of nether Hekate."*[377]

Tibetan Buddhism teaches that *"Death is certain; and the time of
death is uncertain"*, and proposes that the only thing that can help us
as individuals at the time of our death is our spiritual and mental
development. While this is not at all directly linked to the goddess
Hekate, it is a wise approach which initiates of the Mysteries would
have understood. All of us will face death sooner or later, and as
such it is not surprising that customs and practices associated with
the dead and dying can be found in all the regions and cultures in
which Hekate's cult had a foothold.

*"No figure is more closely associated with the returning souls of
the dead than Hecate. Her role as their leader was well enough
established by the fifth century for the tragedians to allude to it
without further explanation."*[378]

---

377 Fragment 249, Aeschylus, 5th century BCE, trans. W Smyth.
378 Restless Dead, Johnston, 1999.

Considering her long history of association with the dead, Hekate's role with the dead is naturally multifaceted. She is called upon in necromantic rites in which efforts are made to interact with the dead, as she was believed to control the domain(s) in which those who had not fully passed into the Underworld dwelled. She was also said to rule over those who died untimely deaths, which included those who died through murder, suicide or another violent act. Described as *"raging among the souls of the dead"* in a fourth-century Hippocratic treatise on sacred diseases.[379] The spirits of these people were thought to do Hekate's bidding with evidence showing that some feared nightly attacks by Hekate's band of ghosts. They were also believed to cause various mental diseases, which were possibly sent to torment those who misbehaved in some way or another, until such time they rectified their action.

The understanding held about death by the priesthoods, devotees and initiates of Hekate's mysteries in the past provides thought-provoking insights on beliefs and customs associated with death. An inscription found on a gravestone from the town of Mesembria, Thrace dated to around the second-century CE tells the story of a devotee of the goddess who died:

> *"I, the goddess Hecate, lie here, as you see. Earlier I was mortal, now, as a goddess, I am immortal and young forever. I, Julia, daughter of the generous Nikias. My native city was Mesembria - the name comes from Melsa and "bria." The stone commemorates the years I lived: in all, three times five, twice over twenty, and, in addition, ten and five."* [380]

It is one of the numerous examples of funeral inscriptions expressing a belief in apotheosis, a process through which the deceased becomes one with the deity. In this case Julia, who was presumably an initiate of the Mysteries of Hekate, becomes the goddess Hekate upon her death. Similar cases exist mentioning the goddess Gaia, the Titan Earth goddess, suggesting that upon death the body does not die, but instead transforms and becomes assimilated into the living body of Gaia[381]. It also brings to mind

---

379 Restless Dead, Johnston, 1999.
380 Inscription, trans. Portefaix, Images of Eternal Beauty by Wypustek, 2013.
381 Eternal Beauty, Wypustek, 2013.

the transformation of Iphigeneia, Aphaia and Queen Hekabe.

With such an understanding there is no death, and there is nothing to fear, as death is understood as a transformation rather than an ending. This may account for the different awareness of death held by initiates of the Mysteries. To them the process of initiation provided a self-transformation from which initiates emerged with a different understanding of death, armed with knowledge on how to transcend death. Additionally, based on inscriptions on some of the Orphic Gold Tablets, initiates may have believed that the knowledge they gained through initiation would provide them with specific privileges after death.

Hekate's association with childbirth brought her into the lives of women at the very liminal time of labour. Not only is childbirth painful, but it is also a dangerous time for both mother and child. Taking into consideration Hekate's role towards the dead, Hekate's role as child-nurse can then be seen to take on additional layers of meaning, where she is seen responsible for helping during birth, and taking into her care those who did not make it through the process.

Speaking to the Dead: Necromancy

Myths, such as that of Odysseus, suggest that the dead are not able to travel into the Underworld until their corpses have been buried with the appropriate funerary rites. The dead who have been given appropriate funerary rites and who have passed into the Underworld were thought to have very limited, if any, capability of interacting with the living. Homer's work suggests that it is only the recently dead who could hear the living. Likewise, Necromancers were more likely to have success with bringing someone back who have not yet received an appropriate funeral.

Re-animation is a form of necromancy where rather than speaking to the disincarnate spirit of the diseased, the practitioner aimed to speak to the diseased using their corpse. Examples can be found in the stories Medea and Lucan's witch Erictho. In both these instances the corpses were prepared by replacing its blood with a brew made by the practitioner. As an aside, it is said that the poet Shelley read Lucan's work to his wife Mary and that this inspired her celebrated work, *Frankenstein*.

Necromancy was also practised by Empedocles, who wrote:

"...and you will fetch back from Hades the life-force of a man who has died."[382]

In *Dialogues of the Dead* Lucian has Diogenes instructing Pollux[383] to find an offering which had been left for Hekate at the crossroads, which would be used in necromantic rites.

"... and, if he anywhere find on the crossroads a supper for Hekate set out, or a purificatory egg, or anything of the sort, let him bring it." [384]

DETAIL FROM AN ENGRAVING SHOWING MEDEA DRAINING THE BLOOD OF AESON IN ORDER TO REJUVENATE HIM WITH HER SPECIAL BREW. BY BAUR, 1659

This suggests a belief that these polluted offerings used in purification rituals gained a different type of power when it was transformed by removing miasma somewhere else. In *Philopseudes* Lucian names the full moon as the best time for necromancy, and notes that the practitioner starts proceedings at about midnight. This highlights the nocturnal nature of these practices. He also notes the digging of a trench which is used to make the appropriate offerings and libations.

"...he would make people fall in love, call up spirits, resuscitate corpses, bring down the Moon, and show you Hecate

---

382 Fragment 111, Empedocles, 5th century BCE, trans. P. Kingsley.
383 Ie. Polydeukes
384 Dialogues of The Dead, 2nd century CE, Trans. M.D. Macleod, 1961.

*herself, as large as life. But I will just tell you of a thing I saw
him do at Glaucias's ... Well, as soon as the moon was full,
that being the time usually chosen for these enchantments, he
dug a trench in the courtyard of the house, and commenced
operations, at about midnight, by summoning Glaucias's
father, who had now been dead for seven months.*

*The old man did not approve of his son's passion, and was very
angry at first; however, he was prevailed on to give his consent.
Hecate was next ordered to appear, with Cerberus in her train,
and the Moon was brought down, and went through a variety
of transformations"*[385]

The Restless Dead: Spells & Charms

The help of the spirits of the untimely and restless dead, under
the control of Hekate, was frequently sought in spells and charms.
One defixiones found in a grave near Paphos, the famous site of
the temple of Aphrodite, petitions Hekate, together with an
extensive list of deities, daimones and the spirits of the dead.
Hekate's help in a legal matter is sought, and the spell aims to
silence the opponent.

*"... O much lamented tomb and gods of the underworld and
Hekate of the underworld and Hermes of the underworld and
Plouton and the infernal Erinues[386] and you who lie here
below, untimely dead and unnamed, EUMAXON, take
away the voice(s)... "*[387]

In a love spell of attraction found in PGM IV. 1390-1495 the
practitioner calls on the help of heroes, gladiators or those who
died a violent death. In this example, the practitioner petitions
Hekate to send forth help from those under her care.

*"...to those who died untimely deaths and those dead violently,
I'm sending food: Three-Headed Goddess, Lady Of Night,
who feed on filth. O Virgin, thou Key-Holding Persephassa,
Kore come out of Tartaros"*[388]

The blood of a person who died a violent death is employed in

---

385 Philopseudes, Lucian, 2nd century CE, trans. H.W. & F.G. Fowler.
386 i.e. Erinyes
387 Curse Tablets and Binding Spells from the Ancient World, Gager, 1992.
388 PGM IV.1390-1495, Betz, 1996.

the creation of a protective charm described in PGM IV:2785-2890, the *Prayer to Selene for any spell* in which Hekate is invoked. The charm, which the practitioner wears while doing the spell, is to be made from a lodestone charm onto which the practitioner should carve a three-formed Hekate, with the head of a maiden, dog and goat. The charm is first purified with natron and water, after which it is dipped into the blood of a person who died a violent death. When it is completed, food offerings are made to it.

HERBS & PLANTS

Hekate's association with the healing arts is often overlooked, strangely so when you take into consideration that she was so closely associated with herbs and the use of plants. More often it seems we are keen to focus on her association with baneful herbs and necromancy, which encourages ideas which are seemingly not compatible with healing.

Plants associated with Hekate

> *"In the furthest recesses of the enclosure was a sacred grove, shaded by flourishing trees. In it there were many laurels and cornels and tall plane trees. Within this the grass was carpeted with low-growing plants with powerful roots. Famous asphodel, pretty maidenhair, rushes, galangal, delicate verbena, sage, hedge-mustard, purple honeysuckle, healing cassidony, flourishing field basil, mandrake, hulwort, in addition fluffy dittany, fragrant saffron, nose-smart, there too lion-foot, greenbrier, camomile, black poppy, alcua, all-heal, white hellebore, aconite, and many other noxious plants grew from the earth. In the middle a stout oak tree with heaven-high trunk spread its branches out over much of the grove. On it hung, spread out over a long branch, the golden fleece, over which watched a terrible snake."*[389]

Today, more often than not, it is the hexing (or baneful) herbs which are associated with Hekate today. These are plants which are typically poisonous, and sometimes have psychoactive qualities. Curiously however, when considering the plants associated with

---

389 Orphic Argonautica, C4th CE, trans. D. Ogden.

Hekate in ancient literature and art, most them are not actually poisonous. Conversely, some were thought to be antidotes to poison, and almost all were better known for their healing qualities.

95 - HEKATE TRIFORMIS, HOLDING A POMEGRANATE TO HER CHEST. 1ST CENTURY CE, ROMAN. SHE WEARS A POLOS AND IS SHOWN STANDING AROUND A CENTRAL PILLAR. THIS IS SIMILAR TO AN IMAGE WHICH WAS DESCRIBED TO BE AT AN ASCLEPION (HEALING TEMPLE) NATIONAL MUSEUM OF ANTIQUITIES, LEIDEN.

This is a table of the plants named in *Hekate's Argonautica Garden*. This is intended as a brief overview of the plants and some of their known uses and associations in the Greek world, not a complete guide.

Plant	Uses
Aconite *(Wolfbane, Monkhood)* **[Poison]**	Legendary plant formed when the saliva of the three-headed hell-hound Cerberus fell onto the earth during a struggle with Hercules. Hekate was said to have discovered the plant. It is one of the most poisonous plants known in the ancient world. It earned its common name, wolfbane, because an extract was used on arrow tips when hunting wolves, and other creatures.

Alcua *(Unknown, but likely a species of Mallow)*	Mallow was used as a cure for many different ailments, due to its astringent, bactericidal and anti-inflammatory properties.
All-heal *(Sicklewort. Prunella)*	As the name suggests, it was used to treat many ailments – including pneumonia.
Asphodel *(Asphodelus Ramosus)*	Planted near tombs as food for the dead. It was also used to produce glue, and eaten as food. Both the Greeks and Romans used to treat a variety of common ailments with it.
Basil, field *(likely Clinopodium vulgare)*	A symbol of mourning in Greece, and was associated with negativity, including abuse, poverty, illness, and death, as well as evil spirits. It was even thought to be a poison! As a result, basil was not used as food in the region until recently.
Chamomile *(likely Chamaemelum nobile)*	Used as a strewing herb, and in washes and baths for women's problems, and for women who were nearing birth.
Cassidony *(Lavandula stoechas, or "French Lavender")*	Named specifically as the healing herb in the Argonautica. It was used for general ailments and to lift moods, physicians recommended anointing the feet or heart with it. It was also used for menstrual problems, cramps, treating insect bites etc.
Cornels *(Cornus Mas. flowering dogwood)*	Used for gout, anaemia, and joint pains. The cherry-like fruit this tree produces, is also used as food, although most varieties require cooking.
Dittany of Crete *(Origanum dictamnus)*	This plant is a native of Crete, and was used to treat stomach problems, and to aid in childbirth. Also as an abortifacient.
Ebony *(Diospyros genus)*	There was a thrice-folding door made from the black wood of Ebony in *Hekate's Garden*. This wood is also linked to the god Hermes in his Chthonic form, and belongs to the Diospyros genus, the name of which derives from *Zeus' Wheat*.
Galangal *(Zingiberaceae, the ginger family.)*	Was used for stomach complaints and as a spice. It has similar qualities to ginger.

Garlic *(Allium sativum)*	This was offered to Hekate as part of Suppers left at the crossroads and in graveyards. Said to provide protection against the restless dead. Used in ancient medicine for purification, menstrual, conception and other womb related problems.
Hedge mustard *(Sisymbrium officinale)*	This was used as an antidote to poison, usually mixed with honey. It was also used to treat throat and voice-related problems.
Hellebore, White *(Veratrum album)* **[Poison]**	The root of this plant is poisonous, affecting the nervous system and paralyzing it. According to one version of the myth it may have been added to wine which led to the death of Alexander the Great.
Honeysuckle, purple *(Lonicera)*	Honeysuckle was a symbol of love in the ancient world, and was used in food and wreaths. The berries are edible.
Hulwort *(Felty Germander, or Teucrium polium)*	This was used to treat epilepsy, which was known as the falling sickness, as well as forms of mental illness (lunacy). Hulwort was also used as an abortifacient and for birth control.
Laurels *(Lauraceae)*	Laurel was famously used to produce wreaths given to the winners in contests, and with which icons were crowned in devotional ceremonies. Laurel is sacred to Apollo, and may have been burned or chewed to help induce trance states for the priestesses who acted as his oracles. It was believed to be able to ward off evil and disease, used for purification, in perfumery and as a flavouring in food.
Lion's Foot *(Lady's Mantle, Alchemilla Vulgaris)*	Used to treat uterine problems, as well as to treat issues related to lactation after birth and menopause.
Maidenhair *(Fern, Adiantum pedatum L.)*	This fern was used to treat respiratory problems, including asthma, blood circulation problems and dandruff. It was also used to menstrual problems, especially to increase flow, and as an abortifacient.
Mandrake *(Mandragora officinarum)* **[Poison]**	The root of this plant has narcotic and hallucinogenic properties. It was used to treat melancholy, and as a surgical sedative by ancient physicians.

Nose-smart *(Lepidium sativum)*	Also known as garden cress, this plant has long been used as a flavouring and garnish in food. The seeds were believed to help heal bone fractures, and to treat nasal issues.
Oak *(possibly the Quercus Ilex, or Holm Oak)*	The oak was sacred primarily to Zeus. The bark and galls of the tree were used to treat dysentery, stomach complaints and as an astringent. It was also used in food.
Plane Tree *(Platanus orientalis)*	This is the famed tree under which Hippocrates, the father of medicine, taught his students. The tree was used in many medicinal preparations, for treating such diverse ailments as stings, ulcers and frostbite.
Poppy black *(Likely horned poppy, Papaver)* **[Poison]**	The sap, extracted from the pods and other parts of the plant, was used for its hypnotic and soporific properties in medicine. An infusion of black poppy in wine or by boiling was used to treat stomach problems. All parts of the plant are poisonous when consumed in quantity, although the seeds of the opium poppy are edible and used as an ingredient in cakes and bread.
Rushes *(Juncaceae)*	The flowers, roots and seeds were used in food. The plant was used in a variety way in medicine.
Saffron *(Saffron Crocus or Crocus sativus,)*	Highly prized (and priced!) red filament strands collected from the crocus. It was used to flavour and colour food, and for its reputed aphrodisiac properties. It was also attributed painkilling and healing qualities. Also used in perfumery.
Sage *(Salvia)*	Sage was used in fumigations, purifying and neutralising smells (much like the 'smudging' done with sage bundles inspired by practices from indigenous North American tribes). Medicinally it was used to treat a wide range of ailments including fevers, infections (esp. of the mouth and throat), for wound-healing and to treat sexual problems.
Verbena *(Vervain)*	Also known as the sacred plant. Used for purification, as well for curing a range of ailments, sometimes within a magical context.

Of all the plants listed as being in Hekate's garden only Aconite, White Hellebore, Poppy and Mandrake are specifically considered poisonous. We don't know exactly what is meant by the reference to *noxious plants,* which may of course indicate other unknown poison plants. Hemlock *(Conium maculatum)* which was well-known for its deadly abilities, was not mentioned and was a major ingredient in potions used to execute those found guilty of a crime in the region. This famously included the execution of Socrates; and knowledge that hemlock was poisonous would have been general knowledge.

96 - ACONITE OR MONKSHOOD (ACONITUM NAPELLUS L.): FLOWERING STEM WITH SEPARATE LABELLED FLORAL SEGMENTS. ENGRAVING BY J.CALDWALL, C.1804, AFTER P.HENDERSON. WITH THANKS WELLCOME IMAGES.

Herbalists who work with fresh plants (gathered from cultivated gardens or the wild) need to be able to tell the difference between a beneficial plant and a poisonous plant of similar appearance, to avoid using the wrong plant. Most of the plants named in the Argonautica as being associated with Hekate has useful medicinal and healing properties, suggesting that far from being associated only with the poison herbs, that her association with plants was a lot wider.

Here it is useful to recall a quote from the Argonautica given earlier in this volume. The young Medea is described as a maiden in the halls of her father Aeetes, and we are told that she was taught to handle all the magical herbs produced on land and in the flowing waters:

> "...the goddess Hecate taught to handle magic herbs with exceeding skill all that the land and flowing waters produce."[390]

Hekate taught Medea the use of all magic herbs, include those with healing, medicinal and culinary properties, not just the few deadly ones.

Herbs and plants, their uses and association with Hekate will be covered in more detail in *Volume III of Circle for Hekate*.

METALS & GEMSTONES

Metals and gemstones were frequently employed for magic, healing and of course everyday use. This is an overview of some of the metals and stones more often associated with Hekate, with some interesting examples.

In the PGM we find one way in which Hekate was entreated for healing. As part of the preparation of this collyrium (a healing eye salve), an image of the goddess Hekate and the magical name *Barzou Pherba* is stamped onto it with an iron ring:

> "Remedies prepared in a magical context could also be stamped, like normal drugs, with an image, but this time explicitly magical. One of the Greek Magical Papyri offers a description of the preparation of a collyrium made of animal and plant material (field mouse, dappled goat, dog-faced baboon, ibis, river crab, moon beetle, wormwood, and a clove of garlic), duly stamped, like regular remedies, but with a ring bearing the image of Hecate and a magical name: Blend with vinegar. Make pills, kolluria, and stamp them with a completely iron ring, completely tempered, with a Hecate and the name Barzou Pherba."[391]

There are numerous carved jasper gemstones with images of

---

390 Argonautica, Apollonius Rhodius, 3rd century BCE, trans. Seaton, 1912.
391 See Gems from Heaven, Chris Entwistle and Noël Adams, 2011.

Hekate from antiquity. Alexander of Tralles, a sixth-century CE Greek physician, gave instructions for a two-part jasper colic-amulet with a special image.

> *"Another red jasper gem in the Bibliothèque nationale, Paris, confirms that these gems were, in fact, used to cure colic several centuries before Alexander wrote down his recipe: Heracles and the lion are partially surrounded by the command: 'Withdraw colic! the divine one pursues you'. On this gem the three kappas (along with an eight-pointed star) lie beneath the feet of the struggling pair, and on the reverse is another common magical image: the tri-form Hecate with the magical names Iao above and Abrasax below."*[392]

97 JASPER STONE CARVED WITH THE IMAGE OF HERACLES AND A LION, SHOWING THE INSCRIPTION, THREE KAPPA AND THE EIGHT-POINTED STAR. THE REVERSE OF THIS STONE HAS AN IMAGE OF A THREE FORMED HEKATE. BIBLIOTHÈQUE NATIONALE, PARIS. PHOTO BY MARIE-LAN NGUYEN / WIKIMEDIA COMMONS

Hekate is also associated specifically with bronze, iron, lead, lodestone (magnetite) and meteoric stones (baetyls).

Bronze and iron nails were used to pierce lead defixiones, and was also used for amulets (including the disk from Ostia showing Hekate and King Solomon). Hekate also had bronze sandals, and magicians wore bronze sandals to show their dedication to her.

The metals and stones associated with Hekate will be considered in more detail in *Volume II, of Circle for Hekate*.

---

392 Gems from Heaven, Chris Entwistle and Noël Adams, 2011.

MAGIC WHEELS & WHIRLINGS

"The sympathetic importance of the sound made by the whirling iynx-wheel fits in with the general importance of sounds in magical or theurgical acts. … magicians believed that the correct pronunciation of each of the seven Greek vowels affected one of the seven astral spheres and therefore aided in invoking and controlling the sphere's divinities…"[393]

Hekate is evoked for her assistance in a well-known love spell published in Theocritus' *Idylls* (circa 270 BCE). Here an iynx is used in an attempt to force a wayward lover to return back to the woman he left, with the chorus accentuating the belief that the iynx is able to lure the individual towards the desired outcome.

"Draw my lover here, iynx (magic wheel)"[394]

More than two hundred years later, Virgil adapted this spell given by Theocritus, in his *Eclogue 8*, *The Sorceress*.[395] Maintaining the style and much of the technique, Virgil removed references to Hekate, changed the name of the protagonist from *Delphis* to *Daphnis*, and made the herb supplier a werewolf, emphasising the malefic nature of the magic.

The word *iynx* is the Greek name for the wryneck bird, a member of the woodpecker family who enjoys feasting on ants. The theory is that the original form in which the iynx wheel was used for magical purposes involved tying a wryneck to a wooden wheel which was then spun. A well-balanced iynx wheel makes a repetitive whirring sound, which somewhat resembles the pulsing call of the iynx bird in the wild.

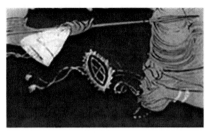

98 - DETAIL SHOWING THE IYNX MAGIC WHEEL LOVE CHARM OF APHRODITE, FROM A CLASSICAL JUG DATED TO CIRCA 330 BCE, SOUTHERN ITALY.

---

393 Hekate Soteira, Johnston, 1990.
394 Idylls 2, Theocritus, 270 BCE, trans. Z. Yardley.
395 Eclogues, Virgil, circa 40 BCE.

The iynx is one of several ritual tools used in the ancient world which was spun in one way or another to produce the desired effect and outcome. In addition to being associated with love magic, it can also be found depicted in death and funerary scenes. It was associated with Hekate, alongside the strophalos, rhombus and bull-roarer.

> "Gow clearly distinguishes the ῥόμβος (rhombus) from the ἴυγξ (iynx), a different Greek instrument consisting of "a spoked wheel (sometimes it might be a disc) with two holes on either side of the centre" strung with a cord and operated between the hands and not swung overhead."[396]

Theocritus also references a bronze *rhombus* whirling[397] which may be a reference to a bull-roarer. These are attached to a piece of string which are whirred in a particular circular motion above the user's head. Bull-roarers were used in the Mysteries of Dionysos as well as those of Kybele. Rhombus may additionally refer to a special type of drum, the *rhoptron,* which was used in rituals by the priests of Kybele, the Korybantes. Mathiesen explains:

> "The bull-roarer might have been called a rhombos not only because of its whirling motion but also because the piece of wood may normally have been cut into a rhombus shape - that is, a shape with four equal sides but only opposite equal angles - to cause it to vibrate more vigorously and thus produce more sound as it whirled through the air. Its mysterious rising and falling pitch, associated particularly with the ceremonies of the priests of Cybele, the Korybantes, was caused by the speed with which the rhombos was spun."[398]

The use of magic wheels in love magic is well attested, with most historical examples of the use of the Iynx being in association with Aphrodite or Eros. In one example a winged Eros is depicted on a gilded bronze ring, seated in a kneeling position while whirring his iynx. The ring is dated to circa 350 BC and is in the British Museum collection. The connection to love magic is emphasised

---

396 The Lost Constellations, Barentine, 2016.
397 Idylls 2, Theocritus, 270 BCE, trans. Z. Yardley.
398 Apollo's Lyre: Greek Music and Music Theory in Antiquity and the Middle Ages, Mathiesen, 1999.

by Xenophon when he wrote of a female courtesan telling Socrates:

> *"I assure you these things don't happen without the help of*
> *many potions and spells and magic wheels."*[399]

Hekate was called on in love spells and was also associated with Aphrodite on a few known occasions. One sixth-century BCE text names Hekate as the attendant of Aphrodite:

> *"the golden-shining attendant of Aphrodite."*[400]

The role of the attendant is one Hekate usually holds in relation to the goddess Persephone in the Mysteries. Aphrodite and Hekate were also worshipped alongside each other on occasion. Pausanias describes a shrine in a porch of a temple of the god *Asklepios* in Titane (Corinthia, Greece) saying that it contained images of Tyche, Dionysos, Hekate and Aphrodite.[401]

In Pindar's *Pythian Odes*, Aphrodite gives an iynx bird and wheel to Jason, which he uses to win Medea's love. By doing this she introduced this form of magic to humanity and encouraged the use of the iynx to manipulate the most famous priestess of Hekate.

> *"The Queen of sharpest arrows,*
> *brought the dappled iynx from Olympus,*
> *bound to the four spokes of the indissoluble wheel;"*[402]

Also see: *The Wandering Goddess, Hekate in the Bosporan Kingdom.*

Marinus, the pupil and biographer of the Greek Neo-Platonist philosopher Proclus, wrote in the fifth century CE that the iynges were used to bring rain when Attica was suffering from a drought. Using the iynges in this way enabled the user to draw down heavenly influence to earth.[403] Similar practices survive into the present day in Europe.

Based on ancient depictions of the iynx-wheel it is evident that there were variations in shape and decoration. Four-spoked wheel and star-like designs appear to have been used most frequently. It is possible that some of the four-rayed wheels which are so

---

399 Memorabilia, 3.XI.17, Xenophon, 4th century BCE, trans. E.C. Marchant & O.J. Todd.
400 Sappho or Alcaeus, Fragment 23, 6th century BCE, trans. Campbell.
401 Description of Greece, Pausanias, 2nd century CE, trans. Jones, 1918.
402 Pythian Odes 4.213-15, Pindar, 462 BCE, trans. C. Faraone.
403 Life of Proclus, Marinus, 5th century CE.

commonly shown with Hekate may represent the iynx, though it is more usual to see the iynx wheel as being attached to a string and with movement implied.

Also see: *Symbols of Her Mysteries, Stars or Wheels*

99 - REPRODUCTIONS OF IYNX WHEELS
PUBLISHED BY GOW IN THE JOURNAL FOR HELLENIC STUDIES 1934.

Extant examples include wheel designs decorated with wryneck birds on the rim facing towards the centre. The holes on these objects allow for multiple strings to be attached, suggesting that this type of wheel was suspended, and twisted into a continuous motion.

The iynges were also employed in conjurations. Eusebius of Caesarea wrote of this in *Praeparatio Evangelica*:

> *"Easily dragging some of these unwilling [divinities] from the Aether by means of ineffable iynges, you lead them earthwards."*[404]

The same text relays Hekate's response to being summoned in this way, signifying that she was successfully evoked with this method.

> *"Why do you call me, the goddess Hekate, here from the swift Aether by means of god-compelling necessity?"*[405]

In later literature, notably the *Chaldean Oracles*, the name Iynges are given to a group of angelic beings. It is possible that in this

---

404 Praeparatio Evangelica, Eusebius, early C4th CE, trans. Des Places.
405 Praeparatio Evangelica, Eusebius, early C4th CE, trans. Des Places.

context the iynx ritual tool was used to somehow communicate with, as well as conjure, these beings. This idea is supported by a reference in the Greek sophist *Philostratus'* work *The Life of Apollonius of Tyana*. In this text is given a description of the King of Babylon's judgement chamber and the iynges are named as *'the tongues of the gods'*:

> *"And it is here that the king gives judgement, and golden iynges are hung from the ceiling, four in number, to remind him of Adrastea, the goddess of justice, and to engage him not to exalt himself above humanity. These figures the Magi themselves say they arranged; for they have access to the palace, and they call them the tongues of the gods."*[406]

The description of the iynges being suspended from the ceiling recalls the design of the wheels with the birds discussed above. Golden iynges were also specifically present in a temple of Apollo in Delphi. These are mentioned by Philostratus and were described as having the same persuasive power as a Siren.[407]

Strophalos comes from the root *to twist* and as such, is an appropriate term for all the variations of twisting ritual tools employed and discussed in this section. The Byzantine historian and philosopher Michael Psellus provide a description of the strophalos dating to the eleventh century CE, many centuries after the Chaldean Oracles. Psellus provides information on different designs of the iynges, describing spherical and triangular objects, covered in symbols which were spun.

> *"The strophalos of Hekate is a golden sphere with lapis lazuli enclosed in its centre, which is spun by means of a leather thong, and which is covered with symbols: as it was spun they [the Theurgists] made their invocations. These spheres were generally called iynges and could be either spherical or triangular or of some other form. And while they were making their invocations they emitted inarticulate or animal cries, laughing and whipping the air. So the Oracle teaches that it is*

---

406 The Life of Apollonius of Tyana, Philostratus the Athenian, early C3rd CE, trans. F.C. Conybeare.
407 See The Song of the Iynx: Magic and Rhetoric in Pythian 4, Johnston, 1995.

the motion of the strophalos which works the ritual, on account of its ineffable power. It is called 'of Hekate' and consecrated to Hekate."[408]

Blue gemstones are specifically associated with the Heavenly Aphrodite, and similar descriptions of stones suspended in gold can be found in association with the Love Goddess.

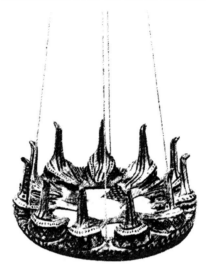

100 - EXAMPLE OF A MAGIC WHEEL DECORATED WITH BIRDS AND SUSPENDED BASED ON A WHEEL IN THE COLLECTION OF THE BOSTON MUSEUM OF FINE ART. ILLUSTRATION FROM THE JOURNAL FOR HELLENIC STUDIES, GOW, 1934

The Neo-Platonist philosopher Damascius also associates Hekate with whirring, saying that:

"The Great Hekate emits a life-generating whir."[409]

And that:

"The life-generating Goddess ... possesses the separated and manifest whirring-forth of the life-generating light."[410]

There are also examples of the god Hermes holding what appears to be an iynx on gemstones, though it possible that he is instead holding a four-spoked wheel attached to a rod. Examples of this can be found on jasper amulets dated to both the first- and second-century CE now in the British Museum collection.

---

408 Psellus commentary on the Chaldean Oracles, C11th CE, trans. D.J. O'Meara.
409 Difficulties and Solutions of First Principles, Damascius, C6th CE, trans. C.E. Ruelle.
410 Difficulties and Solutions of First Principles, Damascius, C6th CE, trans. C.E. Ruelle.

The strophalos may also be a spinning top (strobilus). These were popular toys children enjoyed playing with, as they continue to be today. Spinning tops were often whipped into action, and Guthrie suggests that the Orphic references may refer to a whipping top.

101 - IMAGE OF A SYMBOL NOW KNOWN AS "HEKATE'S WHEEL."

The image above is said to be a *Hekate Wheel*, but is confusingly also named *strophalos* and *iynx* by some contemporary teachers. It is not a modern pattern, but the association of this precise pattern with Hekate appears to date to the twentieth-century CE.

The triskele design can be found in ancient Minoan art, as well as in that of many other cultures. Numerous seal impressions in metal and clay display this[411] and a variety of very similar designs, however the meaning of the original symbols is not definitively known.

Looking at it with modern eyes, we could interpret it as being three labrys axes, the double-headed ceremonial axes which were associated with the feminine divine in Minoan culture, and later with Zeus. The three-fold symbolism also provides a basis for association with Hekate, and the star at the centre can be linked to her stellar nature. It is all enclosed in a circle, which has universal appeal.

---

411 Examples can be found in the Archaeological Museum of Argos and Athens.

Last words

Hekate is a universal goddess with a long and continuous history. Continuous because her history is still being written today - with each new vision and experience shared, new legends and myths are potentially born. It is my hope that this *circle* I offer to Hekate, with examples of some of the mythology and history she inspired others to record in the past, will inspire new stories about her today and into the future. Stories that will widen the understanding held by devotees and researchers alike. Stories that will allow devotees to gain deeper insights into the Goddess of the Crossroads, the torch-bearing guide through the Mysteries, allowing them to gain new insights and understandings in their own work.

It is also my sincere hope that others will be inspired by the history and mythology presented here, and that they will continue the work of making further material about this goddess available for many centuries, maybe even millennia to come.

Circles are intrinsically magical. They symbolise the heavenly luminaries, especially the Sun and the Moon. Circles are beautiful. They represent eternity, as well as the wholeness of a thing. Circles are divine in their perfection – with no beginning and no ending. They are walked alone and with others, and there are circles inside circles. I hope that this *circle* will be one you found both thought-provoking and useful.

With blessings to you on your path,

Sorita d'Este, Glastonbury, 2017

102 - SORITA ON THE STEPS OF THE TEMPLE OF HEKATE, LAGINA. 2015.

About the Author - *Sorita d'Este*

Sorita d'Este is an author, researcher and priestess who has devoted her life to the Mysteries. She is the author of numerous books on both the practice and history of magic, plus mythology, folklore and witchcraft.

In late 2000 she co-founded the StarStone Network with David Rankine, which was dedicated to the study of Initiatory Witchcraft, Ceremonial Magic and the Mysteries of Hekate. With him she co-authored Hekate: Liminal Rites (2009), a compendium of magical practices historically associated with Hekate. With contributions from students, friends and practitioners from around the world she compiled Hekate: Keys to the Crossroads (2006) and Hekate: Her Sacred Fires (2010). In 2010 she wrote the Rite of Her Sacred Fires, a simple devotional ceremony which has become a worldwide annual celebration in honour of Hekate, celebrated at the Full Moon of May each year by many hundreds of people and now translated into 30 languages. She is also the Keybearer and founder of the Covenant of Hekate – www.hekatecovenant.com.

Sorita lives on a hill in Glastonbury from where she works as a publisher and writer. She is often distracted from work by her son, her love of gardening, and interesting visitors from different spiritual and esoteric persuasions.

To find out more about her work visit: www.sorita.co.uk

Selected other works by Sorita d'Este:

(with David Rankine)

Practical Elemental Magick

Practical Planetary Magick

Practical Qabalah Magick

Guises of the Morrigan

Isles of the Many Gods

Visions of the Cailleach

Hekate Liminal Rites

Wicca Magickal Beginnings

Avalonia's Book of Chakras

(Anthologies, Editor)

Both Sides of Heaven

Hekate Her Sacred Fires

Hekate Keys to the Crossroads

Horns of Power

Priestesses Pythonesses & Sibyls

The Faerie Queens

&

Artemis - Virgin Goddess of the Sun & Moon

Go to *www.avaloniabooks.co.uk* for more information.

Suggested Further Reading

There are many books on Greek myth, magic and religious history, the following works are ones I have found most useful and would recommend to students interested in learning more. Not all the books on the list are specifically about Hekate, but she was not worshipped or understood in isolation.

Arcana Mundi, Georg Luck, 1985
Dionysos: Exciter to Frenzy, Vikki Bramshaw, 2013
Hekate Liminal Rites, d'Este & Rankine, 2009
Hekate Soteira, Johnston, 1989
Hekate: Her Sacred Fires, various, 2010
Living Theurgy, Jeffrey Kupperman, 2014
Magic in the Ancient World, Graf, 1997
Roman Religion and the Cult of Diana at Aricia, Green, 2012
The Chaldean Oracles, Mead, 1908.
The Goddess Hekate, Ronan, 1989
The Greek Magical Papyri in Translation, Betz, 1996.
Thracian Magic, Georgi Mishev, 2012

Bibliography

Abrahamsen, V.; Women at Philippi: The Pagan and Christian Evidence, Journal of Feminist Studies in Religion, Vol. 3, No. 2, pp. 17-30; Indiana University Press on behalf of FSR, Inc ; 1987.

Agamben, G.; The Omnibus Homo Sacer; Stanford University Press; 2017.

Aldrich, K; Apollodorus, The Library of Greek Mythology; Kan.; 1975.

Alexander, P. S.; Sepher ha-Razim and the Problem of Black Magic in Early Judaism; in Magic in the Biblical World, p170-90; 2003.

Alexiou, M.; The Ritual Lament in Greek Tradition; Cambridge University Press; Cambridge; 1974.

Ankarloo, B., & Clark, S. (eds); Witchcraft and Magic in Europe: Vol 2 Ancient Greece and Rome; Athlone Press; London; 1999.

Antoniadi, E.M.; On Ancient Meteorites, and on the Origin of the Crescent and Star Emblem; in The Journal of the Royal Astronomical Society of Canada Vol. 33.5:177-84; 1939.

Apuleius & Griffiths, John Gwyn (trans); The Isis-book; Brill; Leiden; 1975.

Aristotle; de Mirabilibus Auscultationibus in Loeb Classical Library; Cambridge (Mass.) and London; 1936.

Arnold, C.E.; The Colossian Syncretism; Mohr Siebeck; Tubingen; 1995.

Arnold, C.E.; Christianity and Folk Belief at Colossae; Siebeck; 1995.

Arnold, C.E.; Ephesians, Power and Magic; CUP Archive; 1989.

Arthur, R. A.; Ps-Dionysus' Angelic Hierarchy and the Chaldean Oracles; in Studia Patristica XLII:23-28; 2006.

Asirvatham, S. R., & Pache, C.O., & Watrous, J. (eds); Between Magic and Religion: Interdisciplinary Studies in Ancient Mediterranean Religion and Society; Rowan & Littlefield; New York; 2001.

Athanassakis, Apostolos N. (trans) & Homer; The Homeric Hymns; John Hopkins University Press, Maryland; 2004.

Athanassiadi, P., & Frede, M. (eds); Pagan Monotheism in Late Antiquity; Clarendon Press; Oxford; 1999.

Athens Info Guide; Church of Agia Fotini; 2016. Online; www.athensinfoguide.com/wtschurches/agiafotini.htm

Audollent, Auguste; Defixionum Tabellae; Minerva; Frankfurt; 1967.

Aune, D.E.; Apocalypticism, Prophecy and Magic in Early Christianity; Mohr Siebeck; Tubingen; 2006.

Babbitt, F.C. (trans.); Plutarch. Moralia Vol. IV. Loeb Classical Library Volume 305. Cambridge, MA. Harvard University Press; 1936.

Babbitt, F.C.; Plutarch: Roman Questions; William Heinemann Ltd; London; 1936.

Beale, G.K..; The Book of Revelation: A Commentary on the Greek Text; Eerdmans Publishing; Grand Rapids; 1999.

Bell, J.; Bell's New Pantheon; Or Historical Dictionary of the Gods, Demi-gods, Heroes, and fabulous personages of antiquity; 1790

Bell, R., Women of Classical Mythology, ABCE-CLIO, 1991.

Brown, R., Semitic Influence in Hellenic Mythology, William and Norgate, 1898.

Berg, W.; Hecate: Greek or 'Anatolian'? in Numen Vol 21.2:128-40; 1974.

Betz, H.D., & Collins, A. Y., & Mitchell, M. M. (eds); Antiquity and Humanity: Essays on Ancient Religion and Philosophy; Mohr Siebeck; Tubingen; 2001.

Betz, H.D.; The Greek Magical Papyri in Translation; University of Chicago Press; Chicago; 1992 & 1996.

Blakely, Sandra; Myth, Ritual, and Metallurgy in Ancient Greece and Recent Africa; Cambridge University Press; Cambridge; 2006.

Bonner, C.; Studies in Magical Amulets, Chiefly Graeco-Egyptian; Ann Arbor; Michigan; 1950.

Botterweck, G.J.; and Ringgren, H.; Theological Dictionary of the Old Testament, Volume 7; Wm. B. Eerdmans Publishing; 1995.

Boustan, Ra'anan S., & Reed, Annette Yoshiko (eds); Heavenly Realms and Earthly Realities in Late Antique Religions; Cambridge University Press; Cambridge; 2004.

Bowden, H.; Cults of Demeter Eleusinia and the Transmission of Religious Ideas; Mediterranean Historical Review, Vol. 22, No. 1, June 2007, pp. 71–83.

Boxall, Ian; The Revelation of St John; Continuum International Publishing Group; London; 2006.

Bramshaw, Vikki; Dionysos: Exciter to Frenzy, Avalonia, London, 2013.

Bremmer, J. N., & Veestra, J. R.; The Metamorphosis of Magic from Late Antiquity to the Early Modern Period; Peeters Publishers; Holland; 2002.

Bremmer, J.N.; Initiation into the Mysteries of the Ancient World; De Gruyter; 2014.

Brouwer, H.H.J.; Bona Dea: The Sources and a Description of the Cult; Brill; Leiden; 1989.

Bryce, A.H., & Campbell, H.; The Seven Books of Arnobius Adversus Gentes; T & T Clark; Edinburgh, 1880.

Butler, Samuel; The Odyssey; Walter J Black; London; 1944.

CBd, Collection of Classical Antiquities of the Museum of Fine Arts, Budapest. Online, www2.szepmuveszeti.hu/

Celoria, F. (ed, trans); The Metamorphoses of Antoninus Liberalis: A Translation With Commentary; Routledge; London; 1992.

Chadwick, J.; The Decipherment of Linear B; Cambridge University Press, 2014.

Chaniotis, A. and Stavrianopoulou, E.; Epigraphic Bulletin for Greek Religion; Kernos; 1990.

Chapman, D. W.; Ancient Jewish and Christian Perceptions of Crucifixion; Mohr Siebeck; Tubingen; 2008

Clarysse, W., & S., A., & Quaegebeur, J., & Willems, H. (eds); Egyptian Religion: the Last Thousand Years; Peeters; Leuven; 1998.

Claudian; Against Rufinus in Loeb Classical Library; Cambridge (Mass.) and London; 1922.

Clauss, J. J., & Johnston, S.I. (ed); Medea; Princeton University Press; New Jersey; 1997.

Clauss, M. The Roman Cult of Mithras: The God and His Mysteries; Edinburgh University Press; Edinburgh; 2000.

Colavito, J.(trans.); Orphic Argonautica, by pseudo-Orpheus. Online; www.argonauts-book.com/orphic-argonautica.html

Cole, S.G.; Theoi Megaloi: The Cult of the Great Gods at Samothrace; Brill; Leiden; 1984.

Collins, B.J.; The Puppy in Hittite Ritual; Source: Journal of Cuneiform Studies, Vol. 42, No. 2 (Autumn, 1990), pp. 211-226.

Collins, Derek; Magic in the Ancient Greek World; Blackwell Publishing; Oxford; 2008.

Conybeare, F.C.; Philostratus: The Life of Apollonius of Tyana; William Heinemann Ltd; London; 2005.

Cook, A.B; Zeus. A study in ancient religion, Part I & II; Cambridge University Press; Cambridge; 1925.

Cormack, J.M.R.; A Tabella Defixionis in the Museum of the University of Reading; in HTR 44:25-34.

Cornell Library Digital Images. Online, www.library.cornell.edu/about/inside/policies/public-domain

Corrigan, Kevin. Reading Plotinus: A Practical Introduction to Neoplatonism, Purdue Univ. 2004.

Cory, I.P. (ed); Ancient Fragments; 1828; Pickering; London; 1951.

Cosmopoulos, M. B.; Greek Mysteries: The Archaeology and Ritual of Ancient Greek Secret Cults; Routledge; London; 2003.

Covenant of Hekate. Online, www.hekatecovenant.com

Craik, E.M.; The Dorian Aegean (Routledge Revivals); Routledge and Kegan Paul Ltd; New York; 1980.

Cunningham, A.; Coins of Alexander's Successors in The East. Part I.—Greeks Of Bactriana, Ariana, And India; The Numismatic Chronicle and Journal of the Numismatic Society.

d'Este, S. (ed.), Various; Hekate: Her Sacred Fires; Avalonia, London, 2010.

d'Este, Sorita & Rankine, David; Hekate: Liminal Rites; Avalonia, London; 2009.

d'Este, Sorita & Rankine, David; Practical Elemental Magick; Avalonia; London; 2010.

d'Este, Sorita & Rankine, David; Wicca: Magickal Beginnings; 2008; Avalonia; London.

d'Este, Sorita; Artemis: Virgin Goddess of the Sun and Moon; Avalonia; London; 2005.

d'Este, Sorita; Triple Horns of the Greek Magical Papyri; 2008; in Horns of Power; p189-94; Avalonia; London

Daniel, Robert W., & Maltomini, Franco (eds, trans); Supplementum Magicum; Westdeutscher Verlag; Opladen; 1990.

Darnell, J.C. and Darnell, D. Theban Desert Road Survey in the Egyptian Western Desert. Volume 1. Gebel Tjauti Rock Inscriptions 1-45 and Wadi el Hôl Rock Inscriptions 1-45. Oriental Institute Publications vol. 119. Chicago: University of Chicago; 2002.

Des Places, E.; Les Oracles Chaldaïques; in ANRW 17.4:2299-2335; 1984.

Dickie, M.; Magic and Magicians in the Greco-Roman World; Routledge; London; 2003.

Dickinson, O.T.P.K.; The Aegean Bronze Age; Cambridge University Press; Cambridge; 1994.

Dillon, M.; Girls and Women in Classical Greek Religion; Routledge; London; 2003.

Ducrey, P.; The Rock Reliefs of Philippi; Archaeology, Vol. 30, No. 2 (March 1977), pp. 102-107; Archaeological Institute of America ; 1977

Duff, J.D. (trans): Lucan: Pharsalia; William Heinemann Ltd; London. 1942.

Dunand, F.; Religion Populaire en Egypte Romaine: Les terres cuites Isiaques du Musee du Caire; Leiden; Brill; 1979.

Edmonds III, Prof. Radcliffe G.; Ephesia Grammata; 2009. Online; www.brynmawr.edu/classics/redmonds/H5-CSTS212.html

Edwards, C.M.; The Running Maiden from Eleusis and the Early Classical Image of Hekate in American Journal of Archaeology, Vol. 90, No. 3 (Jul., 1986), pp. 307-318; Archaeological Institute of America. Online; www.jstor.org/stable/505689 .

Elm, S.; Sons of Hellenism, Fathers of the Church: Emperor Julian, Gregory of Nazianzus, and the Vision of Rome; University of California Press, 2012.

Entwistle, C and Adams, N. (editors); Gems of Heaven - Recent Research on Engraved Gemstones in Late Antiquity, c. AD 200–60o; The Trustees of the British Museum; 2011.

Eunapius, Lives of the Philosophers and Sophists, pp.343-565; English translation; 1921.

Evelyn-White, Hugh G.; Hesiod: The Homeric Hymns and Homerica; William Heinemann Ltd; London; 1941.

Falkener, E.; Ephesus, and the Temple of Diana; Day & Son; 1862.

Faraone, C.A., & Obbink, D.; Magika Hiera: Ancient Greek Magic & Religion; Oxford University Press; Oxford; 1991.

Faraone, C.A.; Ancient Greek Love Magic; Harvard University Press; Massachusetts;

1999.

Farnell, L.R.; The Cults of the Greek States (5 volumes); Clarendon Press; Oxford; 1896.

Felton, D.; Haunted Greece and Rome; University of Texas Press; Texas; 1999.

Fletcher, W.(trans); The Divine Institutes of Lactantius in Ante-Nicene Fathers Vol 7; Christian Literature Publishing Co; New York; 1886.

Fontaine, M. and Scafura, A.C.; The Oxford Handbook of Greek and Roman Comedy; Oxford University Press; 2014

Forlong, J.G.R.; Encyclopedia of Religions or Faiths of Man, vols. 1 through 3, republished through Kessinger Publishing; 2003.

Fowler, H.W. & F.G. (trans); The Works of Lucian of Samosata; The Clarendon Press; Oxford; 1905.

Frazer, J.G. (trans); Pausanias's Description of Greece; MacMillan Company; New York; 1898.

Friedland, Food and Morality: Proceedings of the Oxford Symposium on Food and Cookery 2007 Susan R. Friedland Oxford Symposium, 2008

Fullerton, M.D.; The Archaistic Perirrhanteria of Attica in Hesperia: The Journal of the American School of Classical Studies at Athens, Vol. 55, No. 2 (Apr. - Jun., 1986), pp. 207-217; The American School of Classical Studies; Athens. Online; www.jstor.org/stable/148062

Fullerton, Mark D.; The Archaistic Style in Roman Statuary; Brill; Leiden; 1990.

Gager, J.R.; Curse Tablets and Binding Spells from the Ancient World; Oxford University Press; Oxford; 1992.

Garraffo, S., et al.; Taranto; Institutio per la storia e L'rcheologia della magna grecia, 1995.

Garrison, E. P.; Groaning Tears: Ethical and Dramatic Aspects of Suicide in Greek Tragedy; Brill, 1995.

Garland, R.; The Greek Way of Death; Cornell University Press; 2001.

Getty, A.; The Gods of Northern Buddhism: Their History and Iconography; Dover Publications; 2009

Getty's Open Content Project. Online, www.getty.edu/about/whatwedo/opencontentfaq.html.

Gifford, E.H. (trans); Eusebius of Caesarea: Praeparatio Evangelica; Horatio Hart; London; 1903.;

Goethe, J.W.; The Project Gutenberg EBook of Erotica Romana. Online; www.gutenberg.org/files/7889/7889-h/7889-h.htm

Goldin, O., & Kilroe, P.; Human Life and the Natural World: Readings in the History of Western Philosophy; Broadview Press Ltd; Canada; 1997.

Goodenough, E.R.; Jewish Symbols in the Greco-Roman Period; Princeton University Press; Princeton; 1992.

Goodwin, W.W.; Plutarch's Morals; Little Brown and Company; Boston, 1878. Online, oll.libertyfund.org/titles/plutarch-plutarchs-morals-5-vols

Graf, F., and Johnston, S.I; Ritual texts for the afterlife: Orpheus and the Bacchic Gold Tablets; Routledge; London; 2007.

Graf, F.; Magic in the Ancient World; Harvard University Press; Massachusetts; 1997.

Graf, F.; Roman Festivals in the Greek East: From the Early Empire to the Middle Byzantine Era, Cambridge University Press, 2015

Greaves, A.M.; Miletos: Archaeology and History; Routledge, 2005.

Gregory, Horace (trans); The Metamorphoses by Ovid; Signet Classics; 2001.

Green, C.M.C.; Roman Religion and the Cult of Diana at Aricia, Cambridge, 2012.

Guthrie, W.K.C.; Orpheus and Greek Religion: A Study of the Orphic Movement; Princeton University Press; Princeton; 1966 and 1993;

Hakkert, A.M.; Damaskios; Damascii Successoris; Amsterdam; 1966.

Hall, J. M.; Ethnic Identity in Greek Antiquity; Cambridge University Press; Cambridge; 2000.

Hansman, J.; The Great Gods of Elymais in Acta Iranica: Papers in Honour of Professor Mary Boyce, vol. 1. Leiden; Brill; 1985.

Harlow, M. & Nosch, M.; Greek and Roman Textiles and Dress: An Interdisciplinary Anthology, Oxbow Books; 2014.

Harmon, A.M. (trans); Lucian (8 volumes); William Heinemann; London; 1936.

Harrison, B.; Archaic and Archaistic Sculpture in Agora XI; Princeton: American School of Classical Studies at Athens; 1965.

Head, B. V.; A Catalogue of the Greek Coins in the British Museum; Woodfall and Kinder; London; 1906.

Heidel, W. A.; The Day of Yahweh, Century Co. 1929.

Henry, E.; Orpheus and His Lute: Poetry and the Renewal of Life, SIU Press, 1992.

Hermann, G.; (trans); Orphica; Leipzig; 1805.

Hornblower, Si., & Matthews, E.; Greek Personal Names: Their Value as Evidence; Oxford University Press; Oxford; 2000.

www.persee.fr/doc/paleo_0153-9345_2009_num_35_2_5296.

Isaac, B. H.; The Greek Settlements in Thrace Until the Macedonian Conquest; Brill; Leiden; 1986.

Jackson, Lesley; Isis: Eternal Goddess of Egypt and Rome; Avalonia, London, 2016.

Janouchová, P.; The Cult of Bendis in Athens and Thrace, in Graeco-Latina Brunensia 18; Charles University; Prague; 2013.

Jebb, R. C. (trans); The Characters of Theophrastus; Macmillan; London; 1870.

Johnson, W.R.; Momentary Monsters: Lucan and his Heroes; Cornell University Press; 1987.

Johnston, S.I.; Crossroads; aus: Zeitschrift für Papyrologie und Epigraphik 88 (1991) 217–224.

Johnston, S.I.; Hekate Soteira; Scholars Press; Atlanta; 1990.

Johnston, S.I.; Restless Dead: Encounters between the Living and the Dead in Ancient Greece; University of California Press; 1999.

Johnston, S.I.; The Song of the Iynx: Magic and Rhetoric in Pythian 4, in Transactions of the American Philological Association (1974-), Vol. 125 (1995), pp. 177-206; The Johns Hopkins University Press. Online, www.jstor.org/stable/284351

Julian the Apostate, "Julian the Emperor"; Oration upon the Mother of the Gods; 1888. Online; www.tertullian.org/fathers/julian_apostate_2_mother.htm

Kaibel, G.; Comicorum Graecorum Fragmenta; Apud Weidmannos; 1958.

Kaletsch, H.(Regensburg); Lagina, in Brill's New Pauly, Antiquity volumes edited by Cancik and Schneider. Online; dx.doi.org/10.1163/1574-9347_bnp_e628800.

Karouzou, S.; An underworld scene on a black-figured Lekythos; J.H.S; 1972.

Kater-Sibbes, G.J. F., & Vermaseren, Maarten Jozef; Apis: Inscriptions, Coins and Addenda; Brill; Leiden; 1977.

Kerenyi, K.; Hermes: Guide of Souls;Spring Pub.; 1996.

Kernos. Online, kernos.revues.org/1113

Kingsley, P.; Ancient Philosophy, Mystery, and Magic; Clarendon Press; Oxford; 1995.

Kirk, G.S. and Shewring, W. (trans.); The Odyssey, Oxford World Classics; 2008.

Kirk, G.S., & Raven, J.S., & Schofield, M. (eds); The Presocratic Philosophers: A Critical History with a Selection of Texts; Cambridge University Press; Cambridge; 1983.

Klauck, Hans-Josef & McNeil, Brian; The Religious Context of Early Christianity: A Guide to Greco-Roman Religions; Continuum International Publishing Group; London; 2003.

Klutz, T. (ed.); Magic in the Biblical World: From the Rod of Aaron to the Ring of Solomon; T&T Clark International; London; 2003.

Knight, R.P.;. The Symbolic Language of Ancient Art and Mythology: An Inquiry; Nabu; 2010.

Kotansky, R.; Jesus and the Lady of the Abyss: Hieros Gamos, Cosmogony and the Elixir of Life in Antiquity and Humanity: Essays on Ancient Religion and Philosophy; Mohr Siebeck; 2001.

Kottek, S. S.; Medicine and Hygiene in the Works of Flavius Josephus; Brill; Leiden; 1994.

Kraus, T.; Hekate: Studien zu Wesen u. Bilde der Göttin in Kleinasien u. Griechenland;

Heidelberg; 1960.

Kupperman, Jeffrey K.; Living Theurgy, Avalonia, London, 2014.

Lardinois, A. and Block, J.; Sacred Words: Orality, Literacy and Religion: Orality and Literacy in the Ancient World; M.G.M. van der Poel, 2011

Larson, J. L.; Greek Nymphs: Myth, Cult, Love; Oxford University Press; Oxford; 2001.

Larson, J.; Understanding Greek Religion; Routledge, 2016.

Legge, F.; Philosophumena or The Refutation of All Heresies, formerly attributed to Origen but now to Hippolytus; The MacMillan Company; New York; 1921.

Levi, Eliphas; History of Magic; 1860.

Lewis, C. T.; An Elementary Latin Dictionary; American Book co; 1890.

Lloyd, G. E. R.; Science, Folklore, and Ideology: Studies in the Life Sciences in Ancient Greece; Cambridge University Press; Cambridge; 1983.

Long, C.R.; The Twelve Gods of Greece and Rome; Brill Archive, 1987.

Luck, G.; Arcana Mundi: Magic and the Occult in the Greek and Roman Worlds; John Hopkins University Press, Maryland; 1985.

Luibheld, C. (trans); Pseudo-Dionysus: The Complete Works; New York; 1987.

Maijastina K.; Vettius Agorius Praetextatus – Senatorial Life in Between. Acta Instituti Romani Finlandiae no. 26, Roma 2002. Online; www.maijastinakahlos.net/b/kirjoituksia/praetextatus/vettius-agorius-praetextatus-religion-cults-ch-23/

Mair, A.W. & G.R. (trans); Callimachus Hymns and Epigrams. Lycophron. Aratus; William Heinemann; London; 1921.

Marconi, Clemente & Getty Foundation; Temple Decoration and Cultural Identity in the Archaic Greek World; Cambridge University Press; Cambridge; 2007.

Martin, R.P.; Myths of the ancient Greeks; New American Library; New York; 2003.

Matossian, M.K.; In the Beginning, God Was a Woman in Journal of Social History 6, no. 3 (1973): 325-43. Online; www.jstor.org/stable/3786544.

Mead, G.R.S.; Pistis Sophia; John M. Watkins; London; 1921.

Mead, G.R.S.; The Chaldean Oracles; Theosophical Publishing Society; 1908.

Midwinter, D.; A Voyage Into the Levant, Joseph Pitton de Tournefort; 1741

Mikalson, J.D.; Ancient Greek Religion; John Wiley & Sons; New Jersey; 2011.

Miller, Frank Justus; Seneca's Tragedies Volume I: Hercules Furens, Troades, Medea, Hippolytus, Oedipus; Harvard University Press; Harvard; 1960.

Miller, S.G.; The Altar of the Six Goddesses in Thessalian Pherai; California Studies in Classical Antiquity, Vol. 7 (1974), pp. 231-256; University of California Press. Online, www.jstor.org/stable/25010672

Miller, D.L.; The New Polytheism; Harper & Row; New York; 1974.

Mirecki, Paul Allen, & Meyer, M.W.; Magic and Ritual in the Ancient World, Brill, 2002

Mirecki, Paul Allen, & Meyer, Marvin (eds); Magic and Ritual in the Ancient World; Brill; Leiden; 2002.

Mishev, Georgi; Thracian Magic: Past and Present, Avalonia, London, 2012.

Morgan, C.; Early Greek States Beyond the Polis; Routledge; 2003.

Morgan, M.A. (ed); Sepher ha-Razim: The Book of Mysteries; Chico; California; 1983.

Murray, D.; Reincarnation: ancient beliefs and modern evidence; David & Charles; Newton Abbot; 1981.

Murray, R.D.; The Geography of Strabo. Literally translated, with notes, in three volumes. London. George Bell & Sons. 1903. Online, www.perseus.tufts.edu/hopper/text?doc=urn:cts:greekLit:tlg0099.tlg001.perseus-eng2:14.2

Naveh, Joseph & Shaked, Saul; Magic Spells and Formulae: Aramaic Incantations of Late Antiquity; Magnes Press; Jerusalem; 1993;

Neheti (Sara Croft); Singing for Her. Online, nehetisingsforhekate.tumblr.com/

New Series, Vol. 8 (1868), pp. 257-283. Online, www.jstor.org/stable/42680475

Newton, C. T.; A History of Discoveries at Halicarnassus, Cnidus, and Branchidae, vol. 2, RP Pullan; 1863.

Nisetich, F. J. (trans); The Poems of Callimachus; Oxford University Press; Oxford;

2001.

Noegel, Scott B., & Walker, Joel Thomas, & Wheeler, Brannon M. (eds); Prayer, Magic, and the Stars in the Ancient and Late Antique World; Penn State University Press; 2003.

Nordh, Katarina; Aspects of Ancient Egyptian Curses and Blessings: Conceptual Background and Transmission; Uppsala Studies in Ancient Mediterranean and Near Eastern Civilizations; Uppsala; 1996.

Novak, Ralph Martin; Christianity and the Roman Empire: Background Texts; Continuum International Publishing Group; 2001.

The Numismatic Circular and Catalogue of Coins, Tokens, Commemorative and War Medals, Books and Cabinets, vol. 16, Spink and Son, 1908.

O'Neill, Edward (ed); Plutarch: Moralia; William Heinemann Ltd; London; 2004.

Ogden, D.; Binding Spells: Curse Tablets and Voodoo Dolls in the Greek and Roman Worlds; Witchcraft and Magic in Europe Volume 2: Ancient Greece and Rome; Athlone Press; London; 199.

Ogden, D.; Dragons, Serpents, and Slayers in the Classical and Early Christian Worlds ...; Oxford University Press; 2013.

Ogden, D.; Drakon: Dragon Myth and Serpent Cult in the Greek and Roman Worlds; Oxford University Press; 2013.

Ogden, D.; Magic, Witchcraft, and Ghosts in the Greek and Roman Worlds; Oxford University Press; Oxford; 2002.

Oldfather, C.H. (trans.); Diodorus Siculus ; Loeb Classical Library 279, Library of History, Volume I, Books 1-2.34; Harvard; 1933.

Parisinou, Eva; The Light of the Gods: The Role of Light in Archaic and Classical Greek Cult; Duckworth; London; 2000.

Parker, Robert; Miasma: Pollution and Purification in Early Greek Religion; Clarendon Press; Oxford; 1996.

Petridou, G.; Divine Epiphany in Greek Literature and Culture, OUP; Oxford; 2016.

Petrie, W.M.F.; Ancient Egypt; MacMillan and Co; London; 1915,

Pinch, Geraldine; Magic in Ancient Egypt; British Museum Press; London; 1994.

Pomey, F. and Andrew T., Tooke's Pantheon of the Heathen Gods and Illustrious Heroes, repub. Kessinger Pub, 2010.

Pouilloux, J.; THASOS: Cultural Crossroads in Archaeology, Vol. 8, No. 3 (September 1955), pp. 198-204; Archaeological Institute of America; 1955.

Powell, A.; Athens and Sparta: Constructing Greek Political and Social History from 478 BCE; Routledge; 2001.

Price, S.R.F; Rituals and Power: The Roman Imperial Cult in Asia Minor; Cambridge University Press, 1986.

Price, T.H.; Kourotrophos: Cults and Representations of the Greek Nursing Deities; Brill Archive; 1978.

Price, Theodora Hadzisteliou; Kourotrophos: Cults and Representations of the Greek Nursing Deities; Brill; Leiden; 1978.

Rabinowitz, J.; The Rotting Goddess: The Origin of the Witch in Classical Antiquity. Autonomedia;1998.

Rabinowitz, J.; Hekate's Iynx: An Ancient Theurgical Tool; Alexandria I:321-335, Grand Rapids; 1991.

Ramsay, W.M., The Cities and Bishoprics of Phrygia, Clarendon Press, 1897.

Reed, E.; Persian Literature: Ancient and Modern; Chicago; 1893.

Reeder, E.D.; The Mother of the Gods and a Hellenistic Bronze Matrix, American Journal of Archaeology, Vol. 91, No. 3 (Jul., 1987), pp. 423-4401987. Online, www.jstor.org/stable/505364

Rice, D.G. and Stambaugh, J.E.; Sources for the Study of Greek Religion: Corrected Edition; Society of Biblical Lit, 2012

Rice, D.G. and Stambaugh, J.E.; Sources for the Study of Greek Religion: Corrected Edition, 2012

Rigsby, K.J.; Notes on Sacred Laws; Zeitschrift für Papyrologie und Epigraphik, Bd. 170, pp. 73-80.; by: Dr. Rudolf Habelt GmbH; 2009.

Roberts, Rev. Alexander & Donaldson, James (eds); The Seven Books of Arnobius Adversus Gentes; T & T Clark; Edinburgh; 1871.

Rohde, Erwin; Psyche: The Cult of Souls and the Belief in Immortality Among the Greeks; Routledge; London; 2000.

Roller, Lynn E.; In Search of God the Mother: the Cult of Anatolian Cybele; University of California Press; California; 1999.

Ronan, Stephen (ed); The Goddess Hekate; Chthonios Books; Hastings; 1992.

Ross, Charles Stanley (trans); The Thebaid by Publius Papinius Statius; John Hopkins University Press, Maryland; 2004.

Rouse, W H D. (trans.); Nonnus, Dionysiaca; Loeb Classical Library Volumes 344, 354, 356. Cambridge, MA, Harvard University Press, 1940.

Rouse, W.H.D.; Nonnus Dionysiaca Books 1-48; Harvard University Press; Cambridge; 1960.

Russell, T.N.; Taking the Bull by the Horns: Ideology, Masculinity, and Cattle Horns at Catalhöyük (Turkey); Paléorient Année; 2009; Volume 35, Numéro 2, pp. 19-32. Online;

Rutherford, I.; Pindar's Paeans: A Reading of the Fragments with a Survey of the Genre; Clarendon Press; 2001.

Rykwert, J.; The Dancing Column: On Order in Architecture; MIT Press, 1998.

Ryland, J.E. (trans); Tatian's Address to the Greeks; in Ante-Nicene Fathers Vol 2; Christian Literature Publishing Co; New York; 1886.

Schafer, Peter, & Kippenberg, Hans Gerhard (eds); Envisioning Magic; Brill; Leiden; 1997.

Scholfield, Alwyn Faber (trans); Aelian: On the Characteristics of Animals; Harvard University Press; Harvard; 1959.

Seaton, R.C. (trans); Apollonius Rhodius: Argonautica; LOEB Classical Library; 1990.

Shakespeare, William; Macbeth: A Tragedy in Five Acts; M Douglas; New York; 1848.

Skinner & Rankine, The Veritable Key of Solomon; Golden Hoard Press; Singapore; 2008.

Smith, A.H.; A Catalogue of Engraved Gems in the British Museum; British Museum; London; 1888.

Smith, D.; The Hieropoioi on Kos, Numen, Vol. 20, Fasc. 1 (Apr.,1973), pp. 38-47; Brill. Online, www.jstor.org/stable/3269657

Smith, K.F.; Hekate's Suppers; in The Goddess Hekate; p56-64; Chthonios Books; Hastings; 1992.

Smith, W.; A Dictionary of Greek and Roman Biography and Mythology; Taylor and Walton; 1844.

Southesk, James Carnegie, & Carnegie, Lady Helena Mariota; Catalogue of the Collection of Antique Gems Formed by James, Ninth Earl of Southesk, K.T.; B. Quaritch; 1908.

Strelan, Rick; Outside are the Dogs and the Sorcerors; in Biblical Theology Bulletin 33:148-57; 2003.

Stückenbruck, Loren T.; Angel Veneration and Christology: A Study in Early Judaism and in the Christology of the Apocalypse of John; Mohr Siebeck; Tubingen; 1995.

Sudas. Online; www.stoa.org/sol/

Supplementum epigraphicum graecum (SEG) 42, 1816.

Tavenner, Eugene; Iynx and Rhombus; in Transactions and Proceedings of the American Philological Association, Vol. 64:109-127; 1933.

Taylor, T.; The Eleusinian and Bacchic Mysteries,1891. Online; www.sacred-texts.com/cla/ebm/index.htm

Taylor, Thomas; Iamblichus on the Mysteries (translated from the Greek); Chiswick; 1821.

The Archimedes Project. Online, www.archimedes.fas.harvard.edu/

The Campbell Bonner Magical Gems Database. Online, classics.mfab.hu/talismans/cbd/1571

The Perseus Project. Online, www.perseus.tufts.edu/hopper/

The Red Mullet in Rome. Online;

penelope.uchicago.edu/~grout/encyclopaedia_romana/wine/mullus.html.

Theoi.com. Online, www.theoi.com

Theophrastus; Enquiry into Plants Books VI-IX; Harvard University Press; Cambridge; 1989.

Torijano, Pablo A.; Solomon the Esoteric King: From King to Magus, Development of a Tradition; Brill; Leiden; 2002.

Treister, Michail Yu, & Hargrave, James; Hammering Techniques in Greek and Roman Jewellery and Toreutics; Brill; Leiden; 2001.

Ustinova, Yulia; The Supreme Gods of the Bosporan Kingdom: Celestial Aphrodite and the Most High God; Leiden, Brill, 1999.

Vermaseren, M.J. & Lane, E.N.; Cybelle, Attis and related cults; Brill, 1996.

Vermaseren, Maarten Jozef, & Lane, Eugene; Cybele, Attis and Related Cults; Brill; Leiden; 1996.

Versnel, H.S., & Horstmanshoff, H.F.J., & Singor, H.W.; Kykeon: studies in honour of H.S. Versnel; Brill; Leiden; 2002.

Von Jan, Ludwig (ed); Macrobius: The Saturnalia; Gottfried Bass; Quedlingberg & Liepzig; 1852.

Von Rudolf, Robert; Hekate in Ancient Greek Religion; Horned Owl Publishing; Victoria; 1999.

Webb, P.A.; Hellenistic Architectural Sculpture: Figural Motifs in Western Anatolia and the Aegean Islands; Wisconsin Studies in Classics, Wisconsin University Press; 1996.

West, David R.; Some Cults of Greek Goddesses and Female Daemons of Oriental Origin; Butzon & Bercker; Kevelaer; 1995.

Whiston, William (trans); The Works of Josephus; Hendrickson; 1987.

Willoughby, H. R.; Pagan Regeneration: A Study of Mystery Initiations in the Greco-Roman World; University of Chicago Press; Chicago; 1929.

Wunsch, R (ed); De Mensibus; Teuber; Leipzig; 1898.

Xenophon; Xenophon in Seven Volumes; Harvard University Press; Cambridge; 1979.

Young, F., Edwards, M., & Parvis, P. (eds); Studia Patristica XLII; Peeters; Leuven; 2006.

Index

B

C